Luminos is the Open Access monograph publishing program from UC Press. Luminos provides a framework for preserving and reinvigorating monograph publishing for the future and increases the reach and visibility of important scholarly work. Titles published in the UC Press Luminos model are published with the same high standards for selection, peer review, production, and marketing as those in our traditional program. www.luminosoa.org

Morals Not Knowledge

Morals Not Knowledge

*Recasting the Contemporary U.S. Conflict
Between Religion and Science*

John H. Evans

UNIVERSITY OF CALIFORNIA PRESS

University of California Press, one of the most distinguished university presses in the United States, enriches lives around the world by advancing scholarship in the humanities, social sciences, and natural sciences. Its activities are supported by the UC Press Foundation and by philanthropic contributions from individuals and institutions. For more information, visit www.ucpress.edu.

University of California Press
Oakland, California

© 2018 by John H. Evans

Suggested citation: Evans, John H. *Morals Not Knowledge: Recasting the Contemporary U.S. Conflict Between Religion and Science*. Oakland: University of California Press, 2018. doi: https://doi.org/10.1525/luminos.47

This work is licensed under a Creative Commons CC BY-NC-ND license. To view a copy of the license, visit http://creativecommons.org/licenses.

Library of Congress Cataloging-in-Publication Data

Names: Evans, John Hyde, 1965- author.
Title: Morals not knowledge : recasting the contemporary U.S. conflict between religion and science / John H. Evans.
Description: Oakland, California : University of California Press, [2018] | Includes bibliographical references and index. |
Identifiers: LCCN 2017042858 (print) | LCCN 2017045416 (ebook) | ISBN 9780520969780 (ebook) | ISBN 9780520297432 (pbk. : alk. paper)
Subjects: LCSH: Religion and science—United States—20th century. | Ethics—Social aspects.
Classification: LCC BL240.3 (ebook) | LCC BL240.3 .E925 2018 (print) | DDC 201/.650973—dc23
LC record available at https://lccn.loc.gov/2017042858

27 26 25 24 23 22 21 20 19 18
10 9 8 7 6 5 4 3 2 1

CONTENTS

Acknowledgments — vii

1. Introduction — 1
2. The Religion and Science Advocates in the Academic Debate — 16
3. The Academic Analysts of the Relationship Between Religion and Science — 44
4. The Recent Transformation of Elite Academic and Public Debates — 63
5. Existing Research on the Public — 86
6. Empirical Tests of Knowledge and Belief Conflict for the Religious Public — 119
7. Empirical Tests of Moral Conflict for the Religious Public — 137
8. Conclusion — 160

Notes — 173
Works Cited — 205
Index — 219

ACKNOWLEDGMENTS

As my writing has unfolded over the years it was not until recently that I was able to see the connections between my seemingly varied interests. In retrospect I have always been writing about religion and science, or at least religion and knowledge, but in recent years I became involved with the "religion and science debate." This is an interdisciplinary group of scholars who examine the relationship between these institutions from normative and empirical perspectives. This involvement was largely at the hand of Ron Numbers, who I think I first met at a conference on secularism at Chapel Hill in 2001, and since then he has slowly worked toward bringing me into this academic world, and particularly toward bringing me into conversation with historians. I have greatly enjoyed being a sociologist among the historians, and thank Ron for his sponsorship and friendship.

Over the years, as I have tried to understand this phenomenon sociologically, I have written a number of articles and chapters for books that address various facets of the broader issues examined in this book. Now that I have tried to synthesize all of the earlier partial attempts into one book, my perspective has changed a bit. Themes from these earlier articles survive in this book. While it is primarily only the embryonic ideas from these earlier papers that survive, I have left unchanged some paragraphs from two of the original texts, so as to not reinvent the wheel.[1] I need to acknowledge the intellectual work of Michael Evans (no relation), who co-authored a few of these articles, including one from which a few pages are reproduced in Chapter 4.

The ideas now summarized in this book benefitted greatly from presentations to audiences. Thanks to the audience at the "Beyond the Creation-Evolution Controversy: Science and Religion in Public Life Conference" of the Program on

Science, Technology, and Society, at the Kennedy School of Government, Harvard University (2008); the "Religion Working Group," Department of Sociology, University of California, Los Angeles (2009); the "Religious Responses to Darwinism, 1859–2009" conference at the Ian Ramsey Centre, Oxford University (2009); the conference on "Imagining the (Post-) Human Future: Meaning, Critique, and Consequences" at the Karlsruhe Institute of Technology, Karlsruhe, Germany (2013); the conference on "Religion, Naturalism and the Sciences" at Florida State University (2013); the conference on "Science & Religion: Exploring the Spectrum," at York University, Toronto, Canada (2015); the conference on "The Idea That Wouldn't Die": The Warfare Between Science and Religion," University of Wisconsin, Madison (2015); the "Public Perception of Science and Religion Conference," San Diego (2016); and the "Workshop on Life Sciences and Religion: Historical and Contemporary Perspectives" at the Max Planck Institute for the History of Science in Berlin (2016).

Thanks to Michael Evans and Bernie Lightman for close readings of an early draft. Thanks to Elaine Howard Ecklund and Ron Numbers for close reading of a later draft. As always, the UCSD Sociology Department provided a fertile and collegial place for thought, and the Science, Technology, and Innovation Studies Unit at the University of Edinburgh provided a home away from home.

1

Introduction

If you are going to disagree with your adversary in a debate in the public sphere, I want you to disagree with them for the right reason. A democracy ideally requires knowing the views of those you disagree with, so that your true differences can be negotiated. As a sociologist of religion, I often am bothered by seeing debates in the public sphere when people who are misinformed about American religion—typically nowadays these are social and political liberals—make empirical assumptions about their supposed adversaries that are most certainly false. These false assumptions distort the debate about the motives and predicted actions of adversaries in the public sphere, and often mislead these liberals into wasting their precious resources chasing dragons that do not exist, when they could be focused on effectively achieving their goals, like combatting global warming. Perhaps nowhere are these false assumptions more extreme than in discussions of religion and science.

This book is dedicated to trying to dislodge the myth that there is, in the public, a foundational conflict between religion and science, specifically that there is conflict over "ways of knowing" about the natural world. I know that discrediting this myth will not be easy. In popular accounts, "religion" and "science" have always been at war over knowledge, with the first battle being between Galileo and the 17th century Catholic Church. For example, a textbook on the relationship between science and religion identifies historical landmarks in the "debate" at least four centuries old: the "medieval synthesis," the Copernican and Galilean controversies, debates over Newton's ideas, and Darwinism.[1] This narrative of conflict is classically indicated in the title of an 1896 book by the former president of Cornell University Andrew Dickson White: *A History of the Warfare of Science with Theology in Christendom*.[2]

My argument is that, with a few limited exceptions, even the most conservative religious people in the U.S. accept science's ability to make factual claims about the world. By the end of this book I hope to disabuse the reader of the idea of fundamental conflict over knowledge about nature, while giving the non-religious a more accurate reason to (potentially) disagree with (some) religious people—namely, that religious people's *moral values* are different from those promulgated by science. There is a moral conflict among the public between religion and science.

This is not the perspective you will get from the theologians, scientists, and historians who currently dominate the discussion of religion and science, as they see the relationship—and thus any potential conflict—as primarily about knowledge. Up until very recently social scientists have also shared the knowledge conflict perspective. There are many reasons why these academics see this debate through this lens, which I will discuss in subsequent chapters. But, if we want to understand the relationship between *contemporary* religious people and science, we need to change our lens, or we will seriously misunderstand the situation, and seriously undermine our ability to have reasonable debates in the public sphere about how to move forward with our most pressing social problems.

To see how assumptions of a knowledge conflict are pervasive in the public sphere, consider global warming, one of the great moral challenges to the world. In global warming debates some liberals have created a dragon of religion to chase, wasting time, instead of focusing on what is really wrong about the public debate about climate change. To see the problem, let's look at some of the discourse in the Huffington Post, which is a major source of information for liberals. I looked at all of the Huffington Post articles categorized under "climate denial" that appeared to discuss religion.[3]

To anticipate what I will discuss in much more detail below, what has struck me as totally wrong in liberals' conception of religion and science is the presumption that religious people have a different way of knowing facts about the world than scientists, and that therefore if a religious person does not accept *one* scientific claim, this indicates that they will not accept *any* scientific claim. Therefore, the assumption continues, people who do not accept scientists' claims about human evolution will not accept scientists' claims about global warming.

In looking at these articles, a few have little analysis and yet leave the impression that conservative Protestants, if not all religious people, disagree with scientific claims about global warming because they also believe in religious claims. For example, an article titled "Rush Limbaugh: 'If You Believe In God . . . You Cannot Believe In Man-Made Global Warming,'" reports the comments of the prominent right-wing radio personality who said that "if you believe in God then intellectually you cannot believe in man-made global warming." The reason is that "you must be either agnostic or atheistic to believe that man controls something he can't create."[4] That is, scientific fact claims that climate is a naturalistic process are wrong because climate is actually controlled by God. This implies there are two opposing versions of how nature works and, consequently, two opposing ways of knowing about nature. The article does not explicitly say that ordinary religious people would agree with Limbaugh, but implies it, giving the impression that religious people would have a nonscientific way of knowing if and why the climate is changing.

More analytic posts by academics similarly reinforce these false assumptions. Philosopher and historian Keith Parsons writes about American reverence for science in the 1950s, stating that "something has been lost. Fifty years ago science was king. Science had respect; it was bigger than ideology. No longer." He criticizes postmodern skepticism about truth from the left, and concludes that the biggest enemy of science is "big money."[5] But in his depiction of the right's suspicion of science, he focuses on a religiously inspired conflict over knowledge claims. He writes that "the Texas State Board of Education, which is dominated by religious fundamentalists, prefers the propaganda of ax-grinding cranks over the recommendations of hundreds of qualified scientists and scholars." His example of conflict is evolution: "How, indeed, has it ever come to be thought that there is still a scientific debate over evolution, or that pluperfect nonsense like creationism is worthy of a hearing? How did there come to be a multi-million dollar 'creation museum' in Kentucky, with full-scale models of dinosaurs fitted out with saddles? (Why saddles? So Adam and Eve could ride them around Eden. Duh.)" Everything he writes about Texas fundamentalist Protestant beliefs and creationism is probably true, but the implicit conclusion here is that the industry-funded skepticism of *global warming* science is abetted by the same fact-conflict for evangelicals that leads them to believe that dinosaurs needed saddles. This could only be the case if he presumes that conservative Protestants unwillingness to accept scientific claims about evolution means they will not accept any fact claim from science.

It should be no surprise that the most un-nuanced version of these assumptions comes from a prominent atheist scientist who clearly wants to portray religion in a negative way. In a Huffington Post article titled "The Folly of Faith," the recently deceased physicist and atheist author Victor Stenger starts by writing "religion and science have long been at war with one another."[6] He sees a war of facts: "Religion is based on faith. By contrast, science is not based on faith but on objective observations of the world. This makes religion and science fundamentally incompatible." This is the pure form of the myth: there is a religious way of knowing and a scientific one—and they are mutually exclusive. Moreover, he writes, "nowadays, religious leaders and their political supporters are increasingly, and more stridently, trying to define the real world on their own terms. In the process, they are undermining scientific consensus on issues of great consequence to humans everywhere, such as overpopulation and planetary climate change."

He then provides two pieces of evidence. One is that the Cornwall Alliance, which appears to be an energy-industry funded group of religious right figures, claims that God created a resilient planet that can withstand changes. Second, that there are conservative Protestant climate change deniers who feel that "it is hubris to think that human beings could disrupt something that God created." Stenger implies that these religious-right activists represent "religion."

In a subsequent post titled "Global Warming and Religion," Stenger provides more justification for his claim of a connection between religion and global warming denial.[7] He starts with poll results that showed that, while 58 percent of the religiously unaffiliated believed in global warming, only 50 percent of religious believers do, which is "evidence for a correlation between religion and global warming denialism." Those trained in social statistics will recognize that this is at best a very weak correlation. However, he continues by noting 34 percent of white evangelical Protestants polled believed in global warming. One reason for conservative Protestants not believing in global warming is belief in Armageddon, he says, and then quotes as evidence the view of a Republican house member that climate change is a myth because God told Noah he would never destroy the Earth by flood again. Of course, we have no evidence that typical members of evangelical groups believe in this link between climate change and Armageddon, but again it is implied.

This type of survey data has been more closely analyzed by sociologists. The question is: is it the religion of evangelicals that leads them to be more skeptical of scientific claims about global warming, or some other characteristic that evangelicals tend to have? Evangelicals are anti-elite, and conservative in the traditional sense of the term—suspicious of government. When you take the basic opinion statistics of the type Stenger uses but control for Republican party identification and political ideology, the religion effects disappear and conservative Protestants are just as much believers in global warming as are the non-religious.[8] What does this mean? It means that there is not a religious basis for global warming denial, but rather the basis is other characteristics of evangelicals—probably that they watch too much Fox News. Stenger's assumption about fundamentally different ways of knowing fact claims about the world are distracting his readers from the true culprits that he does identify and that they should be organizing against—the energy industry that funds skepticism of climate change.

In a breath of fresh air, one of the articles I reviewed on Huffington Post does not make the assumption of a knowledge conflict between religion and science, I would guess because the author is familiar with ordinary religious people. In an analysis of why some conservative Protestants reject the claims of scientists, the Reverend Jim Ball, who works for the Evangelical Environmental Network, identifies a number of barriers to action for conservative Protestants.[9] The first is ignorance, with some not knowing "what a serious threat global warming is, especially to the poor and vulnerable." The second barrier he hears about from evangelicals is related to knowledge and is that "the science is not settled." He says that "this dodge is simply unacceptable today," and such a person should "ask God to help you see the truth, to have 'eyes to see.'" The third is "mistrust of the messengers," and here he references moral conflict in the public sphere between groups: "Maybe you feel that scientists have disrespected your faith, or even tried to take your faith away from you, that environmentalists and democratic politicians don't share many of your values or beliefs." The fourth is "fear of lifestyle impacts." The fifth is that people are "immobilized by inaction." The sixth is that it is so big a challenge, "how can you carry another burden like global warming, especially when no one person can solve this problem?"

This list was written by someone who is involved with the on-the-ground evangelical world, and undoubtedly encounters evangelical denialists repeatedly. Yet only one knowledge claim seems prominent enough in that world to make his list, and it is not presented as a knowledge conflict because no alternative religious way of knowing is presented. Indeed, that we should wait for science to settle suggests belief in scientific ways of knowing. He is reporting on a close to the ground conflict that is not about how facts about nature are generated. To anticipate later chapters, Ball's third reason for evangelical lack of action on climate change—mistrust of scientists' values—is the most accurate.

WHAT IS CONFLICT, AND BETWEEN WHOM?

It is amazing that in all of the few centuries of discussion of a "conflict" between religion and science, we have never explicitly been told what the conflict is about. Yes, we know the conflict is about certain scientific claims, like the age of the Earth or whether people can be healed via supernatural force. But, how would you recognize this conflict when you see it?

For the vast majority of scholars in the "religion vs. science" debate, the conflict is about incompatible ideas. For a very large portion of scholars who debate religion and science, the conflict exists only as ideas on a page—and whether these ideas can be logically related. For example, can we assert that Darwinian evolution is true while retaining the belief that God inspired those who wrote the Bible? If these debates simply remained intellectual puzzles at an Oxbridge High Table, nobody would care. But, these academic debates eventually trickle down to the public.

So, what is conflict? At minimum it must be said, and not surprisingly from a sociologist, that I am not focused upon conflict between ideas on a page but rather on social conflict between *people* over *action in the world*. I am not opposed to intellectual debate in the realm of pure ideas, but I should note that the reason so much energy is spent on debates about conflicting ideas is the presumption that these ideas influence ordinary people's actions. For example, many scholars have dedicated a lot of time to showing that Darwinism is compatible with evangelical Protestantism, and the at least implicit hope is that their proposed solution will help ordinary evangelicals operate in the world.

The most consequential conflict is therefore between people. Imagine a fundamentalist Protestant sitting in a pew in East Texas thinking that the Earth is six thousand years old. Since this view is at odds with the scientific consensus, he has the intellectual prerequisite for conflict with science, but is not yet in conflict. He *is* in conflict with science when he goes to the local school board and says out loud that the schools should not teach modern geology, a position that would presumably be opposed by others. Similarly, someone is engaged in religious conflict with science if they cancel their appointment with their oncologist and instead go to a Pentecostal preacher to be healed. And, to turn to moral conflict, a religious person is in conflict with science if they call their congressperson and ask that embryonic stem cell research be banned because their religion teaches that embryos have the same status as born persons. That all said, it is often difficult for social science to observe actual conflict between religion and science, and often all we can measure is the cognitive prerequisites to conflict, such as attitudes. However, what I will choose to empirically examine, and how I interpret what I examine, will be based on my premise that what ultimately matters is human action.

The Importance of the Public Instead of Elites

My concern with debates in the public sphere, and my definition of conflict which requires human interaction, makes the views of the citizens much more important than those of the elites. For my purposes, an elite is anyone who has a social role that allows them to influence the views of other people beyond their immediate acquaintances and family members *on the issue under debate*. So, obviously all academics are potentially elites, as are scientists, politicians, clergy, theologians, church officials, journalists, pundits, TV and movie producers, and leaders of social movements. The public, or citizens as I will often call them, are all of the other members of the public who lack this power. Someone could be elite in one context but not in another. For example, corporate executives are likely elites on the issue of worker pay, but are unlikely to be so for a debate about religion and science. The elites in the religion and science debate are largely academics, scientists, and religious leaders, with a smattering of others we could call public intellectuals.

The reason that the public is more important for debates in the public sphere is that elites cannot, at least in the present day, do too much on their own. The president of the Southern Baptist Convention, an elite, cannot engage in religion and science conflict by banning the teaching of evolution in public schools in Texas. But, he can eventually do so if he gets the public to start a social movement, and this public pressures elected officials. Rush Limbaugh is an elite, and has power because of his role, but his ability to stay on the air, and to influence policy, is dependent on the public. If we are interested in conflict over religion and science as I have defined it—for example, whether children will learn evolution—we need to understand the public.

We know a lot about how the elites in the religion and science debate think, and very little about how the public views religion and science. To anticipate my argument, the elites see the relationship—and thus any conflict—between religion and science as concerning knowledge. Critically, much of what is seemingly known about the public has actually been distorted by extrapolating the views of the elites to the public. But, in the past ten years a new group of scattered sociological studies have been undertaken that do not begin by presuming that the relationship concerns knowledge. We can now see how the entire "religion and science debate" needs to be reconfigured if we are going to talk about the public.

ELITE AND PUBLIC BELIEF SYSTEMS

Before continuing, I must clarify some terminology. A "belief" is a feeling of being sure that something is true, whether or not there is evidence or justification for it.[10] An example would be believing the Earth is four and a half billion years old. "Knowledge" means justified belief. My belief about the age of the Earth becomes knowledge if I also believe that radiometric dating accurately describes the age of rocks, as the radiometric dating is the justification for my belief. It is telling about the status of religion and science in the contemporary age that we do not say "religious knowledge" but "religious belief," because religion is considered to be unjustified by evidence. We do not say "scientific beliefs" but rather "scientific knowledge," which indicates that if a claim is scientific, it is considered to be justified belief.

A belief system is simply the relationship between beliefs. A particular type of belief system relevant to the religion and science debate is what I will call a knowledge system, where beliefs are structured in a hierarchical fashion, with higher-level and more abstract beliefs justifying lower-level and less abstract beliefs. The lower beliefs, since they are now justified, become knowledge.

Scholars see religion and science as knowledge systems, in which people engage in deductive reason from the most abstract justificatory principles down to the most concrete claims.[11] In this elite account, beliefs are like the pyramids in Figure 1. On the ground of the hypothetical pyramid on the right is a belief such as "the Earth is 6,000 years old." To justify this belief, somewhere higher in the pyramid there needs to be a belief such as "what the Bible says is literally true," and above that, perhaps at the top, something like "God can control nature." In the pyramid on the left, a different on-the-ground belief is that the Earth is 4.5 billion years old, which is considered true because the radiometric dating of rocks is true. We know the radiometric dating is true because that which is observed through human senses is true.

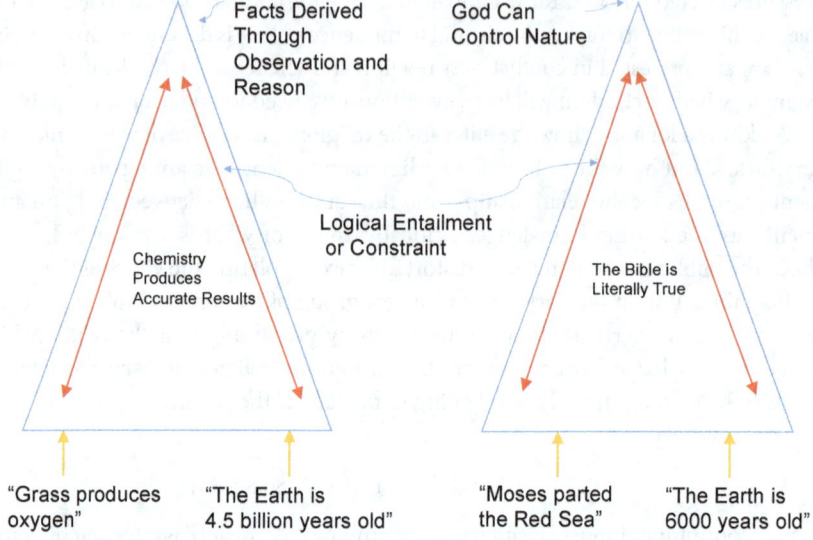

FIGURE 1. Hypothetical Knowledge Systems.

All of the lower parts of the pyramid not only have to be logically consistent with each other, but have to be logically consistent with what is above them. In this view of structure of beliefs, beliefs from the bottom of opposing pyramids such as "Moses parted the Red Sea" and "grass produces oxygen" cannot be held by the same person, because if you follow each claim up through the levels of deductive justification, they end up in logically incompatible places near or at the top of each pyramid. Put simply, in this view, if you believe in the method that produced the statement about grass you cannot believe that the sea parted due to divine intervention. Or, to turn to my introductory example, if you believe God created humans, not evolutionary forces, you cannot also believe scientific claims about global warming. Figure 1 is a depiction of the religion and science conflict as portrayed in the Huffington Post.[12]

Critically, academics and other elites generally hold to these knowledge systems of deductive belief for the issues that they focus upon. Moreover, I would describe the tasks of philosophy, theology, and science as making the vertical and horizontal links in pyramids as logically coherent as possible. In fact, you could argue that this is what academic training *is,* where expertise on a topic is learning to justify your lower-level beliefs with higher-level ones.

Any set of beliefs could be organized in this way. We can imagine that knowledge about baseball could be so organized, and if one listens to sports radio, there are a lot of middle-aged men in America who have intricately organized, logically coherent justificatory belief systems about that sport. That is not how most people view baseball. But, religion and science have historically been defined *as* these pyramids. Peter Harrison persuasively argues that the interaction between science and religion around the time of the 16th Century Reformation led to *both* religion and science being defined by elites as hierarchical belief structures.[13]

Academics and other elites reason in this way because they exist in institutions that reward them for it. The philosophy professor who does not reason in this way will be denied tenure. If this very book has inconsistent fact claims at the bottom, or does not describe its higher-level principles accurately enough, it would not be published. However, and again critically, members of the public are generally not rewarded for formulating logical structures like this about religion or science, or at least do not have logical structures that reach quite as high or have the same degree of coherence. They may have spent the effort to develop such structures in other areas, like sports or politics. I will examine social science research on the coherence of the public's belief systems much more closely in Chapter 5. But, once we no longer assume that the public has a hierarchical justified system of belief back to first principles concerning religion and science—as is assumed in the scholarly literature—we will have to rethink the entire "religion and science debate."

CONFLICT OVER WHAT? THREE TYPES OF RELATIONSHIPS BETWEEN RELIGION AND SCIENCE

We have discussed what conflict *is*, and between *whom* it occurs (public or elites). The final distinction is conflict over *what?* The response from scientists would be—knowledge, of course, because we scientists are only discovering knowledge. However, that turns out to be a very distorted view of the situation. There are three possible relationships, and thus possible conflicts, between religion and science. These are the relationships of systemic knowledge, propositional belief and morality.

The Systemic Knowledge Relationship and Possible Conflict

I use the term systemic knowledge to indicate depictions of relationship and possible conflict that assume people are using hierarchical systems of justified belief like those represented in the pyramids in Figure 1. The vast majority of the claims about conflict are that science justifies concrete beliefs about nature through reason and observation, while religion justifies belief through faith and authority. Systemic knowledge conflict will be most recognizable to readers—in fact, I suspect most would wonder what else the religion and science debate could possibly be about. The common image is of a debate between justifying claims about the age of the Earth by consulting the Bible vs. justifying its age by radiometric dating.

There is a strong and a weak version of the systemic knowledge relationship that depends on what science "is" or requires, which parallels the distinction made by philosophers and historians between the use of methodological and metaphysical naturalism in science.[14] The weak version assumes that the apex of the scientific knowledge pyramid is methodological naturalism, which is "a disciplinary method that says nothing about God's existence," where fact claims are justified through observation and reason.[15] With methodological naturalism, only natural processes can be invoked as explanation, and science cannot use the supernatural in its explanations or methods. But, science would make no claims about that which cannot be empirically investigated, like the existence of God.

In this weak version of the systemic knowledge relationship, people could not believe in a demonstrable scientific claim about nature (e.g., how plants work) and a religious claim about nature that *is* testable (e.g., the Earth is six thousand years old). That is, believing in a young Earth would mean you could not believe in scientists' facts about other topics—and hence there would be conflict. But, this weak version would allow for people who believe in scientific facts about plants to also believe in nonempirical claims like the existence of God, Heaven, the Virgin Birth and so on. This weak version of the systemic knowledge relationship is most commonly portrayed by the elites in the academic religion and science debate, with the assumption that any conflict comes from violating its precepts.

The strong version of the systemic knowledge relationship assumes not only methodological naturalism, but also that science requires *metaphysical* naturalism, where science actively "denies the existence of a transcendent God."[16] This is most recognizable as the position of the scientific atheists. Metaphorically, the apex of the scientific pyramid in this strong version is metaphysical naturalism, which requires that a person could not believe scientific claims based on scientific methodology about why plants move and also believe in a nontestable claim like the existence of God. You could also not believe two on-the-ground fact claims—one religious and one scientific—even if the religious one is never examined by science. For example, a Catholic could not believe in scientific claims about global warming and in the Resurrection, even if there is no scientist who ever makes a claim about the resurrection (e.g. there is no scientific discipline of anti-Resurrection studies).

I will show in subsequent chapters that the elites in the debate assume either the strong or weak version of the systemic knowledge relationship. This is typically indicated by claiming that someone's belief in one fact claim implies belief in another (implicitly, because they are connected by the same justificatory belief above), or by reference to the justificatory beliefs themselves (typically called "method"). The elites' extrapolation of this relationship to the public has hampered our understanding of religion and science. I will show that it is implausible for the public to have such a conflict between religion and science because, as I will discuss below, people do not have the time, motivation, or desire to make their beliefs logically coherent in the way this model demands.

Of course, elites have had the time and have been rewarded. For example, in the infamous 1860 Oxford debate between Bishop Wilberforce and T. H. Huxley over Darwin's claims about evolution, both were elites focused on this issue. Wilberforce knew he would have to respond to Huxley, and logical coherence would have been the standard of who won the debate.[17] Similarly, in the 1925 Scopes trial, William Jennings Bryan knew he would be forced to respond to Clarence Darrow. But, members of the general public are not going to face a Darrow—or a university tenure committee, to mention another social institution that rewards logical coherence. It is important to point out that I am not opposed to systemic knowledge, nor to the academics and organizations that try to create it. I had better not be, as I work in a university that requires it. Rather, I am opposed to assuming that systemic knowledge is used by everyone for all issues, and that the public views institutions only through the lens of knowledge.

Propositional Belief Relationship and Possible Conflict

The relationship concerning propositional beliefs does not presume logical justification or deduction from more general beliefs. A proposition is an assertion without a justification—it is at the bottom of the pyramid in Figure 1 with no logical connections higher in the pyramid.[18] Any agreement or conflict remains at the propositional belief level—such as "science claims the Earth is billions of years old, but my religion tells me the Earth is 6,000 years old." No one who is rewarded to argue in terms of logical systems of ideas—such as a university professor—would reason in this way. But, it is quite plausible for the general public, who are not rewarded for using tightly connected logically coherent structures of justified belief, to do so. This relationship is not described in the current religion and science literature, which assumes a systemic knowledge relationship, but it is the best description of the public's orientation to religion and science derived from the sociological studies that I will report below.

In this model, since people do not reason up to higher-level justificatory beliefs, there is no reason why people in a tradition that has conflicting propositional belief claims with science would be in conflict over *all* scientific knowledge. For example, a believer in a six thousand-year old Earth could accept most of the claims in the field of chemistry, because chemistry contains few or no propositional statements that conflict with any religious claims. They would presumably, however, avoid the parts of science that make many conflicting statements, like geology. I will show in later chapters that there *is* evidence for this type of conflict with *some* religious groups. The question is how pervasive this more limited conflict really is, and I will suggest that it is probably limited to a very small group of religious people in the U.S. Later, I will describe the social effect of such a conflict, which is much less dramatic than would be the case if the religious public were engaged in systemic knowledge conflict with science.

Moral Relationship and Possible Conflict

I think that the moral relationship between religion and science, which often results in conflict, is dominant in at least the contemporary U.S. While academics use the term "morality" in many ways, I will follow cultural and historical sociologists who use it to mean "relating to human character or behavior considered as good or bad . . . [or] the distinction between right and wrong, or good and evil, in relation to the actions, desires, or character of responsible human beings."[19]

This relationship between religion and science is rarely if ever talked about directly, and is obscured by our focus on knowledge conflict. The relationship in many cases is one of agreement—both religion and science believe in the moral value of the relief of human suffering and that it is good to acquire knowledge about the world. This relationship is also obscured because scientists typically claim that they do not advocate for a morality. Instead, they are engaged in the morally neutral analysis of nature. However, a better way to describe the work of a chemist who is trying to understand how electrons move is that this work *does* promote a moral perspective that "inquiry into the functioning of nature is of value." Similarly, cancer research presumes the moral value that suffering is bad. It is just that there is moral consensus about these scientific activities, so they are not even considered to concern morality.

But, there are also many instances of contemporary moral conflict. For example, is it morally acceptable to take the mitochondrial DNA out of one human egg and put it in another? Is it acceptable to engage in embryonic stem cell research? More abstractly, does Darwinian theory implicitly teach a moral lesson to children? Critically, these debates are independent of any conflict over knowledge, and many religious people have been opposed to scientists on each of them.

Even if scientists do not take a public moral stance such as "destroying embryos is acceptable," scientific research and technology itself is often morally expressive. As bioethicist Erik Parens points out, technology is not morally neutral, but pushes people in particular moral directions.[20] For example, inventing a test to see whether a fetus or embryo has Down syndrome presumes that people should avoid having children with Down syndrome. Of course, people can refuse the test, but the existence of this test, and the fact that doctors are supposed to discuss it with pregnant woman, expresses the moral message.

I am not the first to see the importance of moral conflict between science and religion. Some of the historians who have been able to get a bit closer to the views of the religious public have shown how the public often has both knowledge and moral conflict with science. For example, Ronald Numbers' canonical book about creationism shows that creationist activists were often not so concerned about the fact claims of Darwinism, but rather that Darwinism was teaching youth a particular moral lesson.[21] For example, the defender of the creationist view in the Scopes trial, William Jennings Bryan, was concerned about "the paralyzing influence of Darwinism on the conscience. By substituting the law of the jungle for the teachings of Christ, it threatened the principles he valued most: democracy and Christianity." He thought that this teaching had led to both German militarism and the German decision to declare war in World War I.[22] However, historians have generally not theorized this moral conflict. I will argue that this moral conflict is more relevant to today's public than is knowledge conflict.

SUMMARY OF SUBSEQUENT CHAPTERS

This book should definitely not be considered the last word on this subject, but more like a provocation. I am pulling together information from diverse fields to lay the groundwork for my claims, and in the data analytic chapters I rely upon a myriad of data that was not originally designed to test my thesis. I want to convince others that this thesis demands further investigation.

I should be clear at the outset that I am focusing on the U.S. in order to keep a sprawling topic under control, as well as due to a lack of data from other countries and, frankly, my own limited knowledge of non-Anglophone cultures. Some of the academic debate I will be summarizing includes Britain, which has had an influence on American debates and has a strong history of an elite debate between religion and science. Moreover, besides a few brief discussions of Judaism, I am not focusing on religious minorities in the U.S. because, again, there are almost no contemporary data, primarily because each minority group represents two percent of the population or less. Therefore, my analysis is primarily about different types of Christians and the nonreligious.[23]

In Chapter 2, I start to outline the assumptions in the academic religion and science debate. I examine the academic *advocates* in the debate, the scientists and the theologians, as well as dialogue associations that share the views of the theologians, and show that they assume that the relationship between religion and science concerns systemic knowledge. The most extreme are the scientific atheists who assume the strongest version of the systemic knowledge conflict thesis—that a person who believes in any scientific facts cannot believe in any religion. I review the liberal Christian theological synthesizers, who also assume that both religious and scientific knowledge are systems, but who also think they can be synthesized into one knowledge structure. I also explain why these groups hold the positions they do.

In Chapter 3, I continue to describe the academic debate by turning to the *observers or analysts* of the debate of the scientists and theologians, who are primarily historians and sociologists. They too share the view that any relationship is based on systemic knowledge. If my entire thesis is correct, we would expect that the sociologists who study the contemporary public to see moral conflict, so I focus on the source of the sociologists' blinders.

In Chapter 4, I start to develop my overall explanation for why the participants in the academic debate assume the public is also in systemic knowledge conflict. Put simply, radical changes to the religion of the American public over the past fifty years have not been accounted for. For example, it turns out the sociology debates examined in Chapter 3 that assume systemic knowledge conflict are based on much older theories. In this chapter I examine more contemporary definitions of religion, debates about secularization, and the sociology of science and show that these all portray religion and science as *not* in knowledge conflict. Moreover, the history literature examined in the previous chapter, produced by professional historians, was largely of elite debates from fifty or more years ago. Looking at the recent history of public debates between religion and science, largely not written by historians, we see debates that are fixed resolutely on morality, not knowledge. I conclude this chapter by showing how the exemplar case of contemporary religion and science debate—Darwin and evolution—is primarily about morality.

In Chapter 5, I turn to existing research on the public to show that it is extremely unlikely that the *contemporary* religious public thinks their religion is about knowledge claims about nature, or that science is exclusively about nature. This makes systemic knowledge conflict unlikely. I begin with a history of American religion and science and conclude that it is really only in the conservative Protestant tradition that the religious public could be taught a knowledge conflict with science. I continue by examining contemporary social science research that suggests, to somewhat overstate the case, that members of the general public do not have knowledge systems—which would make systemic knowledge conflict impossible.

I continue by discussing research on the contemporary American religious public showing that conservative Protestantism is decreasingly concerned with truth and doctrine. The tradition is also becoming increasingly therapeutic—concerned with the happiness and well-being of the individual. Moreover, religious Americans in general are increasingly assembling their religious beliefs from different religious systems with less concern for what the elites would consider incompatibilities. All of this suggests that conservative Protestantism is not concerned with systemic knowledge about nature. Finally, I turn to what we know about the public's view of science and scientists, and show that it is unlikely that the public views scientists as morally neutral observers of nature, but are rather more likely to see them as morally questionable outsiders who potentially need to be controlled. This disparate research on the public provides the grounds for being skeptical that we will find systemic knowledge conflict between religious citizens and science.

In Chapter 6, I put the conflict narrative to an empirical test and do not find any religious groups where the members are in systemic knowledge conflict with science. I do find that most Christian traditions are, to varying degrees, in propositional belief conflict with science over a few fact-claims about the world—fact-claims that do not matter to the everyday lives of the vast majority of Americans. Finally, I engage in some speculation as to why—given that I did not find systemic knowledge conflict—religious people would be disproportionately engaged in propositional belief conflict. Of all the possibilities, I focus for the rest of the analyses in this book on the idea that this more limited belief conflict is actually driven by moral conflict with science.

Chapter 7 puts the moral conflict theory to an empirical test. Data that can be used to examine moral conflict between religion and science are limited because the scholars who develop data sources have presumed that science is about knowledge. However, I outline three types of moral conflict which I can indirectly examine. The first is conflict over which institution will set the meaning and purpose of society. Will we have faith in science or religion? I show that religious Americans, and conservative Protestants in particular, are in conflict with science over which institution our society should have faith in. The second is conflict over the implicit morality embedded in some scientific claims, such as Darwinism. I find that conservative Protestants are in moral conflict with science over scientific claims in the public sphere. The third conflict is over technology, such as medical technology having to do with embryonic stem cells or the genetic modification of humans. I find that conservative Protestants are in moral conflict with scientists over technology to modify the human body. I finish the chapter with a close look at interviews with religious people about reproductive genetic technology. This analysis suggests a subtle moral conflict exists over the use of this particular set of technologies.

Chapter 8 is the conclusion, and I finish by discussing the contribution of sociological analysis of the contemporary public relationship between religion and science to other disciplines in the religion and science debate. If we are to have an improved debate, we need a social location, and I ponder the possibilities. I finish by describing the research agenda necessary for this new direction in the field.

2

The Religion and Science Advocates in the Academic Debate

Unsurprisingly, the academic religion and science debate involves advocates of religion and science—theologians and scientists. In this chapter, I show that almost the entire debate involving scientists and theologians assumes that what is under debate is systemic knowledge. That is, to examine one strand, the debate is whether religion and science have always been locked in "warfare" over how to make claims about the natural world. Scientists point to Galileo's persecution by the Catholic Church for arguing that the Earth is not the center of the universe. On the other side, theologians work to resolve any conflict by making sure that there is no disagreement between the fact claims of science and that of religion. I will also explain why science and technology focus on a systemic knowledge relationship, and not on a moral relationship. Finally, I will, when possible, show that these elites assume that the public has the same relationship between religion and science as they do. They are never explicit about this. When it is not possible to determine if they are extrapolating their views to the public, the elite views remain important for us to consider because they are trying to teach the public a particular relationship between religion and science.

The scientists and the theologians create two problems for a healthy debate about religion and science in the public sphere. First, by writing as if all conflict is about knowledge, the public who consumes this material is taught that religion and science are in knowledge conflict and not moral conflict. Second, by not acknowledging that the concern with coherent knowledge is an elite activity, these writers imply that the public has systemic knowledge concerns, when in actuality the religious public may only be in propositional belief conflict with science.

Before I get to the specific reasons that members of these two groups would view themselves as engaged in a systemic knowledge relationship, let me address two general explanations. First, to reiterate what I wrote in the Introduction, these two groups comprise academics and/or have a large amount of academic training, and are rewarded for thinking extensively on this exact topic. Therefore, all else being equal, they will have worked out systemic knowledge because, to oversimplify, that is what academia trains people to do.

Second, that academics would see the specific institutions of religion and science as both systemic knowledge systems is over-determined, and indeed has its origins before the sixteenth century Reformation. From the Greeks forward, religion, and science for that matter, were virtues of the individual. Historian Peter Harrison describes an early Christian author as seeing religion as "not a system of beliefs and practices but of godliness, modes of worship, a new kind of race, and a way of life." By the time of the Reformation, the meaning of "religion" begins to shift. The "interior virtues of scientia and religio" change. While catechisms had once been understood as techniques for developing an interior piety, they now came to be the essence of some objective thing—religion. In Harrison's words, "religion was vested in creeds rather than in the hearts of the faithful." That is, "religion" shifts from an "interior disposition" to "beliefs themselves." Protestant reformers further contributed to this idea by insisting that Christians be able to articulate the doctrines, and do so in propositional terms. The printing press also contributed to this process, as Protestant clergy stressed the importance of the inculcation of religious doctrines—now available more broadly. Indeed, catechisms came to embody the content of the Christian religion.[1]

Now conceptualized as a system of beliefs, religion could be "true" or "false." With this new idea of religion as a system of belief comes the idea that religion can be rationally justified. Harrison almost perfectly depicts my pyramid metaphor when he writes that for idealists, "the perfect religion would be a body of propositions, firmly established by ironclad logical demonstrations." At this point, he continues, "belief could be described as the act of giving intellectual assent to propositions."[2]

Ironically from the contemporary perspective, the "sciences" of the seventeenth century—called natural history and natural philosophy—were given the task of providing some of the general warrants to justify the new propositional religion, which reinforces the idea that religion should be understood as "a system of beliefs" that requires rational support. With this definition, religion was now capable of conflict with science because, in Harrison's words, "religion consists of factual claims that should be subject to scientific confirmation." The end result is that religion is "characterized by propositional beliefs, which, on par with beliefs in other spheres, require rational justification."[3]

There is general truth in the common wisdom that Protestantism is concerned with proper belief and Catholicism is concerned with proper practice, so this is a particularly Protestant way of looking at religion. But, it was Protestants who were at the center of these changes, and it was Protestantism that dominated the public square, academia, and public life in the U.S. until the mid-twentieth century. This idea of religion as a hierarchically justified system of belief and facts became the elite conception of what "religion" was, and thus influenced debate from that point forward.

So, any academic should be prone to seeing both religion and science as systemic knowledge. I will argue in later chapters that the "religion" described by Harrison as emerging before the Reformation and continuing to today either was never held by the ordinary members of these religions, or has run its course and is being changed into something else, at least in the U.S. For the remainder of the chapter I will examine how academic scientists and theologians view their own beliefs and the relationship to the beliefs of the other institution. Besides their own self-image of producing systemic knowledge, I will also explain why they see themselves in systemic knowledge *conflict* with the other, and why the possibility of moral conflict never seems to be discussed.

CONTEMPORARY SCIENTISTS IN THE DEBATE: WE ONLY PRODUCE KNOWLEDGE

Obviously one important set of elites in any debate between religion and science are contemporary scientists. They generally believe that any conflict with science by the public, religious or otherwise, is about a lack of knowledge by the public. For there to be a "religion and science" debate there must be scientists, but having them in a debate means accepting their premise that any conflict with them is only about knowledge.

The field of science communication offers us some studies of academic scientists in general, which offer background for my later examples of scientists in the religion and science debate itself. These studies *do* evaluate what these scientists think the public's views are, and reveal that scientists think that any conflict between them and the public—religious or otherwise—is about knowledge of the natural world. One study concludes that "almost universally" scientists "believe the public is inadequately informed about science topics." Further, scientists believe that, "the public is uninterested in becoming more knowledgeable," and that scientific illiteracy is at the root of opposition to new technologies and adequate science funding. The authors also summarize several studies that find that "scientists view the public as non-rational and unsystematic in their thinking such that they rely on anecdotes." That is, the public is accused of not using a system of knowledge. Other studies have found that scientists see the public as emotional, fear prone, focused on the sensational, self-interested, and "stubborn in the face of new evidence."[4]

Similarly, a survey of members of the American Academy for the Advancement of Science found that 85 percent thought that "the public does not know very much about science" and this was a "major" problem "for science in general." When scientists were asked about public engagement, studies suggest that scientists view engagement as chiefly about information dissemination rather than dialogue. Moreover, "the primary argument that scientists give for public engagement is the need to increase citizen knowledge . . . or allay unfounded fears," with engagement usually "framed in terms of providing information." That is, communication with the public, religious or otherwise, is about knowledge. Anticipating my later point that conflict may actually be about morality, these studies show that the key difficulty for scientists in public engagement "may be that scientists often believe public debates should turn on logic and cost-benefit-analysis accounting whereas the public wants consideration of factors such as fairness, ethics, and accountability." The study authors' overall conclusion is that "scientists believe the public knows little about a range of scientific issues and that they see this knowledge deficit as shaping risk perceptions, policy preferences, and decisions." Scientists "emphasize a need to educate the public so that non-experts will make policy choices in line with the preferences of scientists."[5]

In other words, scientists are in the thrall of what communications scholars consider to be one of the great myths about public communication—the knowledge deficit model.[6] This is the belief, largely held by scientists, that "ignorance is at the root of social conflict over science. . . . Once citizens are brought up to speed on the science, they will be more likely to judge scientific issues as scientists do and controversy will go away."[7]

The knowledge deficit model held by scientists dismisses any possibility that the relationship between religion and science, and any possible conflict, is moral. Indeed, it can lead scientists to redefine obvious cases of moral conflict as being about knowledge. For example, Sir Peter Medawar commented on public fears of genetic manipulation in the 1970s by ignoring the obvious moral conflict between scientists and the public and attributing conflict to a lack of knowledge. He wrote that "I find it difficult to excuse the lack of confidence which otherwise quite sensible people have in the scientific profession . . . for their fearfulness, laymen have only themselves to blame and their nightmares are a judgement on them for their deep-seated scientific illiteracy."[8]

Scientists Who Reflect on the Public's Views of Religion and Science

I lack a survey of the scientists who are engaged in the religion and science debate, so I will instead conduct a small case study of a group of elite scientists engaged in a religion and science event. The assumption by scientific elites that systemic knowledge conflict also organizes the thought of the religious public is quite evident in the 2005 Terry Lectures at Yale. That year was the 100th anniversary of the prestigious lectureship devoted to "religion and its application to human welfare in the light of scientific knowledge and philosophical insights."[9]

This makes a good case study because the prominence of the event meant that some of the more influential scientists who had focused on the religion and science debate were invited to speak, and because they were asked their views of the religious public. The fact that it was held under the auspices of the Yale Divinity School suggests that if anything the scientists would be more restrained in what they would otherwise say about religion.

The Yale selection committee decided to ask the question why the controversy between science and religion in the public "continues with such force."[10] The organizers asked a philosopher of religion, a historian of religion and science, a sociologist of religion and three scientists to each provide an explanation for the continued conflict in the public. What resulted is that all of the lecturers assumed that "controversy" was about knowledge claims, except, as we might expect, the sociologist, who had more knowledge of the contemporary religious public's views.[11] The scientists in particular reinforced the idea that the public's conflict was about knowledge claims.

Paleontologist Keith Thomson introduced the series of lectures by repeating the systemic knowledge conflict narrative, saying "there is bound to be a debate because science and religion are two very different entities with different ways of arriving at 'truth.' Both have claims on both our reason and our intuition." One disadvantage for religion in this debate is that it is seen as "imposing a body of truths that must be accepted on faith and revelation rather than discovery and analysis." In case this was not clear enough, he then wonders what science's greatest liability is "when it comes to public understanding and acceptance." He concludes that the limit on public acceptance is that science "proceeds by making a changing and progressively more uncommon sense out of common sense . . . People distrust a science that gives changing, more refined, answers."[12] Conflict for Thomson is driven by the powerful knowledge-making apparatus of science.

Another scientist on the panel, Lawrence Krauss, at first sounds like he sees moral conflict as the cause of the "continued debate," when he says that conflict is the result of "fear of the moral implications of science and its perceived challenge to religion." However, he also says that debates about evolution are a "straw man," and "what people are challenging is science itself and the methods by which it investigates the universe." So, he sees the religious public as in systemic knowledge conflict with science. It turns out the link to morality for Krauss is that the loss of epistemic standing of the "God caused nature" perspective leads to thinking that science "is inherently atheistic, and thus immoral."[13] So, any moral conflict is simply the result of the fact that the supernatural is not allowed as a justification for fact claims. In fairness to Krauss, he was focusing on the intelligent design movement, and this is one place where both sides are talking about knowledge, with intelligent design advocates trying to overthrow the scientific pyramid that has methodological naturalism at the top.

The first two scientists appear to see a strong version of the systemic knowledge conflict between the religious public and scientists. The final scientist, Kenneth R. Miller, assumed the weak version of systemic knowledge relationship, probably because he is a Catholic who uses Catholic theology to talk about religion and science. Early in his talk he acknowledged that opponents of Darwin often give moral reasons for their opposition, that "Darwin's great idea is indeed seen as the foundation of everything wrong in society, including lawlessness, abortion, pornography,, and the dissolution of marriage."[14] However, his chapter is not about moral conflict but rather primarily shows that Intelligent Design claims are scientifically false.

He finishes with a section that argues for the standard Catholic account of systemic knowledge compatibility based on a science that assumes methodological naturalism. "Nothing could be worse for people of faith than to defer to the Bible to [sic] as a source of scientific knowledge that contradicted direct, empirical studies of nature" he begins. Saint Augustine "warned of the danger inherent in using the Bible as a book of geology, astronomy, or biology . . . to Augustine, the eternal spiritual truth of the Bible would only be weakened by pretending that it was also a book of science." Opposing atheist advocates of the strong version of systemic knowledge conflict, where science requires metaphysical naturalism, he rejects their attempts to claim that "science alone can lead us to truth regarding the purpose of existence."[15] In sum, Miller does not see conflict between his version of science and his religion, but the relationship he depicts is nonetheless the relationship between two forms of systemic knowledge. As we will see in a few pages, he would fit in well with the theologians in this debate.

Scientific Atheists and Their Allies

By far the group of scientists engaged in the religion and science debate with the biggest soap box are the scientific atheists. For example, an incredible 21.4 percent of a random sample of Americans claim to have heard of Richard Dawkins, undoubtedly the most influential scientific atheist, whereas only 4.3 percent claim to have heard of evangelical scientist Francis Collins, who we will meet later in this chapter.[16] In general, the scientific atheists have a greater influence on the public's views of religion and science than any other type of academic.

The systemic knowledge conflict view is evident in their writings. They portray both religion and science—among elites and the public—as iron-clad hierarchically structured systems of belief. On the science side, science requires metaphysical naturalism, and therefore any conflict between religion and science is the strong systemic form. That is, if you believe in one scientific knowledge claim that has been institutionalized by the scientific community you must believe in them all, and you certainly cannot believe any knowledge claim that is "non-scientific" such as the existence of God. For the scientific atheists, religion must fit into the scientific pyramid or be declared false, starting with what they take to be a fact claim about the world demonstrable through scientific observation—whether God exists.

Regarding values, scientists are not promoting any, but are simply investigating nature. Religiously derived values appear, but they are driven by what the scientific atheists consider the central knowledge claim—the existence of God. Were this false knowledge claim to be eliminated, then the faulty values of the religious public would also be repaired.

This belief in pure logical coherence and hierarchical justification up to first principles is exemplified by Dawkins' admitted theological ignorance. From the view of religious critics of Dawkins, he needs to know something about what he is criticizing. In my terms, religious people complain that Dawkins does not know anything about the middle of the religious pyramid—what Christians really think about creation, miracles, the human and so on. This critique was most evocatively stated by Terry Eagleton in his review of Dawkins' book *The God Delusion:*

> Imagine someone holding forth on biology whose only knowledge of the subject is the *Book of British Birds,* and you have a rough idea of what it feels like to read Richard Dawkins on theology. Card-carrying rationalists like Dawkins, who is the nearest thing to a professional atheist we have had since Bertrand Russell, are in one sense the least well-equipped to understand what they castigate, since they don't believe there is anything there to be understood, or at least anything worth understanding. This is why they invariably come up with vulgar caricatures of religious faith that would make a first-year theology student wince. The more they detest religion, the more ill-informed their criticisms of it tend to be.[17]

But, this ignorance is not a problem if religion and science are assumed to be perfectly coherent hierarchical structures of knowledge or belief, where all lower-level beliefs are dependent on the top belief. Indeed, Dawkins has admitted that he has not bothered to learn much theology because it is all irrelevant. In reaction to the critique that he does not know very much theology, Dawkins wrote "Yes, I have, of course, met this point before. It sounds superficially fair. But it presupposes that there is something in Christian theology to be ignorant about. The entire thrust of my position is that Christian theology is a non-subject. It is empty. Vacuous. Devoid of coherence or content. . . . The only part of theology that could possibly demand my attention is the part that purports to demonstrate that God does exist. This part of theology I have, indeed, studied with considerable attention. And found it utterly wanting."[18]

He has effectively defined religion as a hierarchical logical structure of knowledge with "God exists" at the apex. Knocking out this apex leaves us with the only logical conclusion, that all claims below it on the pyramid are false. Moreover, science and religion are coherent knowledge structures that you have to believe *all* of, because you agree with the first principles, and since these first principles are incompatible, you cannot believe any components of the opposing structure.

Dawkins and other scientific atheists have often been accused of being fundamentalists, but the reasons offered for the similarity with Protestant fundamentalism are varied. If we focus on what the scientific atheists think structures of knowledge are, Dawkins is like a Protestant fundamentalist pastor. Both believe in iron-clad hierarchical knowledge in science and religion. Fundamentalist elites simply insert a different belief at the top and utterly reject any scientific claim that does not fit with that top belief, such as the age of the Earth. Critically, both Dawkins and his fundamentalist adversaries are teaching the public the idea that any conflict between religion and science concerns the strong version of systemic knowledge.

We can also consider the views of Jerry A. Coyne, who is probably the most influential American scientific atheist. The first page of his book *Faith versus Fact* reveals the base assumption of what the debate is about when he writes that the book "is about the different ways that science and religion regard faith, ways that make them incompatible for discovering what's true about our universe. My thesis is that religion and science compete in many ways to describe reality—they both make 'existence claims' about what is real—but use different tools to meet this goal." In my terms, he thinks both religion and science are primarily methods for making claims about the natural world. Indeed, he sees that "the truth claims religion makes about the universe turns it into a kind of science, but a science using weak evidence to make strong statements about what is true." "Science and religion, then, are competitors in the business of finding out what is true about our universe."[19] A lot of his book consists of arguments that religion is about knowledge generation and not about something like moral values. This seems critical to his argument, because if religion is not about knowledge production, then as a scientist he has no argument against it.

Like Dawkins he spends a lot of time on the fact claim that God does not exist because, without an empirically verifiable deity, the entire logically deductive pyramid of religious belief below it collapses. His assumption is that these beliefs are logically coherent. For example, he says the reason that elite scientists are less likely to be religious is that "science's habit of requiring evidence for belief, combined with its culture of pervasive doubt and questioning, *must* often carry over to other aspects of one's life—including the possibility of religious faith." I emphasize the word "must" in the quote to focus on the assumption he is making about logical consistency. He further demonstrates his assumption by saying that some people can wall off this logic: it is the religious scientists who "happen to be the ones who can compartmentalize two incompatible worldviews in their heads."[20]

What is most striking about Coyne's book is not the fairly standard scientific atheist assumptions about what religion is. Rather, it is that he so deeply assumes systemic knowledge conflict that he apparently does not realize that his book makes the case that the actual conflict between science and religion is over morality. In his final chapter titled "Why Does It Matter," he talks about the harms that come from the public using religion to make claims about the natural world. He starts with an extreme and rare case to stand in for all religion, which is "those sects that reject medical care in favor of prayer and faith healing, and enforce this belief on their children," by which he is primarily referring to Christian Science and Jehovah's Witnesses.[21] Like the Huffington Post bloggers we met in the first few pages of this book, he also claims that religion leads to denial of climate change by citing the religious claims of conservative politicians and an energy industry-funded evangelical think tank. As we will see in Chapter 6, this claim is just based on the assumption that people who do not believe science in one instance cannot believe it in another. This one extremely rare claim and one empirically false claim *are* about knowledge conflict.

But, the main reasons he thinks that religion should be gotten rid of is that he does not like its moral agenda. In addition to faith healing and climate science, there are "several other areas where science clashes with faith in the public arena." The first is embryonic stem cell research, which has been limited because of religious beliefs that embryos are equivalent to persons. The second is vaccination against the virus that causes cervical cancer, which is spread by sexual contact. Because "many Christians oppose any sex outside of marriage" they oppose the mandatory vaccinations because they think it will encourage sex outside of marriage. Another harm that springs "from the morality claims of faith, claims that flout both science and reason" is "opposition to assisted dying." Most people think it is "merciful to euthanize our dog or cat if it's suffering terribly" but followers of many religions reject this because humans are "the special creation of God, and uniquely endowed with souls."[22]

While these religious moral claims are all dependent on facts to the extent that religious morality is dependent on a belief in God, these facts are very far up the pyramid. That Coyne's primary opposition to religion appears to be moral can be seen in the fact that the religious opponents of embryonic stem cell research, sex outside of marriage, and opposition to assisted dying would agree with all of the scientific claims about these phenomena. They would agree with embryologists' claims of how many cells an embryo has and what would happen if you were to let it continue dividing. They would agree with how viruses cause cervical cancer. They would agree with descriptions of how people die and how their dying could be assisted. They would just disagree over what we *should* do about these things.

These moral debates in the public sphere would be much more efficient if Coyne would just define the morality of science and directly argue about morality.

There are too many scientific atheists to conduct an analysis of each one. I will conclude this section by examining the historian Ronald Numbers' contribution to the Yale conference described above, in which he compiled the views of religion of famous scientific atheists. Numbers is making a point about intelligent design theory, but I repurpose his compilation to show that the scientific atheists not only assume that religion only concerns knowledge claims, but that disproving one knowledge claim by religion through science invalidates the entire knowledge structure—including belief in God—because each piece of knowledge is logically dependent on each other.

Numbers writes that atheist Daniel Dennett has "portrayed Darwinism as 'a universal solvent, capable of cutting right to the heart of everything in sight'—and particularly effective in dissolving religious beliefs."[23] This is only possible if all religious beliefs are so utterly dependent upon the fact claim that humans did not evolve from lower life forms, or more generally that events do not happen in the world for random reasons, that removing this one piece of the knowledge pyramid causes its collapse.

Scientific atheists also make it clear that science and religion are only about knowledge by comparing knowledge claims from the two. Co-discoverer of the structure of DNA and Nobel prize winner Francis Crick wrote that "the view of ourselves as 'persons' is just as erroneous as the view that the Sun goes around the Earth. . . . In the fullness of time, educated people will believe there is no soul independent of the body, and hence no life after death." Oxford chemist Peter Atkins notes appreciatively that science abrogates to itself "the claim to be the sole route to true, complete, and perfect knowledge." Harvard biologist E. O. Wilson writes that "the final decisive edge enjoyed by scientific naturalism will come from its capacity to explain traditional religion, its chief competition, as a wholly material phenomenon. Theology is not likely to survive as an independent intellectual discipline." The late William Provine, who was a biologist and historian at Cornell, wrote that "modern evolutionary biology tells us loud and clear [that] there are no gods, no purposes, no goal-directed forces of any kind. There is no life after death . . . There is no ultimate foundation for ethics, no ultimate meaning to life, and no free will for humans either."[24]

In all of these claims against religion by famous scientists, religion only concerns knowledge about the natural world, and therefore is not only in conflict with scientific knowledge, but is doomed to extinction once it is shown that scientific knowledge is superior. Most critically, religion and science are each logically coherent systems of fact claims reaching up to first principles (reason and observation vs. faith), so you cannot believe in one component of a system without believing in them all.

Why Scientists Assume Any Relationship Concerns Systemic Knowledge

To explain why the scientists see religion and science as both systemic knowledge structures, and that these are then in conflict, we must start by reiterating what I wrote at the beginning of this chapter. That is, post-Reformation definitions *do* portray religion as a set of hierarchically oriented beliefs, so we can see why scientists who are not familiar with the religious public would assume that for ordinary religious people "religion" means hierarchically structured beliefs about knowledge. I think science *is* a systemic knowledge system, although I will argue that it is also a moral system.

In addition to this general explanation, over the years scholars have pointed out that promoting the idea that they are in knowledge conflict with religion is critical to scientists' self-identity and is a way to gather resources. In a seminal series of articles during the emergence of the field of the sociology of scientific knowledge in the early 1980s, Thomas Gieryn and colleagues examined the boundary drawing that scientists have historically engaged in against pseudoscience, mechanics and religion. Drawing such boundaries was useful for scientists' professional goals, such as "acquisition of intellectual authority and career opportunities."[25]

For example, referring to the efforts of John Tyndall in Victorian England, Gieryn writes that "because religion and mechanics thwarted (in different ways) Tyndall's effort to expand the authority and resources of scientists, he often chose them as 'contrast cases' when constructing ideologies of science for the public."[26] In a later application of these ideas to American court trials over teaching creationism in the classroom, Gieryn and his colleagues conclude that the relationship between religion and science was used to advance the goals of justifying investments in scientific research and education, and the monopolization of "professional authority over a sphere of knowledge in order to protect collective resources for scientists."[27]

Historian Peter Harrison also sees that the emergence of what we would now recognize as science in the nineteenth century was partially accomplished by "drawing sharp boundaries and positing the existence of contrast cases" including "science and religion." "Religion is what science is not: a kind of negative image of science" writes Harrison, and "the conflict myth continues to serve the role for which it was originally fashioned in the late nineteenth century, of establishing and maintaining boundaries of the modern conception 'science.'"[28]

Scientists then promote the myth of an enduring and timeless knowledge conflict between religion and science, with scientists promoting the idea of Galileo being an early martyr for science at the hands of religion. Galileo never went to jail—to paraphrase the title of a book meant to disabuse scientists and others of the conflict myth—but it is in the interests of scientists to continue to say that he did.[29]

In a fascinating analysis of how scientists describe the Galileo affair in textbooks and other texts, communications scholar Thomas Lessl finds that the stories about Galileo "reflect the master narrative of 'warfare between science and religion' that has been such a prominent feature of scientific rhetoric during the past century." In the common scientific narrative, Galileo was not only the first person to use empiricism to make discoveries about nature, but this was at the core of his conflict with the Catholic Church. Lessl cites Stephen Hawking's *A Brief History of Time*, which states that "Galileo, perhaps more than any other single person, was responsible for the birth of modern science. His renowned conflict with the Catholic Church was central to his philosophy, for Galileo was one of the first to argue that man could hope to understand how the world works, and, moreover, that we could do this by observing the real world." Such statements frustrate historians to no end, because they are not fully true. Galileo was not persecuted for his methods or his rationalistic assumptions, and defended his views as descriptions of the world created by God.[30]

We could go on and on with this, as historians show that the myths of the conflict between religion and science of Galileo, Darwin and many others, often promulgated by scientists, are incredibly persistent. The frustration of historians has reached the point where Jon Roberts calls the idea of a universal knowledge conflict between science and Christianity the "idea that wouldn't die."[31] The question is why scientists keep repeating these false statements. One reason is that contemporary science finds it useful as a way of saying what makes science distinctive and thus worthy of public investment and trust. Another plausible answer is that the myth is a type of identity-work, a set of myths that define the community of scientists in ways that are useful. For example, if older scientists want to teach new scientists that science is rational and disinterested, then it is useful to have an "other" with which to contrast yourself. In Lessl's words, "the presumed irrationality, credulity, and intellectual self-interest attributed to Galileo's opponents in the Church appear in these folk narratives as inversions of the rationalism, skepticism, and disinterestedness of science. Such dramatic demarcations attach distinctive virtues to the scientific culture and at the same time ratify its claims to institutional autonomy". Moreover, with the Galileo legend "the features of the scientific ethos that set it apart from religion are lionized, grounds for the scientific culture's professional autonomy are given an historical rationalization, and a social-evolutionary vision of science as the triumphant road to the future is dramatically visualized."[32]

THEOLOGICAL SCIENCE-RELIGION SYNTHESIZERS

The second group in the academic religion and science debate to examine are the theologian synthesizers, who, after the scientific atheists, are the most prominent.

As we would expect, most of these theologians are liberal Protestants and Catholics, and many also have a PhD in a science field and/or are practicing scientists.

They assume that the relationship between religion and science concerns systemic knowledge, and therefore any conflict is due to the failure to synthesize the fact claims of religion and science into one hierarchically structured logically coherent pyramid. They reject the view that science requires metaphysical naturalism, and take the more mainstream view that science only requires methodological naturalism. That is, science cannot address non-demonstrable claims like the existence of God, but science should address demonstrable claims about the natural world like the age of the Earth. The goal of the synthesizers is then to avoid the weak version of systemic knowledge conflict by making religious knowledge claims consistent with scientific knowledge claims generated through methodological naturalism. For example, they want to interpret their religious tradition to make the Genesis narrative consistent with scientific discoveries about the Big Bang. I will examine the writings of a few of the more influential theological synthesizers to show that in their striving to avoid conflict they deeply presume that the relationship between religion and science concerns systemic knowledge.[33]

Again, I do not want to give the impression that these efforts are wrong. Indeed, you could argue that this task of synthesis is what theology *is*. Rather, my goal is to point out that this perspective cannot be extrapolated to the public.

Ian Barbour's Four Relationships Between Religion and Science

To see the most common academic depiction of the relationship between religion and science, we should start with the late Ian Barbour, who was one of the modern progenitors of discussions of the relationship between religion and science. Wikipedia, which is undoubtedly a primary information source for the public, claims that Barbour was "credited with literally creating the contemporary field of science and religion." In the citation nominating him for the Templeton Prize, which he won in 1999, John B. Cobb wrote that "no contemporary has made a more original, deep, and lasting contribution toward the needed integration of scientific and religious knowledge and values than Ian Barbour. With respect to the breadth of topics and fields brought into this integration, Barbour has no equal."[34]

Note that, like many of the other academics discussed in this chapter, he does not explicitly make a distinction between elite arguments and what the public would think. While he and others in this group would probably acknowledge a difference, by not being explicit the reader is left to assume that his claims are true for all religious people.

For Barbour, the relationship between religion and science is resolutely about knowledge. Actually, science is only about knowledge, and religion sometimes has to change its theology due to new knowledge, or scientific knowledge raises ethical debates that religion can contribute to. But the reaction by religion is always to the knowledge produced by science, not to any of the social or moral aspects of science. Finally, knowledge is or should be coherent within each of the two systems, which reinforces the systemic knowledge conflict perspective.

The capstone book of Barbour's career is *When Science Meets Religion: Enemies, Strangers or Partners*, published in 2000, in which he reiterates his typology of possible relationships between religion and science. He says early on that this "typology was developed for fundamental science as a form of knowledge, not for applied science in its impact on society and nature." There are four possible relationships between religion and science: "conflict," "independence," "dialogue," and "integration." That all of these relationships are about knowledge is clear from the second sentence of the book: "Most of the founders of the scientific revolution were devout Christians who held that in their scientific work they were studying the handiwork of the Creator." That is, these early scientists were making fact claims about nature, and they saw these fact claims as logically consistent with their theological belief. The second paragraph emphasizes that what is important is that science is a knowledge producer, and that knowledge challenges religion: "New discoveries in science have challenged many classical religious ideas. In response, some people have defended traditional doctrines, others have abandoned the tradition, and still others have reformulated long-held concepts in the light of science."[35] Again, this is important activity for the elites, but Barbour does not mention that the public might have a different set of priorities, or that religion may be about more than facts about the natural world.

The book is structured around five of "the most widely debated questions," over which science and religion could have a relationship. These are all about knowledge—and all are knowledge claims by scientists that religion has to react to. First, science has shown that the Big Bang occurred, and religion should discuss what this means. Second, quantum physics has shown inherent uncertainty in the universe, and theology can think about what this means for theological thought—in my terms, what quantum physics means for the entire pyramid of theological belief. Third, Darwinism has shown a number of facts about where humans came from, and theology has developed to consider a more immanent God who creates over a long period of time through evolution. Fourth, scientists have suggested that due to genetics and body chemistry, freedom is an illusion. This calls into question the soul and the mind vs. matter distinction, but some theologians have begun to re-think those ideas in light of the science. Fifth, scientists have shown that nature works through rules, but some theologians have taken to showing that this can be made compatible with God acting in the world in a way that does not violate scientific views. Every one of these questions portrays a science that is producing knowledge, and thus religion must react to that knowledge either by changing the system of religious belief or interpreting the meaning of that knowledge for the scientists. The debate is most certainly not about the morals promulgated by scientists.

This framing of the relationship as *only* concerning knowledge is even more clear when we turn to his four possible relationships, which assume that both science and religion are separate, logically coherent belief structures. The first relationship, "conflict," is narrated through debates between Christian Biblical literalists on the one side and materialist Darwinists on the other, where the debate is about "scientific evidence" for evolution.[36] So, for Barbour, explicit "conflict" is clearly about knowledge claims about nature.

"Independence" holds that science and religion "refer to differing domains of life or aspects of reality," answering "contrasting questions," that science asks "how things work and deals with objective facts;" while "religion deals with values and ultimate meaning."[37] This is akin to what was perhaps even more famously depicted as "non-overlapping magisteria" by Steven J. Gould.[38] This describes two pyramids that reach to the apex of their respective core beliefs. Independence is violated when religion makes scientific claims, such as when fundamentalists make claims about the age of the Earth, or science makes religious claims, such as when scientists promote naturalistic philosophies.

The "independence" relationship is technically advocating no relationship between religion and science, but conflict could be about systemic knowledge (if religion unjustifiably makes knowledge claims) or about morality (if science unjustifiably makes moral claims). However, when he describes the relationship in more detail and applies it to various scientific debates, the primary concern is religion trespassing into knowledge generation, not science trying to develop a moral program. Moreover, his description of the task of religion is not about morality, but usually about a different way of perceiving reality.[39]

The "dialogue" relationship is not only about knowledge, but really emphasizes that science and religion are separate logically coherent knowledge systems. One component of dialogue is talking about knowledge beyond the limits of the abilities of the conversation partner—the "limit questions" which are "raised by science but not answered within science itself." An example would be "why is there a universe at all?"; answering such a question with religion does not impact the nature of scientific knowledge itself. Another component of dialogue is "a comparison of the methods of the two fields." For example, religious ideas of what cannot be observed, like God, may help scientists develop methods for unobservable subatomic particles. Science can take from religion whatever metaphors and models may be useful for integration into its system of knowledge. Science properly remains a logical unity only beholden to its own epistemology, as in this relationship the two sides are "respecting the integrity of each other's fields."[40]

Finally, "integration" is a partnership of religion and science, and this partnership is about knowledge claims, referencing the natural theology tradition that sought proof of God in the facts of nature. For example, Stephen Hawking has claimed that "if the rate of expansion one second after the Big Bang had been smaller by even one part in a hundred thousand million million, the universe would have recollapsed before life could have formed." To Barbour, this suggests a force controlling the universe, and God "caused" scientific facts, so the system of scientific beliefs should be modified to accept this religious belief. He also references the "theology of nature" tradition, wherein theological ideas are reformulated to fit with scientific facts, such as the idea of original sin, which needs to be "reformulated in the light of science."[41]

While the point here is to mix knowledge claims between the two institutions, this integration view is even stronger in teaching people that religion and science must be logically unified entities. In the end they remain separate but each has become even more logical by not ignoring the fact claims made by each other.

Barbour actually does not advocate the "independence" relationship, which would block off religion from making any contribution to fact claims about the natural world and block off science from making religion more accurate. Independence "avoids conflict, but at the price of preventing any constructive interaction," he writes. His "own sympathies lie with Dialogue and Integration," and especially integration[42]. In general, Barbour's description of the four possible relationships between religion and science reinforces the idea that everyone holds elite standards of logical coherence of belief, and that to believe in any science is to believe in logically coherent empirical knowledge back to the apex of the knowledge pyramid described in Chapter 1. The possibility of propositional belief conflict is also never considered as it is presumed that beliefs are nestled in hierarchical systems of justification (e.g. systemic knowledge).

Alister McGrath

The dominance of the portrayal of the relationship between science and religion as conflict between logically coherent systems of belief or knowledge can be seen in the work of other influential synthesizers. For example, the prolific Alister McGrath, who has doctoral degrees in molecular biology and theology, is currently the Andreas Idreos Professor of Science and Religion at Oxford University. This long-time participant in these debates titled a 1999 book simply *Science and Religion: An Introduction*. "Science and religion" is implicitly the history of elites trying to synthesize the knowledge systems of religion and science. The debate is about how one would know anything about the world—a concept high in each pyramid—and the book delves extensively into the philosophy of science and religion, debates over creation, natural theology as well as issues like whether God acts through the indeterminacies in quantum theory.[43] It is not acknowledged that this is a history of elite debates, and it is either presumed that this is what the religion and science debate "is," or that the public views the debate the same as the elites.

Another book by McGrath is titled *The Foundations of Dialogue in Science and Religion*. Were this focused on the contemporary American public, the foundations of dialogue might concern embryonic stem cell research and be a dialogue about whether scientists should consider other values besides the relief of suffering in their moral calculations. But, given that the dialogue between science and religion is the (unacknowledged) elite debate between theologians and scientists, the book is purely about systemic knowledge. For example, one chapter asks what the differences are between religion and science in how "information about the world is obtained and its reliability assessed."[44]

He does write that attention has been paid to "ethical matters," such as "whether recent scientific developments (such as genetic engineering) raise fundamental religious and moral issues." However, systematic engagement with issues like ethics "rests upon a prior substantial engagement with questions of *method*—including such issues as the way in which knowledge is gained and confirmed, the manner in which evidence is accumulated and assimilated, and particularly the manner in which the world is represented."[45] That is, ethics first depends upon knowledge, and knowledge is therefore more important.

John Polkinghorne

Among the most famous of these theologian-scientists is John Polkinghorne, a theoretical physicist who later became a theologian and Anglican priest. Later knighted by the Queen, and a recipient of the Templeton Prize, like other theologian-scientists his goal is to make scientific and religious knowledge compatible and logically consistent. For example, the Bible does not say anything about quantum mechanics, but quantum mechanics can be made consistent with Christian theology. A long quote gives a sense of his concerns:

> Quantum theory was the first branch of physics to make it plain that the laws of nature do not always have a tightly predictive character rather, sometimes they can take only probabilistic form. . . . Unpredictability is an epistemological property, for it concerns what we can know about what is going on. How we relate what we know to what is actually the case is a central problem in philosophy, and perhaps the problem in the philosophy of science. . . . In the case of quantum theory, this realist strategy has been followed almost universally. . . . In the case of the intrinsic unpredictabilities of chaos theory, the realist option has been a far less popular move so far. Only a minority of us have made it. . . . We have done so not only because it accords with a certain scientific instinct but also because we see here the possibility of the metaphysical gain of describing a physical world whose process is not only subtle but also supple, in a way that may offer a glimmer of hope of beginning to be able to accommodate

our basic human experiences of intentional agency and our religious intuition of God's providential interaction with creation.[46]

This dialogue is not about moral values. Nor is it about propositional belief claims where one fact-claim in the Bible contradicts a fact-claim of science. Rather, this dialogue is about whether entire systems of knowledge built up over the centuries are consistent with the scientific system of knowledge.

Why Theologians See Conflict as about Knowledge and Belief

I have three basic assertions for why these theologians see conflict as concerning systemic knowledge. The first is seemingly obvious, which is that theology is defined as "a system of religious beliefs or ideas,"[47] so obviously those who are experts in theology will talk of systems of related beliefs or ideas. But, that does not explain the focus on knowledge. Indeed, there is another type of theologian that is not considered to be part of a religion and science debate, who are, to use the Christian terms, moral theologians (Catholic) and Christian Social Ethicists (Protestants). The fact that the second type of theologian is not thought to be engaged in a "religion and science debate," even when they debate ethics with scientists, shows the utter dominance of the knowledge perspective.

A second reason why the synthesizing theologians only see knowledge conflict is because they are focused on *dialogue* with scientists—and scientists only think of themselves as engaged in discovering knowledge. Indeed, many of the most prominent of these synthesizers started their careers as academic scientists and only later became theologians. Science is clearly the dominant partner in this dialogue, as theology is reacting to scientific developments, not the inverse. Even if theologians were to recognize various moral conflicts between religion and science, they would not be able to get scientists to focus on morality because this is not what scientists think science "does."

The final reason is that theologians do not have any systematic way of getting input from the ordinary members of their religions—theology is not known for using the sociology of religion as a source. I will argue below that the conflict for the religious public is more concerned with morality. The one-way flow from theologian to the pews means that the public's view of religion and science that would contradict the theologians' natural inclination cannot reach its target.

DIALOGUE ASSOCIATIONS

Associations that try to produce dialogue and understanding between scientists and religious people are very similar to the theological synthesizers. The organizations are largely led by religious scientists. These are probably the most public face of the religion and science debate because of their websites and their educational materials produced for a general audience. And, to continue the narrative of this chapter, they portray any relationship between religion and science as about knowledge, not about morals or values.

However, the fact that these associations try to interact with the public allows me to begin to develop my argument about the public's views. Segueing into my analysis of later chapters, I will show that the closer these associations get to interacting with the religious *public*, and not just the elites, they unreflectively start describing the relationship—and conflict—as moral and not about knowledge. I examine two associations that are arguably the most visible—one because of its founder and topical focus, and the other because of its association with the most prominent scientific organization in the world.

BioLogos

BioLogos is concerned with integrating scientific claims about biology and evolution with evangelical Protestant belief. Part of its centrality to the debate is the result of its focus on the most prominent disagreement between religion and science. BioLogos began in 2006 when geneticist Francis Collins, then Director of the Human Genome Project, wrote a book about his own faith and the compatibility of evangelical belief with science.[48] The publicity around the book spurred him to start BioLogos in 2007, which he led until he was appointed Director of the National Institutes of Health in late 2009, which forced him to step down. BioLogos has continued with leadership from well-known evangelicals involved with religion/science issues.[49]

One can only imagine what it is like to be Francis Collins. One of the most influential scientists in the world, at the pinnacle of influence as Director of the Human Genome Project . . . and yet he claims to be a member of a religious tradition that many elite scientists think is opposed to scientific knowledge. The article reporting on his nomination to head the NIH in *Science* magazine reported that "some are concerned about his outspoken Christian faith," and prominent atheists wrote in the *New York Times* suggesting that his religion disqualified him from the post.[50] Given that Collins is a scientist, an elite, and surrounded by scientists, we can see why these knowledge conflict issues are central to his concerns, as they are in his popular book.[51]

This centrality is designed right into BioLogos. Its five "core commitments" include: "We embrace the historical *Christian faith*, upholding the authority and inspiration of the Bible." This indicates a standard evangelical yet nonfundamentalist orientation toward the Bible, and points high up the knowledge pyramid. The second is "We affirm *evolutionary creation*, recognizing God as Creator of all life over billions of years." This idea, also called theistic evolution, is that evolution occurred as science describes, but was caused by God, or God produced Creation through evolution. Again, this is a belief high in the pyramid. If you hold that science only requires methodological naturalism, this knowledge claim does not conflict with science because it is not demonstrable with science. BioLogos' concern with knowledge is also made clear in the third commitment, which is that "We seek *truth,* ever learning as we study the natural world and the Bible." This seems a reference to a long-standing evangelical conception of the two books of God: nature and the Bible, both of which are true.[52]

A more extensive eleven-point "What We Believe" section fleshes this out further. The Bible is clarified as the "inspired and authoritative word of God." The two books of God concept is emphasized, in that "God also reveals himself in and through the natural world he created . . . Scripture and nature are complementary and faithful witnesses to their common Author." Consistency of belief with the scientific consensus is re-emphasized in statements such as "we believe that God created the universe, the earth, and all life over billions of years," and "we believe that the diversity and interrelation of all life on earth are best explained by the God-ordained process of evolution with common descent. Thus, evolution is not in opposition to God, but a means by which God providentially achieves his purposes." Science—at least of the methodological naturalist variety—remains a logically coherent system where you need to accept all of the knowledge claims of science. It is just that the religion in which one should believe is an evangelicalism that does not conflict with any of these knowledge claims.

Finally, BioLogos argues that science requires methodological naturalism and not metaphysical naturalism—using the terms "Materialism" and "Scientism" to represent metaphysical naturalism. BioLogos writes "We believe that the methods of science are an important and reliable means to investigate and describe the world God has made. In this, we stand with a long tradition of Christians for whom Christian faith and science are mutually hospitable. Therefore, we reject ideologies such as Materialism and Scientism that claim science is the sole source of knowledge and truth, that science has debunked God and religion, or that the physical world constitutes the whole of reality."[53] In my terms, BioLogos works to avoid weak systemic knowledge conflict through synthesis and rejects the definition of science that could produce the strong systemic knowledge conflict.

A large portion of their website is devoted to answering questions about evolutionary creationism. These questions are centrally concerned with avoiding conflict between the knowledge claims of scientists and conservative Protestants, or within conservative Protestantism, with nearly none having any referents to value conflict.[54]

One way to describe BioLogos is that it is part of the ongoing struggle between evangelicalism and fundamentalism, with BioLogos trying to teach the conservative Protestant public the evangelical version of knowledge about the natural world. The creation of a systemic knowledge structure that accounts for theology and science is part and parcel of the evangelical worldview. And, I am sure that people affiliated with BioLogos recognize moral conflict with science. My point is that by not emphasizing that the evangelical public might not have a systemic knowledge relationship with science—and may be focused on a moral relationship with science—people who encounter BioLogos might be misinformed about how ordinary evangelicals view science.

The American Academy for the Advancement of Science (AAAS)

Another prominent dialogue association is the "Dialogue on Science, Ethics, and Religion" (DoSER), founded in 1995 by the American Academy for the Advancement of Science (AAAS).[55] Its prominence stems from its sponsor. AAAS, founded in 1848, is the world's largest general scientific society, including 261 affiliated societies and academies of science, serving 10 million individuals. It publishes *Science* magazine, which is the largest paid circulation peer reviewed general science journal in the world, with an estimated readership of one million people. AAAS is the embodiment of institutional science in the U.S.[56]

DoSER was established to "facilitate communication between scientific and religious communities." But, communication about what? The statement continues that "DoSER builds on AAAS's long-standing commitment to relate scientific knowledge and technological development to the purposes and concerns of society at large," which suggests this communication is about knowledge claims. However, their overview page describes the dialogue as not about knowledge, saying that "issues of value and ethics are raised by the appearance of technologies not even imagined by earlier generations. Questions of meaning and religion emerge from our deepening understanding of the natural order. Issues of value and meaning are grounded in the disciplines of ethics and religion." This is then an endorsement of what Barbour called an "independence" relationship, and Gould called "non-overlapping magisteria." The religious citizens can be relieved that the AAAS is not putting its weight behind metaphysical naturalism in order to eliminate religion as the scientific atheists would want. Rather, science requires only methodological naturalism, and religion takes up matters of value.[57] At first glance, the website suggests that science is about knowledge, religion is about morality, so there can be no moral conflict as long as science does not talk about its morality.

As we dig deeper, we see DoSER describing the relationship between religion and science as the theological synthesizers do, making sure religion does not contradict scientific knowledge claims. Of the two substantive goals of DoSER, the first is to "encourage an appreciation among scientists, religious leaders, and religion scholars of the ethical, religious, and theological implications of scientific discoveries and technological innovations."[58] This repeats the idea that science produces knowledge, and this knowledge has implications for religious and theological beliefs. The second goal is to "improve the level of scientific understanding in religious communities." Note that there is not a matching goal of "improving the level of theological understanding in scientific communities," suggesting the influence of the knowledge deficit model. This is a one-way dialogue: scientific knowledge has implications for religious belief, and if religious leaders can learn the science, the religious system of belief can be modified.

A report of the DoSER "thematic areas" makes the emphasis on synthesizing religious and scientific knowledge more clear. One theme is "Physics & the Cosmos," and the description of this theme is dominated by discussion of quarks, quasars and quantum mechanics and other physics facts, which "provoke intriguing physical and metaphysical questions."[59] The theme of "Neuroscience, Brain & Mind," similarly starts with a compendium of fact claims in this area.[60] Moral challenges, presumably for religion to work on, are included. For example, "many recent advances in neuroscience also highlight ethical questions with both societal and personal consequences" as science invents things to react to, such as whether people should be mandated to take drugs for neurological problems.

As in the other themes, these scientific facts need to be systematized with religious beliefs. DoSER talks of the spiritual ramifications of neuroscience:

> such as the relationship between the human brain and mind. Interdisciplinary research in neuroscience, physics, biology, philosophy and even cosmology has sparked interest in the conversation regarding determinism and free will. The premise is that if actions of minute atoms can be measured with such a high degree of certainty, then can larger aspects of the universe which are comprised of these atoms also be determined with a keenly devised prescription? Do these predictions extend to choices we make, our personalities, and our future? Can we assume biology, conditioning, and probabilistic calculations have declared moot our ability to choose? Theologically speaking, do these determined actions affect our ability to choose good from evil?[61]

This points fairly high up the religious belief pyramid to central concepts like free will. So far we see that DoSER sees a relationship of systemic knowledge between science and religion, where religious and scientific knowledge needs to be synthesized, primarily by religion changing its claims to make them consistent with modern science. While mentioning that religion is concerned with morality and meaning, DoSER does not see a relationship between science and religion over morality because religion has been exclusively given that task. Thus, implicitly, science does not promote a particular morality.

DoSER and the Public

DoSER, unintentionally in my opinion, gets closer to accurately describing a relationship between religion and science among the public that concerns morals when it moves away from elite perspectives focused on knowledge and gets input from regular religious citizens and non-elite scientists who have not spent much time pondering this issue. A recent project of DoSER was the "Perceptions" project, intended to break down false perceptions of scientists by the religious and false perceptions of the religious by scientists.[62] It primarily focused upon evangelicals, and was conducted in partnership with the National Association of Evangelicals and the American Scientific Affiliation. The National Association of Evangelicals is the largest and most influential coalition of evangelical denominations and organizations in the U.S., and the American Scientific Affiliation is, roughly, an association of evangelical scientists.

The project seems to have started with an assumption of conflict over knowledge or beliefs, with one document stating that "while some evangelicals may be skeptical of scientific theories and worry about the impacts science may have on their communities, some scientists feel that evangelical Christianity hinders the growth of scientific literacy and argue that religion should stay out of public discourse."[63] The project held community-based workshops that brought together local scientists and local religious leaders. While not the general public, these people were a lot closer to being general members of the public than the elites discussed so far in this chapter, in that these local leaders were not experts in this debate.

Encountering a group much closer to the public seemed to necessitate talking about morality. A discussion guide for the local dialogue groups offered three choices for the relationship between religion and science.[64] First, "Explore shared values and promote understanding," which may include the values of "service, compassion, and perseverance." This is the rare mention of the fact that scientists have values too, and while DoSER wants to highlight agreement, obviously such values could conflict as well. The second is to "Work together to confront common concerns," such as "health, education, poverty, environmental stewardship, and human rights." This too builds on a shared value—the "common concern for the well-being of others"—and also presumes that scientists have values they promote. The third possibility is to "Ensure civility and minimize confrontation" through separation, with the motto being "good fences make good neighbors." It is striking how the premise of this project is that tensions can be lowered by by-passing elite concerns about fact-claims about the world, and focusing upon the shared values of scientists and the religious community.

Geared toward dialogue about issues other than knowledge claims about the natural world, it became clear at these workshops that the moral conflict between science and religion was two-way, wide, and deep. At a meeting between local evangelicals and scientists in Denver, they talked about renewable energy—presumably a topic over which it would be almost impossible to find knowledge conflict, given that there is nothing in the evangelical tradition that would be opposed to any of the science required for solar panels. One pastor said "It was good to reach into the world of people who are opposed (and sometimes outright hostile) to my worldview, to understand and remember that each one is a person with very real needs."[65]

At the Atlanta workshop, again focused on evangelicals and scientists, the report indicated that "other topics—human origins, evolution, stem cell research, and human sexuality—were identified as areas around which it will be more difficult to find agreement." Two or three of these are fact-claims and one or two of these are moral claims—depending on what the discussion of human sexuality was about.

The pastor of a Baptist church near Atlanta said he was "surprised to learn that a lengthy ethical review process governs all publicly funded research. I had assumptions that were not correct. In one instance, we were talking about the sanctity of life. The traditional view among many evangelicals is that scientists really have very little to do with 'sanctity of life'. . . But to hear them say, 'No, life is very important,' and to understand why they're doing what they're doing was eye-opening."

Clearly, this pastor thinks that scientists have a particular moral stance in public debates about embryonic life, and that "scientist" means "those who do not follow standard moral norms," not "those who discover knowledge." Another participant described another scene from the workshop where a biologist quipped, seemingly to break the tension, that "We have morals, too!"[66] The biologist's quip suggests a deep assumption on the part of the religious participants that scientists are amoral or immoral people. Debates about knowledge seemed to be quite secondary.

The program director reported in a newsletter of the AAAS what I will show in subsequent chapters: that evangelicals are not rejecting scientific facts because of how these facts were generated, but because they oppose the moral message that comes with these facts. The director wrote:

> In fact, a deeper probe shows that it is actually the underlying basic philosophical concerns of religious citizens toward science that can lead to responses of either enthusiastic support for science or else rejection of scientific data in ways that can be sometimes baffling to scientists.
>
> One evangelical leader who advises the project points out that people within his constituency are often more concerned with the "package" that they perceive may be coming along with science, rather than any particular result. For example, it may not be "the fossil record" or the age of the universe that troubles, but rather the perception that "evolutionary science implies godlessness" or the concern that "if my child is taught evolution in school, will it come wrapped in a package of atheism?"

In other words, Conservative Protestants are not opposed to the scientific method per se, but do not like the ideologies that seem to come implicitly wrapped in those scientific claims, such as the metaphysical naturalism of the atheist scientists. When the project leadership encountered the religious public, they saw that conflict was not primarily about knowledge claims, but was about values or morals.

While this moral conflict was glancingly identified, it was not highlighted, presumably because all of the leaders of the project had knowledge conflict in their minds. When the perceptions project later turned back to the elites who ran it, predictably the conflict reverted to being about knowledge. This is exemplified by the fact that, after the dialogue workshops, DoSER produced a booklet targeted to evangelical congregations called "When God and Science Meet: Surprising Discoveries of Agreement," produced in conjunction with the National Association of Evangelicals. Critically, the majority of the leaders and writers for this project were either elite leaders of religious groups or academics. The advisory team for this booklet included the president of the National Association of Evangelicals, a program officer for DoSER (who is also a scientist who works for NASA), the Dean of Natural and Social Science at Wheaton College (a flagship evangelical institution), the director of the American Scientific Affiliation, and a pastor in the Washington area. They asked a number of people who were both "committed Christians" and "credentialed scholars" to write very short essays. With the concerns of elites returning to the forefront, this booklet is all about systemic knowledge conflict.

The president of the National Association of Evangelicals sets the tone in the introduction by making it clear that this is all about fact claims. "We hear our doctor describe a life-threatening diagnosis in scientific terms and then rush to the hospital chapel, where we pray for divine intervention. We listen to a pastor's sermon from the Bible and wonder how it fits with the latest article in *Time* or *National Geographic*. We are dazzled by the discoveries about tiny DNA or massive galaxies and are humbled by the simplicity of the Bible's opening line that 'God created the heavens and the earth (Genesis 1:1).'" He offers a solution to knowledge conflict by quoting Saint Augustine: "Let every good and true Christian understand that wherever truth may be found, it belongs to his Master," which is often paraphrased as "All truth is God's truth."[67]

In the rest of the essays there are a few passing references to scientists pushing metaphysics and moral values. There are warnings about "scientists who arrogantly puff up their knowledge of nature into materialistic metaphysics, or who claim that science trumps all non-scientific moral restraint," or of science implicitly teaching naturalism beyond the lab. However, by and large the ten other short essays reiterate a version of the systemic knowledge conflict narrative. For example, the two books of God perspective is ubiquitous, such as where the booklet claims that scientific skills "provide real knowledge of God's real world, not to be overruled by theological or church authority."[68]

In sum, when DoSER is focused on elites, it reinforces and reflects the elite view of a systemic knowledge conflict. However, when it encounters the public, in this case by facilitating conversations between local pastors and scientists, it turns out that moral conflict is just as important as knowledge conflict.

THE TEMPLETON FOUNDATIONS

Readers who are familiar with these debates will note that nearly every person and organization discussed in the synthesizer and dialogue sections of this chapter—and numerous people who would fit in those categories but who were not mentioned—are involved with the Templeton foundations in some way. There are three foundations: The John Templeton Foundation, the Templeton World Charity Foundation, and the Templeton Religion Trust.

Sir John M. Templeton (1912–2008) was an early innovator in the mutual fund industry, making a large fortune along the way. His upbringing was in both the Cumberland Presbyterian Church (generally an evangelical Protestant denomination) and, seemingly paradoxically, the Unity Church.[69] The Unity School of Christianity (Unity Church) was founded by Charles and Myrtle Fillmore in 1889, and is a metaphysical and mystical blend of Christianity and pantheism. This group emphasizes that the mind controls healing, that God is an impersonal principle, that God is in everything, that the divine exists within everyone, there is no Heaven or Hell, and that Jesus was an exemplar of spiritual truth, not the Christ.[70]

Templeton had a very strong view of the abilities of science, seeing that it was primarily through scientific research that religion could make "spiritual progress." It is quite clear from his voluminous writings that in his life he was primarily concerned with discovering the truth of reality. While clearly science was to be used to discover truth about nature, Templeton was clear that there was much reality beyond nature. Such truth was not to be found through at least present-day science or through religion, but through a religion that used science to discover more truths. Scientific research would "supplement the wonderful ancient scriptures" that were limited by their time.[71] Thus, both science and religion are about true knowledge.

He was obviously not an advocate of a science that required metaphysical naturalism, given that he thought science could be used to show the details of what God truly is. He *was* an advocate of a science that requires methodological naturalism—God is not part of a scientific explanation, but scientific findings can help us understand God. That is, he was the ultimate advocate of synthesis, where science would proceed using a secular method, and religion would learn from that science, adjusting its doctrines as it approached spiritual truth.

This is clear in his long-time advocacy of a "humble approach in theology and science." The problem was that while scientists were humble, the theologians were not. He wrote that "as part of a historical legacy of the scientific method, most scientists have learned to avoid the stagnation that comes from accepting a fixed perspective.... They have learned to become epistemologically open-minded, always seeking to discover new insights and new perspectives." However, "often theologians, religious leaders, and lay people can be blind to obstacles they themselves erect. . . . Many do not imagine that progress in religion may be possible, perhaps by appreciating ways that sciences have learned to flourish and by being creatively open to a discovery-seeking and future-oriented perspective. For so many religious people, the future of religions seems nothing much beyond the preservation of ancient traditions."[72]

He clearly envisioned scientific research in fundamental physics, such as quantum mechanics, as providing spiritual insight into the "mind of God." Another approach to spiritual progress was to use science to determine whether there was evidence of "universal purposes in the cosmos." Other fields like human evolution could tell us about the spiritual practices of Neanderthals, which could give us spiritual insight today. Another Templeton program examined "conceptually expansive ways of understanding the world," as a way to "connect science with concepts of divinity," and included research in "quantum information theory, quantum chaos, game theory and ethics, emergence of order, timetabling, consilience, the nature of mathematics, the limits of knowledge, aesthetics, the theology of artificial intelligence, and the theology of extraterrestrials."[73] Templeton, and his foundations, were also strong advocates of the idea of dialogue between religion and science.

To return to my terminology, Templeton was, like the theological synthesizers, an advocate of the weak version of the systemic knowledge relationship between religion and science. Religion and science were in conflict over fact claims, but his hope was to avoid conflict by synthesizing the two pyramids into one coherent one that would actually be an improvement on both. Critically, science and religion are not centrally concerned with morality, but rather, and ideally, both are concerned with determining spiritual truth.

Templeton and his foundations did not create the synthesizers and the dialogue promoters—those were part of academia long before Templeton came on the scene. And, again, this sort of research is totally legitimate and is, in fact, what theologians are supposed to be doing. What Templeton and his foundations did was to amplify these ideas, involve more people than would otherwise be involved, and make these ideas much more publicly prominent than they otherwise would be. Like the other debaters in this and the following chapter, it would have been better for public debate about religion and science if Templeton grantees had been required to emphasize in all of their output that what is being discussed may not be how the general public views religion and science. Moreover, an implication of the later pages of this book is that the Templeton foundations might consider whether moral conflict is stopping many religious people from accepting the science that Templeton thought was required for spiritual progress.

CONCLUSION

The overwhelming assumption among scientists and theologians in the academic religion and science debate, as well as the dialogue associations, is that there is a systemic knowledge relationship between religion and science. This is almost a statement of faith among scientists who think that since they are only producing knowledge, the only reason anyone else would be in conflict with them would, of course, be about knowledge. This reaches its apotheosis in the form of the scientific atheists who are assuming a different scientific belief system than most other scientists—a metaphysical naturalism instead of just a methodological naturalism—which makes holding any religious idea at all incompatible with science.

Fundamentalist Protestant Biblical inerrantists ironically agree with the scientific atheists about knowledge conflict, but simply reverse the conclusion: it is scientific knowledge that needs to be modified because it is incompatible with fundamentalist Biblical exegesis. The theological synthesizers also see any relationship as concerning systemic knowledge, but to avoid conflict they aim to change the religious knowledge system so that knowledge conflict does not exist. This perspective has been amplified by funding from the Templeton foundations. Critically, all of those discussed in this chapter are implicitly teaching systemic knowledge conflict to the public.

3

The Academic Analysts of the Relationship Between Religion and Science

In addition to scientists and theologians in the academic debate, there are a number of other academics who are analysts or observers of the relationship between science and religion who, I will show, are also teaching the public the systemic knowledge perspective. In this chapter I will focus on the two most active groups, the historians and the sociologists. Historians show, for example, that Victorian era scientists often thought they were investigating the details of God's creation, and thus there was harmony in religious and scientific knowledge. Sociologists assume that the spread of scientific knowledge is a cause of the loss of religious belief. As in the previous chapter, I will also offer an explanation of why these fields see the relationship in this way. I will particularly focus upon explaining this view within the field of sociology, given that it often focuses on the general public, and I am claiming that the public does not use systemic knowledge to understand science and religion.

HISTORIANS OF RELIGION AND SCIENCE

In recent decades, historians have been on a quest to debunk the claim of the inevitable conflict between religion and science over knowledge about the world. They want to replace the universal knowledge conflict narrative with descriptions of the limited times and places such conflict has occurred, and emphasize the other times and places where there was no conflict over knowledge.[1] While debunking the simplistic view of universal conflict, the historians nonetheless inadvertently reinforce the idea that the relationship, and any conflict, is by definition about systemic knowledge.

It is difficult to generalize about the complexity that historians see in the relationship between religion and science. Metaphorically, imagine two stages facing each other. On one is a cast of one hundred characters, each representing a different religion in a different time and place. On the other is a cast of one hundred characters, each representing a different conception of science in a different time and place. As the numerous combinations of characters stand one at a time at the front of each stage and face the other, historians may write about that relationship. For example, the character representing mid-eighteenth-century American science looks little like the science character today. That character could face a mid-nineteenth-century Catholic religion character, an evangelical Protestant religion character, a Jewish religion character and so on—each of which would have a different relationship with that particular version of science. Only some would be in conflict, and others would be in perfect harmony. Given these historical particularities, we can see that there was not a universal conflict in the Middle Ages, for example, because Isaac Newton was religious. Similarly, in the late Victorian era there was not universal knowledge conflict because many Anglicans agreed with Darwin about evolution. And, in early twentieth-century America, there *was* conflict between Darwinism and many conservative Protestants.

Again, this link across the stages is almost always about knowledge claims about nature, thus reinforcing the knowledge conflict narrative. There are also social, political, personality, disciplinary, and other conflicts described, but these are usually part of explaining a knowledge conflict. There are sometimes instances of moral conflict identified, particularly for the twentieth-century debates, but these are not separately theorized, and I will focus on discussing these in Chapter 4.

I start with the extremely influential late twentieth-century summary statement of historical work in this area, John Hedley Brooke's encyclopedic history *Science and Religion: Some Historical Perspectives*. The book starts in the sixteenth century and generally proceeds chronologically. As we go through Galileo to Darwin and so forth, it is quite clear that the relationship between science and religion—be it supportive, conflictual, subsuming, or anything else—is about systemic knowledge. To take but one of the innumerable possible examples, he discusses Isaac Newton's "apprehension lest a fully mechanized universe might cripple divine activity." We can almost see Newton trying to make consistent and systematize all of the knowledge in his pyramid when Brooke describes Newton's dilemma:

> His disenchantment with the cosmology of Descartes was partly due to the boldness with which the French philosopher had presumed to show how an organized solar system could develop from a disorganized distribution of matter. Newton insisted that organization could not result from disorganization without the mediation of an intelligent power. As if to defuse the deistic tendencies of Cartesian philosophy, Newton scrutinized the universe for evidence of divine involvement. . . . Because his voluntarist theology allowed events in nature to be explained both as the result of mechanism and of the divine will, there was a difficulty in determining what kind of event would most demonstrate divine involvement.[2]

Anticipating my claim about late twentieth-century elite moral debates about science, which I will examine in the next chapter, the final 10 of the 347 pages in the book are about "science and human values" in the twentieth century. In that section, portrayed as a very recent development in the long history of religion and science, but prefigured in various ways, Brooke discusses controversies surrounding human reproductive technologies and the moral problems supposedly caused by Darwinism. He is largely not discussing history, but what were at the time of his writing current events. Like other historians who view this development in the current time or very recent history, it is not seen as a change in the relationship between religion and science, and not the imminent decline of debates about knowledge, but more like an additional wrinkle that has emerged in recent decades.[3]

We could use any other of the histories of science and religion to describe conflict over systemic knowledge. But one of my favorite examples comes from Peter Bowler, who examines debates about religion and science in early twentieth-century Britain, and shows heroic attempts at iron-clad logical consistency in knowledge and belief by the elites of the time. One debate was about whether materialism, a belief high in the scientific knowledge structure, could be changed to make room for religion. Some solutions included the idea that "matter itself was mysterious, and thus offered no suitable foundation for the kind of materialism that sought to eliminate mind and purpose from nature." Another was that "ether theory" would allow for a worldview "that was still in touch with science, but which transcended materialism and allowed the scientist to believe that the universe as a whole was a divine construct." The general idea was to take abstract scientific beliefs like materialism and make them compatible with religious belief and vice versa.[4]

Given the voluminous output of historians, it is difficult to easily demonstrate the utter dominance of their assumption that any relationship between science and religion concerns knowledge of the natural world at minimum, and a systemic knowledge relationship at maximum. I will make my case by summarizing the 103-chapter encyclopedia titled the *History of Science and Religion in the Western Tradition,* published in the year two thousand, which contains chapters from most of the prominent historians of religion and science of the time.[5] The table of contents give us the general story. Part 1 is titled "The Relationship of Science and Religion," and there is not an entry titled "Morality" or "Moral Debates." However, there are fourteen entries that all refer to knowledge, such as "Natural Theology" and "Views of Nature."[6] These are followed by "Biographical Studies" of Galileo, Pascal, Newton, and Darwin—who we know of because of their roles in major transformations of our understanding of knowledge of the natural world.

The next section is titled "Intellectual Foundations and Philosophical Backgrounds." These twenty-six chapters are even more clearly focused on knowledge generation, with topics such as "Cartesianism," "Baconianism," and "German

Nature Philosophy."[7] Part 4 contains twelve chapters concerning "specific religious traditions and chronological periods."[8] The encyclopedia then turns for the final forty-seven entries to the history of groups of disciplines making fact-claims about nature. These are grouped under the headings of "Astronomy and Cosmology," "The Physical Sciences," "The Earth Sciences," "The Biological Sciences," "Medicine and Psychology," and "The Occult Sciences."

This is not to say that moral conflict is unmentioned in the over six hundred tightly packed pages of this encyclopedia. Rather, it is not central and not theorized. The first two framing essays are telling. In the first, historian David Wilson examines the historiography of science and religion, and it is clear that the historiography up to that point was about the relationship between science and religion over knowledge about the physical world.[9] The next chapter is a summary of all historical studies on the conflict with science and religion, and historian Colin Russell outlines the "issues of contention." The first is purely systemic knowledge, "in the area of epistemology: Could what we know about the world through science be integrated with what we learn about it from religion?" An example involves "the Copernican displacement of the earth from the center of the solar system." The second issue is also purely systemic, and has been in the realm of methodology, between a "science based on 'facts' and a theology derived from 'faith.'"[10] So far he is describing conflict over ways of knowing facts—a belief far up each pyramid.

Russell identifies another conflict, which he calls "social power." Here he points to historiography of religion and science that concerns knowledge conflict, but the explanation for the conflict is that the debate is not really about knowledge, but an attempt to undermine the power of institutional religion or science in society. His example is the efforts of the scientific naturalists associated with Thomas Henry Huxley and their attempt to overthrow the hegemony of the English church.[11] This is still concerned with knowledge conflict, it is just that the motive for the conflict is not truth itself.

The final conflict he identifies is "in the field of ethics," and this unintentionally demonstrates that historians have almost exclusively focused on knowledge conflict. The final conflict seems to contradict my claims in this section. However, unlike the other conflicts he identifies, and like Brooke, he turns from the historical literature to contemporary society, saying "most recently this has been realized in questions about genetic engineering, nuclear power, and proliferation of insecticides." Again, like Brooke, he gestures to the few nineteenth century cases that have been discussed by historians—such as debates about the morality of vaccination and anesthesia and moral reaction to Darwin—but then turns back to the present, writing that these have been replaced by "conflict over abortion and the value of fetal life." He then distances historians from this version of conflict by writing that "in nearly all of these cases, however, it is not so much science as its application (often by nonscientists) that has been under judgment."[12] I take this to be an oblique reference to present-day reality, but also an acknowledgment that historians have largely not focused on this type of conflict. Historians have seen the same social phenomena as I have in the contemporary world, but they have not worked out its implications.

Explaining Historians' Focus On Knowledge Conflict

Historians are not wrong, but their claims need to be restricted to history and not the present day. The first and most important reason the historians are correct is that historians largely study and write about the elites who spent time thinking about religion and/or science, and such persons are more concerned with systemic knowledge. Ronald Numbers writes that historians have had little to say about popular views of religion and science, and even regrets that two of his own edited volumes have neglected the views of the public.[13] There are good reasons for this neglect. One is, especially for historical studies before the nineteenth century, that what the actual "common folk" thought was irrelevant to what was going to happen in society and to the evolution of debates about religion and science. These societies were not democratic in the same way we think of them today, with no public spheres to provide input from the governed to the governors. Illiteracy was widespread, and the vast majority of the people in a country would have been primarily concerned with their own survival. In fact, most social elites did not even have the time to understand science. An early historian of the Royal Society wrote that Descartes and Newton's mechanistic view of the universe, "could be known but only to those, who would throw away all their whole Lives upon it. . . . It was made too subtle, for the common, and gross conceptions of men of business."[14]

Moreover, the historians have focused on elites, and thus on systemic knowledge conflict, because the common folk, in Numbers' explanation, "left little evidence of their thoughts, and much of what we have is filtered through the writings of those who observed them."[15] Of course, historians have tried to get as close to the public's views as possible. Peter Bowler's book is almost exclusively about elites, but he tried to get some information about the public by examining how many books were sold to the public. For example, he examined sales of popular novels by HG Wells, but unfortunately this cannot tell us too much about what ordinary people were thinking.[16] Bernard Lightman has similarly written about the popularizers of science in the Victorian era, and these popularizers, while elites, were one step closer to the public than other elites.[17] James Secord was able to painstakingly compile evidence of readers' responses to the *Vestiges of the Natural History of Creation,* a naturalistic pre-Darwin British account of human origins. Letters, diaries, publicity for events, and even handwritten marginalia were all obtained—but this sort of study is the exception, not the rule, because these data rarely exist, and certainly would be extremely fragmentary before the nineteenth century.[18]

The second reason that historians have focused on knowledge conflict, besides their necessary focus on elites, is that it is quite plausible that the farther one goes back in time, the more the debate between religion and science *was* about systemic knowledge for both the elites and the public. As Harrison and other historians have so convincingly shown, what "science" and "religion" have been over time has changed. The rise of our contemporary version of science in the nineteenth century, and its separation from religion, has meant that science is responsible for the vast majority of knowledge about the world. I would argue that while religion used to see one of its tasks as explaining the natural world, religion in the U.S. has moved away from this task, and that this long process has accelerated within the lifetimes of many of the current scholars in the religion and science debate—or so I will argue in Chapter 5. So, the focus of historians on knowledge conflict may not only be due to the focus on elites, but because there *was* knowledge conflict fifty or more years ago.

SOCIOLOGY AND SYSTEMIC KNOWLEDGE CONFLICT

If I am right about the differences in reasoning between elites and the public, we would expect that since social scientists often study the contemporary public, they will *not* describe conflict between religion and science as between two hierarchically organized knowledge systems. However, they have, up until the most recent years, assumed the same conflict that other academics see. In part this is because, at least historically, many of the social science studies of religion and science have been of elite scientists. However, even those who study public opinion surveys have assumed systemic knowledge conflict. As I will explain later in this section, this is a result of the deep assumptions of social science derived from its origins in the nineteenth century. While a variety of social scientists have contributed to these debates, and I will touch upon this variety, the debates about religion and science in the industrialized West have been dominated by sociologists.

Before engaging in my interpretation of the impact of the sociological literature, I should acknowledge the one study that more directly examines the extent to which social scientists believe in, and pass on to students, the idea of a systemic knowledge conflict between religion and science. An empirical examination of the content of contemporary anthropology textbooks shows that they depict a situation where "science and religion have always been, and will continue to be, bitter adversaries." The author did not design his study to examine knowledge vs. moral conflict, but it is quite clear from his quotations that these anthropology textbooks depict the irredeemable conflict as concerning knowledge. For example, when anthropology textbooks depict religious reaction to Darwin, depictions include "the intense conflict between the new evolution paradigm in science and an outmoded static worldview in religion" and "evolution and the principle of common descent demolished the scientific plausibility of creation and design for the universe." This conflict is depicted as continuing to this day, as "evolution remains an active source of debate in many societies due to the fundamental contradictions between religious interpretation and scientific investigation."[19] The author's investigation of sociology textbooks reaches a similar conclusion.[20] At least these two social sciences directly teach the systemic knowledge conflict to their students.

Sociological Theory

The tendency to depict the relationship between religion and science, and therefore any conflict, as concerning knowledge has been most marked in sociological theory. To be fair, most of this high theory is making historical claims, or was written long ago, and knowledge conflict may well have been the situation in the past. However, without exposure to studies of contemporary religious people, students learning these theories will presume that the depiction of religion and science is accurate today.

Consider as an example the theory of the rationalization of religion. German social theorist Max Weber, writing at the turn of the twentieth century, viewed religion as becoming more rationalized with time, and believed that the Protestantism of the Reformation was a particularly strong example of this process. In the words of Peter Berger, one of the most influential interpreters of Weber's sociology of religion:

> The Catholic lives in a world in which the sacred is mediated to him through a variety of channels—the sacraments of the church, the intercession of the saints, the recurring eruption of the "supernatural" in miracles—a vast continuity of being between the seen and the unseen. Protestantism abolished most of these mediations. . . . This reality then became amenable to the systematic, rational penetration, both in thought and in activity, which we associate with modern science and technology. A sky empty of angels becomes open to the intervention of the astronomer and, eventually of the astronaut. It may be maintained, then, that Protestantism served as a historically decisive prelude to secularization, whatever may have been the importance of other factors.[21]

Rationalization in religion had resulted in a situation where mysterious forces and powers were replaced by the calculation and technical means embodied in modern science. This then leads to religion reducing the number of truth claims about the world that are not compatible with the "systematic, rational penetration" that we "associate with modern science and technology." This may well be an accurate depiction of how religions have changed in the West over time. Note that in this account religion is resolutely about knowledge, and a religious perspective on how the world operates is in conflict with the scientific perspective.

Studies of the Religiosity of Scientists

Many participants in the historical or theological debate about religion and science will be most familiar with the sociological studies of the religiosity of scientists, which have been the most consistently used research design in the sociology of religion and science over the past fifty years. These studies not only presume that any conflict between science and religion is about knowledge, but are testing for the presence of the strong version of the systemic knowledge relationship between religion and science. They assume that scientists are metaphysical naturalists, holding a rigidly coherent belief system up to first principles—a similar strength of coherence that Dawkins demands where believing in scientific fact-claims means you cannot have one non-scientific belief (such as the existence of God). Thus, this research design is used to determine if scientists have *any* religious belief. Since it is assumed that the most elite scientists are those who have thought the most about how scientific knowledge is justified, the assumption of this research is that they should then be much less religious than the public.

Early twentieth-century studies of the religious beliefs of scientists found that scientists were less religious than were the public, and that higher-status scientists were the least religious of all.[22] A study of graduate students in the early 1960s also came to the same conclusion, and found that the students who were better educated and who were doing what was necessary to achieve higher scientific status were less involved with religion.[23]

But later studies found that social scientists were even less religious than natural scientists, despite their being less "scientific."[24] While this evidence still supported the knowledge conflict thesis, it subverted the linearity of the model, and being more scientific did not necessarily mean being less religious. Scholars explained this variously as an effect of "scholarly distance from religion," or as a "boundary posturing mechanism" by social scientists trying to appear more scientific by being less religious.[25]

Current research suggests that while scientists are less religious than the public, just as in the early twentieth century, religiosity (in varying forms) is persistent among scientists.[26] Elite scientists at top research universities remain much less conventionally religious with, for example, 28 percent of the population being evangelical but only 2 percent of elite scientists identifying with this tradition. Similarly, 27 percent of the population but only 9 percent of elite scientists are Catholic. More generally, 16 percent of the public but 53 percent of elite scientists do not have a religious identity.[27] (Studies of super-elite scientists, such as members of the National Academy of Sciences, find very few who believe in a personal God.)[28] Differences in religiosity across the scientific status hierarchy are lessening, so that being in a more "scientific" discipline is a less useful predictor of the religiosity than many other characteristics of the scientist, such as age, marital status, and childhood religious background.[29]

Ecklund and Scheitle critique the literature in this tradition by writing that it "supports the perception there is a conflict between the principles of religion and those of science, such that those who pursue science tend to abandon religion, either because of an inherent conflict between knowledge claims or because scientific education exerts a secularizing force."[30] This literature then presumes that religious people will not only avoid areas of science that make contrary claims to religion—as is the case with conservative Protestantism and biology—but all science, because people are assumed to be logically consistent and cannot believe one scientific claim without believing in all of them.[31] This literature has traditionally been part of the debate about the causes of secularization, because it was thought to be a test of whether scientific belief leads to a decline of religious belief.

The most recent studies of elite scientists have begun to look for reasons beyond the idea that religion and science are conflicting knowledge systems where the conflict is relieved by abandoning religion. For example, more recent studies by Ecklund and her colleagues have shown that religiosity of the home when one is a child is the most important predictor of present religiosity among elite scientists, that science is more like an identity that is threatened by a religious identity, and that most elite scientists do not perceive a conflict between science and religion.[32]

Sociological Survey Researchers

In later chapters, I will be showing evidence from surveys about whether contemporary religious people are in different types of conflict with science. However, up until very recently it has not been possible to demarcate types of conflict due to a lack of data on anything beyond the amount of scientific knowledge held by a religious respondent. Moreover, sociological survey researchers have been able to determine whether contemporary religious people *avoid* science in various ways, but do not know why avoidance is occurring. The dominant assumption in this research is that which sociology inherits from its intellectual origins and the broader academic debate—avoidance is due to systemic knowledge conflict, where religious people avoid science because they disagree about some scientific facts and do not want their belief system to be threatened.

When survey researchers generalize, this conflict is often described as the strong version of systemic knowledge conflict, where religion and science are incompatible at the highest level of the pyramid. For example, sociologists Ellison and Musick, before critiquing the view, summarize the dominant academic assumption about the incompatibility of *any* religious belief with science:

> Over the years, many observers have asserted that scientific materialism, as the guiding ideology of the scientific community, is ontologically and epistemologically

incompatible with conventional Western religious belief . . . In simplest terms, scientific materialism holds (1) that matter (or matter and energy) is the fundamental reality in the universe, and (2) that the scientific method is the only reliable means to disclose the nature of this reality. . . . In contrast, Western religious traditions generally assume that the universe and its inhabitants have been created by, and often are guided by, a supreme intelligence that transcends the material world. . . . Moreover, religious adherents embrace these tenets despite the lack of (a) public data, (b) experimental testing, and (c) standard evaluative criteria for ascertaining their validity.[33]

Empirical sociologists tend to limit their claims to particular religious groups, and have focused on conservative Protestants because the elites in this tradition have had the most public conflict with science. The assumption is that conservative Protestants are in systemic knowledge conflict with science because they reject the very basis of all science and instead look to God's revelation for truth about the natural world. The best place to view this assumption is in the social science literature on educational attainment, where one central question is: why is there a somewhat lower level of obtaining undergraduate and graduate degrees among conservative Protestants?

In general, the exact reason cannot be assessed due to lack of data, so instead scholars determine if people from particular religions really do have different attainment, and then speculate about why, based on what is otherwise known about society. (This is a common approach in social science.) The traditional explanation is that conservative Protestants have less educational attainment because they want to avoid scientific knowledge, which they are in conflict with. For example, sociologist of religion Darren Sherkat, who generally claims that conservative Protestants "view secular knowledge with considerable suspicion and disdain," writes that:

> In line with fundamentalist orientations towards knowledge, assessments of validity are most often generated a priori—requiring little assessment of the relative fit between events or data and abstract concepts. For many committed fundamentalists the "truth" is known based on understandings and interpretations of fundamentalist Christian sacred texts. . . . The orientation towards knowledge which tends to permeate conservative Christian belief systems precludes a systematic examination of the complexities of human conflict or the natural world. . . . abstract processes like disease, plate tectonics, or the scientific method can have diminished cognitive consequence, since ultimately the gods are responsible for the dynamics of earthly matter.[34]

Again, this is not propositional belief conflict where religion and science only conflict over a few fact claims. Rather, religious people's lack of belief in scientific claims is due to their different method for justifying claims, which is systemic knowledge conflict.

A slightly different argument is that conservative Protestants are opposed to knowledge acquisition not generated through the method of biblical exegesis, and thus would not want to learn about any science. In explaining what leads people to obtain a graduate degree in science, two economists posit that conservative Protestants will be less likely to obtain such a degree because "to the extent that science is incompatible with a set of core Christian beliefs, and/or is antagonistic to beliefs about the Bible as an inerrant source of truth, differences in belief among individuals about the truth content of the Bible can generate differences in the utility and cost of acquiring a science education."[35] The authors continue by claiming that conservative Protestants will be opposed to obtaining any knowledge itself, and particularly any knowledge based upon materialism.[36]

Similarly, Sherkat writes that "according to some activists and adherents in conservative Christian communities, the search for knowledge is often equated with a sinful predisposition toward self-love and pridefulness—and juxtaposed with the fundamentalist ideal of faithful and unquestioning servitude."[37] Again, this is a claim of conflicting *systems* of belief, not individual fact-claims, as it is claimed that conservative Protestants are opposed to all secular knowledge, because of how it was generated, not just claims that contradict fact claims conservative Protestants see in the Bible.[38]

Most of the sociological data cannot distinguish between knowledge and moral conflict, so scholars offer explanations that reflect their assumptions. If what I say in subsequent chapters is correct—that the dominant form of conflict among the religious public is moral—it would be surprising if the sociologists who study contemporary members of the general public did not see moral conflict at all in the data. What we find is that these sociologists, particularly in more recent years, unreflectively combine what I am calling knowledge conflict and moral conflict explanations. My approach in later chapters will be to pull apart these two explanations and test them separately.

As an example of this unreflective and untheorized mixing of explanations for conflict, sociologists Andrew Greeley and Michael Hout imply that knowledge conflict leads to moral conflict. In a survey analysis, they find that conservative Protestants are less likely to agree that "science will solve our social problems," and more likely to agree that "science makes our way of life change too fast," "scientists always seem to be prying into things that they really ought to stay out of," and that "science breaks down people's ideas of right and wrong." Each of these statements is not about knowledge or facts about nature, but about the moral effect of science. However, they interpret the responses to these moral questions not as moral conflict, but as indicators of knowledge conflict. They write that "it is hardly unexpected that the conservatives are skeptical about science" and "conservative Protestants take their stands not because they are uneducated but because they hold strong religious beliefs that take precedence over scientific facts."[39] In this passage, not only do religious beliefs take precedence over scientific facts—the knowledge conflict assumption—but the moral conflict is actually a knowledge conflict.

In another example of such mixing of explanations, Sherkat theorizes that he will find that conservative Protestants are less scientifically literate. The reason is their opposition to scientists' claims about evolution, which are in conflict with biblical claims, and "unscientific views of seismic events" like Pat Robertson claiming that an earthquake hit Haiti because Haiti made a pact with Satan. But in Sherkat's argument for why conservative Protestants have less scientific knowledge, he unreflectingly includes disagreements that have nothing to do with knowledge claims, such as "opposition to embryonic stem cell research," and that the students avoid "not only basic science courses, but also courses in social studies and literature that may question conservative Christian values about tolerance, social relations, sexuality and gender roles, and cultural diversity."[40]

Similarly, a study of religion and wealth, unable to distinguish the mechanism connecting the two phenomena, unreflectively asserts both moral and knowledge conflict in explaining what is seen as a pattern of conservative Protestants attaining less education. The author writes that conservative Protestant "cultural orientations tend to be at odds with the approaches of nonreligious schools and universities that propagate secular humanist values . . . and promote scientific investigation rather than acceptance of divine truths."[41]

Sociologist Kraig Beyerlein *does* offer a moral conflict explanation for a lack of educational achievement for conservative Protestants in which the basic conflict is the culture of universities more broadly. Beyerlein, citing Sherkat, says that one possible reason conservative Protestants avoid college is "the scientific method practiced in state colleges and universities threatens such conservative Protestant world views as a creationist understanding of human origins and a literal interpretation of scripture." But, he then adds a moral reason, which is that "the emphasis on emancipation from traditional authority stressed in public institutions of higher learning undercuts a variety of core theological and familial precepts of conservative Protestantism, especially submissiveness of children to God and to their parents."[42]

Like the others in this research area he lacks the data to determine which conflict is actually keeping conservative Protestants from college, but his conclusion undermines the idea that it is only knowledge conflict. He finds that evangelicals have the same level of educational attainment as mainline Protestants as well as higher attainment than fundamentalists or Pentecostals. This he attributes to the fact that the "the cultural traditions of fundamentalist Protestantism and Pentecostal Protestantism advocate withdrawing from the broader culture," while "the cultural tradition of evangelical Protestantism generally stresses engaging the broader culture."[43]

THE ORIGINS OF SOCIOLOGICAL BIAS TOWARD SEEING KNOWLEDGE CONFLICT

I will spend more time on explaining sociological bias toward seeing knowledge conflict than I spent on the other academic fields because sociology appears to be such an anomaly. Assuming that the analysis I report in later chapters is correct, and the contemporary religious public is primarily concerned with a moral relationship with science, why have the sociologists who study the public not seen moral conflict?

It is important to recognize that social science thinks of itself as a *science*. Many social scientists do not like that term because it implies they have the same positivist epistemology as natural scientists. However, social science can be interpretivist or positivistic; its analyses quantitative or qualitative; its methods observation, interview, survey, or the summation of records—but social scientists share with the natural scientists the basic Enlightenment ideal of making claims on the basis of observation and reason.

Therefore, it is not just that social scientists observe a relationship between *natural* science and religion—they have their own relationship as a science with religion. Using my pyramid metaphor in Figure 1 in Chapter 1, there would be a social science pyramid and a religion pyramid, and as I will show below, the inherited theories of social science presume that social science is in an extreme form of systemic knowledge conflict with religion. Both social science and religion are seen as systems of justified beliefs about the world, with methods and theories halfway up each pyramid. Therefore, when sociologists see *natural* science in relationship with religion, they presume that religion is a hierarchical system of belief about the *super*-natural, and that empirically observed facts about the world by science will undermine the foundations of this belief. Put simply, both natural and social science see religion as a really inaccurate system of developing fact-claims about the world. How did social science—and sociology in particular—develop this view?

The answer is that sociology was born with the strong version of systemic knowledge conflict in its DNA—akin to that of the scientific atheists—and thus this perspective is built into sociological theories. Like the scientific atheists, sociology depicts religion as a hierarchical system of justified belief that can be shown to be false by (social) science. With this assumption built into sociology, it is hard for sociologists to see any debate involving religion and science that is about morality.

To understand this bias in sociology, we should remind ourselves of the distinction between the strong and weak systemic knowledge conflict—between methodological naturalism ("a disciplinary method that says nothing about God's existence") and metaphysical naturalism (which "denies the existence of a transcendent God.")[44] Sociology was born in the Enlightenment era, assuming both methodological and metaphysical naturalism.

The social science version of methodological naturalism is that a social scientist cannot invoke the supernatural in explanations of social behavior. For example, a social scientist cannot claim that God causes wars. The social science version of metaphysical naturalism is that if we believe social scientific explanations of social behavior we also cannot believe that God exists. With metaphysical naturalism built into sociology, it is easy to see why sociologists have not seen moral conflict with science. Like other scientists, they define religion as that which makes (false) knowledge claims about the world.

The Origins of Social Science and Methodological and Metaphysical Naturalism

Historically, the *natural* sciences adopted methodological naturalism, and much later a small subgroup of atheist scientists began to promote metaphysical naturalism. In contrast, social science was born as a challenge to religious authority, and thus began by assuming metaphysical naturalism. Metaphysical naturalism presumes or subsumes methodological naturalism. Social scientists, not natural scientists, were the original scientific atheists.

For our purposes, the origin of social science is in the Enlightenment of seventeenth and eighteenth century Europe. One of the central concepts in Enlightenment thought was that people should use their own senses and reason to evaluate the physical and social worlds, and not tradition, faith, or religious authority. The first proto-social scientists were Enlightenment figures such as Montesquieu, Smith, Condorcet, and Herder, whose work was premised on the idea that history was caused by human action. While this seems obvious today, this was a change from earlier conceptions in which humans influenced history but history was ultimately under God's control. By the early nineteenth century all of reality, including what had previously been seen as immutable and unchanging, came to be seen in contextual historical terms.[45]

Building on earlier Enlightenment ideas, the "scientific" aspirations of the first social scientists were the result of the natural science triumphs of the era. Natural scientists had been seen as successful in explaining all sorts of natural phenomena, and the proto-social scientists wanted to transplant those successes to understanding the social world. For example, French philosopher Auguste Comte (1798–1857) is often portrayed as the founder of both sociology and positivism. He looked to natural science as an inspiration for understanding society, and invented "sociology" to "complete the scientific revolution by bringing human phenomena within the orbit of positive study." Moreover, reflecting the metaphysical naturalism of the Enlightenment-era social scientists, he tried to make positivism a "new world-religion to replace Christianity," complete with an ecclesiology—with social scientific experts at the apex of priestly authority. His metaphysical naturalism—which held that religion is a set of beliefs about the world that are false—was clear in his depiction of the stages of history, stages that reflected standard nineteenth century beliefs about progress. The first stage, infancy, was based in theology that assumed religion is about claims to nature ("the anthropomorphic projection of fictive causes"). The second, adolescence, is based on metaphysics, the rule of abstract ideas. The third, maturity, is "positive," and based on "evidential knowledge having the form of laws."[46] In this scheme, belief in transcendent force is evidence of a backward society.

Enlightenment-era social scientists gathered social facts in the pursuit of moral causes. Social science was designed to "liberate humankind from ignorance and oppression," with Jean-Jacques Rousseau, for example, arguing against inequality and for the dignity of the person.[47] As contemporary sociologist Malcolm Williams writes, there was an important "difference between the natural and social sciences in the nineteenth century—even at their most avowedly scientific. The latter were not just about how the world 'is' but how it 'ought' to be."[48] One of these "oughts" was demonstrating that religion is false.

Anthropology is like sociology in its presuppositions about religion and indeed, "throughout its entire history as an academic discipline, anthropology has been perceived as having an ethos that is predominantly hostile to religious convictions, especially those of Christianity." Founding anthropologists of the time shared Comte's view of progress and the idea that religion was based on false claims about nature. Edward Tylor, the first person to hold a faculty appointment in anthropology and often called "the father of anthropology," saw three stages of human history: savage, barbaric, and civilized. In his theory, "religion is fundamentally the erroneous thought of 'savages' that has continued into civilized contexts by sheer, unreflective conservatism, even though its false intellectual foundations have now been exposed." In fact, "anthropology should be a 'reformer's science,' which actively worked to eradicate religion from modern civilization."[49]

The most famous anthropologist of the generation after Tylor was James Frazer, whose stages of history were magic, religion, and science. Religion and science were locked in a battle over true knowledge, as he thought that "religion gives primitive, irrational answers to questions correctly answered by science." He too saw one purpose of this social science as demonstrating that religion is a set of false beliefs, believing that "anthropologists should work to ensure that science would increase and religion decrease," writing that "it is for those who care for progress" to aid the final triumph of science as much as they can in their day."[50]

The first sociological theorists, building on Enlightenment thought, developed more elaborate theories that promoted metaphysical naturalism, using social science reasoning to explain how religious belief was false, and actually reducible to social forces. Karl Marx (1818–1883), Max Weber (1864–1920), and Emile Durkheim (1858–1917) later became known as the "classical theorists" of sociology or, pejoratively but tellingly, the "holy trinity" of classical sociological theorists. These three would ultimately be more directly influential than the earlier Enlightenment figures, and were clearly engaged in an agenda of metaphysical naturalism.

What these three shared was an assumption that individual humans were alienated from the objective world, and that therefore people do not realize that the social forces that act upon them are actually the result of human activity. The central purpose of the classic sociologists was then "demystification"—to make people aware of humanity's own control over itself. Critically, religious belief was one of the primary institutionalized ideas that people needed to become aware was not a force outside of humanity, but something that humans had invented. For example, for Marx, religious beliefs are caused by the relations of the means of production in a particular era, and religion is one aspect of false consciousness that humanity needs to see through in order to experience true liberation. In its bumper-sticker version, religion is the "opiate of the masses" depriving humanity of the correct perception of who is oppressing them.

Durkheim similarly argued that people do not realize that it was they who created religious symbolism, not some transcendent force, and that religion was a metaphorical representative of the society. If people would agree with Durkheim's insight that sacred symbols were *actually* a reflection of social relationships, this fact would undermine religion in the same way that showing humans had evolved from lower primates would do. The general goal of the classic sociologists was to show "that the force believed in as divine entities were merely reflections of social experience."[51] Classical sociology argued that not only should social science use methodological naturalism, but also that social scientists have an obligation to promote metaphysical naturalism to further human freedom. Social science and religion were not compatible or capable of synthesis—the point of social science was to show that religion is false. To this day, sociology PhD programs in the U.S. begin the first semester with a class devoted to these classical theorists.

Sociology in America

At the same time the classical sociologists were writing in Europe, on the west side of the Atlantic social science was coming into its own. Historians point to this period, between the end of the American Civil War and World War I, as a transformative time for naturalist thought in American academia. Before this period, American natural scientists tended to believe that science described the details of God's creation, and thus science was ultimately supportive of theological claims.[52] But, "increasingly after 1870," write historians Jon H. Roberts and James Turner, "scientists preferred confessions of ignorance to invocations of supernaturalism."[53] It helped that the dominant version of Christianity in academia of the time was what would now be called liberal Protestantism where, for example, the Bible was not thought of as literally true in all details.

The growing specialization within academia contributed to the emergence of distinct social science disciplines, and what we would now consider social science was at the time embedded in courses on moral philosophy. Specialization meant carving off the social aspects of the field of moral philosophy, and the proto-social scientists of the time thought this specialization was critical for their future growth in the universities.[54] The proto-social scientists allied themselves with the increasingly powerful natural sciences which, by this time, were reaching consensus on methodological naturalism. Roberts and Turner describe it well:

> As disciplines that self-consciously sought to ally themselves with the natural sciences, the human sciences were in a very real sense born with a commitment to methodological naturalism, as . . . the natural sciences had already rendered exclusion of the supernatural from discourse quite conventional. Indeed, the notion that it was essential to restrict discourse and patterns of explanation to natural agencies and events had become one of the reigning assumptions in conceptions of what it meant to do science. Disciplines with aspirations to anchor themselves within institutions dedicated to scientific inquiry and production of knowledge could ill afford to incur the taint of "speculation" by incorporating God into their analysis.[55]

American sociologists reached back to European figures like Comte, and built metaphysical naturalism and systemic knowledge conflict into the bedrock of American sociology. Ironically, American sociology started as a field that collected social data for the Social Gospel movement—a late nineteenth-century religious social reform movement.[56] As Northern Baptist pastor and influential social gospel advocate Walter Rauschenbusch wrote, "we need a combination of the Kingdom of God and the modern comprehension of the organic development of human society . . . So directing religious energy by scientific knowledge that a comprehensive and continuous reconstruction of social life in the name of God is within the bounds of human possibility."[57] These religious social reformers were methodological but not metaphysical naturalists. As contemporary sociologist Michael Evans writes, "most Social Gospel writers committed themselves to scientific approaches and knowledge without committing to the underlying secularism of Comte or Spencer."[58]

A competing faction of sociologists that wanted to be seen as forwarding an objective science of society regarded any association with religion as detracting from that goal.[59] This made *metaphysical* naturalism attractive. Moreover, nearly all of the scientific sociologists in America during the discipline's establishment "were personally hostile to religion per se," writes contemporary sociologist Christian Smith. "These were skeptical Enlightenment atheologians, personally devoted apostles of secularization."[60]

The motivation for promoting metaphysical naturalism was a combination of the personal anti-religiosity of the founders and the need to draw very strong intellectual boundaries against the competing group of religious social gospel sociologists. By delegitimating religious belief writ large, this latter faction could be convincingly defeated and sociology could be a "science," given that natural scientists, with their naturalistic assumptions, controlled what was considered to be legitimate knowledge in universities.

In his examination of sociology textbooks published from the 1880s through the 1920s, Christian Smith concludes that they were devoted to the idea that religious knowledge-claims were false. In the words of a nineteenth-century textbook writer, emphasizing that religion is about knowledge claims about nature, "All . . . phenomena are now satisfactorily explained on strictly natural principles. Among people acquainted with science, all . . . supernatural beings have been dispensed with, and the belief in them is declared to be wholly false and to have always been false." Echoing Comte, another textbook states that religion is the anthropomorphic projection of "savages," and that this projection constitutes "the basis of all religious ideas." Smith concludes that the textbooks claim that "religion is concerned with the spiritual realm, which is beyond sociology's ability to examine, but . . . all religions are finally reducible to naturalistic, material, and social causes, and are clearly false in their claims."[61]

In sum, while metaphysical naturalism is not dominant in the natural sciences, the European social scientists such as Comte advocated for metaphysical naturalism, and this was adopted by American social science. Later European theorists like Marx, Weber and Durkheim reinforced this vision. American social science was born with methodological naturalism in its DNA, and sociology was born with a commitment to advocating metaphysical naturalism as well.

Committed to showing that religious *beliefs* are false, sociologists saw religion as about knowledge about the world, and therefore any conflict with science must be about knowledge. Moreover, it was not just a few religious beliefs that were false, but the entire religious system of knowledge, further encouraging sociologists to see systemic knowledge conflict. Of course, most sociologists are not consciously engaged in promoting metaphysical naturalism or cognizant of the systemic knowledge assumptions embedded in classic sociological theory. Rather, when needing to go beyond their data, they must turn to theoretical assumptions to complete their claims, and they turn to theories which assume systemic knowledge conflict.

CONCLUSION

In the previous chapter I showed that the elite scientists and the theologians—the advocates—are having a debate about systemic knowledge conflict. In this chapter

I showed that the academics who are observing or analyzing the conflict between science and religion also see systemic knowledge conflict. Historians primarily examine elites from the past, so it is not surprising that they have primarily observed systemic knowledge conflict. This could be because they inevitably study elites, or because religion and science in the past *were* engaged in systemic knowledge conflict.

We might expect that sociologists, who do study the public, would not portray the religion and science relationship as one of systemic knowledge conflict. What we find is that theories that originated a hundred or more years ago, but are still influential to this day, promote the idea that any relationship concern systemic knowledge. These have left a legacy of difficulty in seeing anything but knowledge conflict.

Elites in the literatures portrayed in the past two chapters are portrayed as resolutely concerned about knowledge conflict. However, the historians are studying debates of more than fifty years ago, and the sociological theories I reviewed are similarly aged. If we look at elite debates of the past fifty years, we will see a presentation of religion and science that does not imply conflict over knowledge, a transformation that has not been recognized. I turn to this examination in the next chapter.

4

The Recent Transformation of Elite Academic and Public Debates

My claim is that the religion of the American public has changed in the past fifty years—within the lifetimes of many current participants in these debates. Moreover, the public's view of science as primarily a means of generating facts about nature has similarly changed. These changes have resulted in the current relationship between religion and science being primarily concerned with morality. In this chapter I will show that religion and science conflicts of the past fifty years, as well as sociological theory developments in the same time frame, have already demonstrated the same change—although this has not been recognized by scholars. I cannot demonstrate that the public's new view changed the elite debate or vice versa, but when the information in this chapter is combined with that of the next, we will see that overall the relationship between religion and science has indeed changed.

I first examine the recent history of academic sociology debates that are not about religion and science per se, and are therefore not beholden to existing categories, but which do suggest that sociology is unconsciously moving away from the systemic knowledge conflict perspective. I then turn to the recent history of public debates between elite scientists and theologians, akin to the bulk of historical studies of religion and science, and show that these are primarily about morality, with the religious accepting the knowledge claims of science as true.

Of course, nobody tripped a historical switch in 1967 that transformed society. The antecedents of this moral debate existed for a century, as has been recognized by historians, particularly those examining debates about Darwin. However, since historians do not examine the present, they have largely not seen that these were indeed antecedents of a transformation that is only evident from looking at contemporary society. I therefore re-narrate the history of debates over Darwin from a moral perspective.

In the systemic knowledge conflict account, the supposed clash in the seventeenth century between Galileo and the pope over claims about the physical world is a totemic object. To be provocative, the recent conflicts between science and religion described in this chapter will eventually be a replacement for the Galileo account—a shorthand way to say that history shows there has "always" been an "inevitable" conflict between religion and science over morality.

RECENT SOCIAL SCIENCE THEORIES
Definitions of Religion That Do Not Focus on Knowledge of Nature

The definitions of religion that are used when people see types of knowledge conflict are those that see religion as concerning distinctions between "nature" and "super-nature," or, more commonly, the "supernatural." Since science is tasked with explaining nature, this ends up defining religion as that which is not science, thus setting the stage for seeing systemic knowledge conflict. However, since the 1960s there has been a competing family of definitions of religion which opens the possibility that contemporary religion is not centrally about knowledge-claims about nature. If the authors of these competing theories are reflecting the beliefs of ordinary religious people, this suggests that "religion" is ultimately something that does not clash over knowledge.

There are two dominant traditions in defining religion: the substantive and the functional.[1] Substantive definitions divide the world into sacred and profane, where the profane world is explicable by human reason. The sacred world operates outside of the power of human reason (e.g., science) to explain it—this is typically called the transcendent or supernatural. Thus, substantive definitions of religion generally "refer to transcendent entities in the conventional sense—God, gods, supernatural beings and worlds, or such metaempirical entities," with Max Weber defining religion as "a cumulative rational systematization of ideas concerning the supernatural."[2]

This results in religion being defined as the "irrationalities," as the "not-science." Defining religion as that which is not demonstrable with human reason fits quite well with metaphysical naturalism, and focuses the analyst on claims about the natural and supernatural world. With this definition in hand, religion is about beliefs and knowledge claims, and therefore any conflict with science is bound to be over beliefs and knowledge claims.

This is what religion "is" in the religion and science debate. If religion is based on fact claims about nature, as that which is above or beyond nature, then it is easy to see religion as a failed attempt to explain the natural world. As the new atheists are fond of pointing out, a fundamentalist Protestant exegesis of the Bible makes a conflicting fact claim about the natural world—the age of the Earth—and a superior system called science has come along to show that religion is a faulty system of explanation.

In contrast are functional definitions of religion, which became more influential in the 1960s, where religion is any cultural system at its most abstract. Functional definitions of religion identify a religion as that which does certain things for a group of people, independent of content, transcendent, or otherwise. One of the most influential of these definitions among sociologists is that of anthropologist Clifford Geertz, who in the late 1960s defined religion as "(1) a system of symbols (2) which acts to establish powerful, pervasive, and long-lasting moods and motivations in men (3) by formulating conceptions of a general order of existence and (4) clothing these conceptions with such an aura of factuality that (5) the moods and motivations seem uniquely realistic."[3]

Geertz further explains each of these elements in his definition. "A system of symbols" is like a program "for the institution of the social and psychological processes which shape public behavior" that is based in a social group. "Moods and motivations" are about how we are supposed to live, our sense of direction, and what we aspire to. Religious symbols "express the world's climate and shape it," shaping it "by inducing in the worshiper a certain distinctive set of dispositions (tendencies, capacities, propensities, skills, habits, liabilities, pronenesses) which lend a chronic character to the flow of his activity and the quality of his experience." Religions formulate "conceptions of a general order of existence," where the entire world and our values make sense.[4] Creating an "aura of factuality" that makes the "moods and motivations seem uniquely realistic" are, for my purposes, that these socially oriented moods and motivations are come to be thought of as true through social interaction. In this definition, religion is not about knowledge of the natural world.

Others, such as sociologist Peter Berger, published similar and equally influential conceptions of religion during this same era.[5] Religion in these functional definitions is a combination of understanding the social world and telling us what we should do in the social world. Again, religion is not about facts of nature.

I could be easily convinced that premodern religion concerned fact claims about nature, since surviving in nature was probably central to most people's experience. However, in the contemporary Western world, nature is not the problem for our survival, but our social relationships are. Therefore, using this definition of religion, religion is much more about morality and social relationships than it is about facts. For example, from this perspective on what religion is, while an evangelical will tell you that the Genesis account of creation is true, that does not really matter in their life, and this ritual enactment of this truth actually exists to deliver a social or moral lesson, such as "we are not God." Did Job of the Hebrew Bible and Christian Old Testament exist? Some churches would say yes to this fact-claim, but that does not matter to an ordinary congregant as much as the fact that the collective belief in Job teaches the community a social and moral message about suffering.

A study of secularization on a Danish island nicely demonstrates how changing the definition of religion can allow the analyst to see a relationship between religion and science in the public quite differently than has historically been portrayed. Anthropologist Andrew Buckser concluded that the decline in religious activity on the island was not because of science. Rather, it was due to how social relationships on the island had changed due to agricultural mechanization, which had, in turn, reduced the population of villages and weakened social ties. He concludes that the problem with using the then-dominant secularization theory to understand his case is that it uses a definition by which religion is "a method of explaining the physical world through the supernatural." But, he concludes, citing Geertz, that "in any religion, explaining the physical world is only a subordinate task; it is explaining the social world, giving it meaning and moral value, which is religion's primary concern."[6]

While the established and older definition of religion was pushing him to see systemic knowledge conflict, by adopting the newer functional definition of religion he saw that any conflict between religion and science was social or moral. To the extent that this definition of religion was generated through observing the most recent religious public, this strand of social science theory suggests that we are right to question whether the contemporary religious public is in knowledge conflict with science.

Questioning Science as Neutral Knowledge

From the other side of the religion-science relationship, scholarship in the field of the sociology of science evolved in the mid 1970s to challenge the idea that science is a value-free investigation of the truth of nature independent of influence from the social and moral worlds. Intellectually, this was largely a reaction to a Whiggish historiography of science, which portrayed today's scientific truths as inevitably coming to be realized. Sociologists and other academics involved in the nascent field of science studies came to agree with Hegel, who wrote that "truth is not a minted coin which can be given and pocketed ready-made."

One of the basic insights of the late 1970s Edinburgh School of science studies was that social situations and interests influenced the fact claims about nature that are made by scientists. While there is an extremely strong version of this view that suggests that truth does not exist, I think most academics would agree with the milder form, which is that truth does exist, but that human access to truth is limited and influenced by our social relationships. Part of the intellectual strategy of the Edinburgh School was to bracket whether a truth claim was later agreed to be true by scientists, and to show how scientists had to use various social mechanisms to convince their colleagues of claims that would eventually be considered true (the double-helix structure of DNA) and false (phrenology).

The early academic statements in this field made the case that the establishment of a scientific knowledge claim as true was a social achievement, not something that would just emerge on its own.[7] Severed from the truth of nature, science had to make efforts to establish truth and authority, not unlike how religious leaders had to establish truth and authority. There have been sporadic studies in science studies that do not start with the assumption that the science is correct and the religion is incorrect. For example, one set of studies examined how scientists struggled to demarcate "science" from "non-science," and therefore establish social authority for their knowledge claims.[8]

The eventual term for this academic field—the sociology of scientific knowledge—indicates that while science was still thought of as concerning knowledge, it certainly also was about social relationships and morals, in service of creating authentic knowledge. This field, developed within the past fifty years, reflects the post-1960s public skepticism about all institutions, and suggests that the public might not be as confident as they were in the past that scientists are only engaged in the morally neutral discovery of truth about the natural world.

New Secularization Theory Without Systemic Knowledge Conflict

Recent secularization theory also has shifted away from a focus on knowledge. The classic studies of secularization presumed systemic knowledge conflict—that the growth of certain types of rationality embodied in modern science—were central to secularization. In one summary, "the era of the Enlightenment generated a rational view of the world based on empirical standards of proof, scientific knowledge of natural phenomena, and technological mastery of the universe. Rationalism was thought to have rendered the central claims of the Church implausible in modern societies, blowing away the vestiges of superstitious dogma in Western Europe."[9]

The most explicit version of this knowledge conflict account of secularization comes from Anthony Wallace, who saw science as directly causing secularization. He wrote that "the evolutionary future of religion is extinction. Belief in supernatural beings and supernatural forces that affect nature without obeying nature's laws will erode and become only interesting historical memory.... Belief in supernatural powers is doomed to die out, all over the world, as the result of the increasing adequacy and diffusion of scientific knowledge."[10]

However, a twenty-first-century strand of secularization theory avoids assuming that religion is centrally concerned with knowledge about the world, but focuses on religion as an institution with multiple tasks and interests, struggling against other institutions. The focus here is on power and agency of individuals within institutions, and empirical study of public interactions supports a different view that is incompatible with knowledge conflict. Secularization is not the result of a creeping habit of thought but rather due to secularizers—people who have an interest in discrediting religion.[11] Since it is not science per se that has a secularizing effect, these secularizers do not need to be scientists. For example, journalism as a profession secularized as subjective religious perspectives in newspapers were jettisoned in order for the media to have an impact on public education.[12]

The recent use of rational choice secularization theory also ignores science. This strand of theory was developed as a reflection of social reality—it was developed in part to explain the empirical reality that science had not destroyed religion in the U.S., one of the most scientifically advanced countries in the world. This theory assumes a constant demand for religion from the public, and secularization happens where religious organizations do not effectively meet this demand.[13] Europe is then more secular than the U.S. because of its religious monopolies, as represented by national churches, which result in lazy, ineffective religious suppliers. America is then more religious because our diverse and competitive religious market maintains efficient religious organizations.[14] Secularization is then not the result of science.

Even secularization theories that seem based on religion being a faulty understanding of nature have been tweaked to make them not about nature per se, but about the typical human response to nature. For example, Norris and Inglehart created a theory of secularization based on existential security where, in traditional societies, a lack of existential security comes from nature, and thus religion explains nature. However, in the U.S., a lack of existential security comes from society, where people could die due to a lack of healthcare. The existence of religion in the U.S. would then be due to this social threat, and the reason the U.S. has not secularized like Western Europe is, essentially, the absence of a welfare state. Scientific knowledge does not cause secularization per se, rather science causes secularization by allowing for the technology that provides existential security. This appears to be a clear case where a theory reflects society, in that the persistence of religion in the U.S.—in spite of claims that science should have wiped it out—led to a new theory that does not include science per se.[15]

The secularization literature has been the location of much of the sociological work on the relationship between science and religion. The earlier tradition assumes systemic knowledge conflict between science and religion, with an increase in science mechanically leading to a decline in religion. Secularization theories of the past fifty years no longer presume that the decline of religion is due to the spread of scientific knowledge. This suggests that when these theorists examine the contemporary religious public they do not see a religion centrally concerned with knowledge.

THE RECENT HISTORY OF ELITE SCIENTISTS AND THEOLOGIANS IN CONFLICT

We have extensively examined the historical literature in the previous chapter. How about the recent history of the past fifty years, which is typically not covered by historians? We saw evidence in the previous chapter that when historians more informally shift to discussing the contemporary era, they unreflectively start describing moral conflict, not knowledge conflict. In my examples below, we see conflict that lacks any knowledge component whatsoever, and only concerns morality. These conflicts are often prefigured in earlier periods. If it was true that pre-1960s American religious elites were in conflict with elite scientists over knowledge, I would argue that scientists won that contest, and scientists are now moving on to try to take the one remaining jurisdiction of theology—morals or values.

Scientists Trying to Produce Meaning for Humanity

What should be the source of the social norms that underpin a society? In the West these underpinnings have been religion. But, at various points in the past 100 years scientists have gained a level of confidence to assert that science should be the source of the norms that undergird society. By the late nineteenth century, a number of elite scientists and other intellectuals had created the rationale for a pseudo-religious "ethic of science" that would replace religion—what intellectual historian David Hollinger calls "the intellectual gospel."[16] This ethic of science included disinterestedness, objectivity, universalism, and veracity, and sociologists will recognize the similarity with what Robert Merton in the early 1940s considered to be the norms of science.[17] This ethic, epitomized and replicated by the best of the scientific community, could have religious potential for the society.[18] In one particularly evocative formulation of the advantage of this religion of science, an advocate wrote in 1916 that "the truly scientific mind 'cannot be brought within the bounds of a narrow religious formulary . . . yet it is essentially devout, and it influences for good all with whom it comes into contact.'" As a popular book written by a biologist stated in 1922, "'the scientific habit of mind' would 'satisfy the ethical and philosophical desires which have been hitherto formulated as religion and theology.'"[19] Intellectual historian Andrew Jewett writes that this group "reasoned that, because science carried with it a set of ethical resources, it could ground a democratic culture in the absence of a central religious authority, and thereby take over the core political functions of the pan-Protestant establishment."[20] Hollinger implicitly endorses my thesis that this moral conflict has largely been ignored by historians when he writes that "the intellectual gospel may not have been an episode in any 'warfare' of science and religion, but it did function in a real struggle between rival claimants to the cultural leadership of the United States."[21] Quite obviously, this has little to nothing to do with knowledge.

There was a very similar elite debate between religion and science from the 1950s forward that has also not been described as a debate between religion and science. Like the earlier "ethics of science" debate, the reason for its invisibility is probably that it was not about fact claims about nature, but about morality, so it did not fit into scholars' conception of what an actual religion and science debate is.

This 1950s and 1960s era debate between theologians, scientists, and others eventually became what is now called the "public bioethical debate." In previous texts I have examined the history of this debate, and what is most important for my present purposes is that I am unaware of any instance in all of that deliberation where a theologian challenged a scientist or physician about a fact claim about the natural world.[22] Instead, the theologians wanted to discuss either the morality behind, or the moral implications of, the scientists' activity.

Starting in the 1950s, scientists and physicians had made huge progress with the degree to which they could intervene in the human body. Scientists came to think that they would soon be able to engage in mind control, human cloning, human genetic engineering, test-tube babies, parthenogenesis, human/animal chimeras, organ transplantation, and much more. This led to deeper questions, such as what a human was and when would you know someone was actually dead so that you could remove their organs. Some of the elite scientists of the time were not content with making fact claims about nature, but were trying to have science answer the questions that had typically been associated with theology.

As Robert Edwards, co-inventor of in-vitro fertilization would later recall, "many non-scientists see a more limited role for science, almost a fact-gathering exercise providing neither values, morals, nor standards. . . . My answer . . . is that moral laws must be based on what man knows about himself, and that this knowledge inevitably comes largely from science."[23] Similarly, Jacob Bronowski would state in 1962 that "I am, therefore, not in the least ashamed to be told by somebody else that my values, because they are grounded in my science, are relative, and his are given by God. My values, in my opinion, come from as objective and definitive a source as any god, namely the nature of the human being."[24] Like the advocates of the "intellectual gospel" before them, elite scientists argued that science could set the morals of society.

Some of the theologians of the time recognized that they were being challenged on moral grounds by biologists. For example, Methodist theologian Paul Ramsey was opposed to some of the planned activities of the scientists on moral grounds, but was primarily opposed to the moral system being promoted by the scientists, recognizing that these scientists posed a challenge to theology's jurisdiction over determining meaning and morality. He was opposed to what he called the "surrogate theology" of the "cult" of "messianic positivism" of the scientists. Reacting to scientists like Edwards and Bronowski, he thought the scientists' goal was not to be an "exact science" of knowledge generation, but to provide the meaning of life:

> Taken as a whole, the proposals of the revolutionary biologists, the anatomy of their basic thought-forms, the ultimate context for acting on these proposals provides a propitious place for learning the meaning of "playing God"—in contrast to being men on earth.
> [The scientists have] "a distinctive attitude toward the world," "a program for utterly transforming it," an "unshakable," nay even a "fanatical," confidence in a "worldview," a "faith" no less than a "program" for the reconstruction of mankind. These expressions rather exactly describe a religious cult, if there ever was one—a cult of men-gods, however otherwise humble. These are not the findings, or the projections, of an exact science as such, but a religious view of where and how ultimate human significance is to be found. It is a proposal concerning mankind's final hope. One is reminded of the words of Martin Luther to the effect that we have either God or an idol and "whatever your heart trusts in and relies on, that is properly your God."[25]

Scientists soon realized that they had over-reached, and many influential scientists called for an end to scientific claims to remake humanity for fear that such talk would threaten funding for the science that most scientists wanted to do. For example, Harvard bacteriologist Bernard Davis agreed with the other scientists that science had "replaced earlier supernatural and animistic explanations of the universe" and thus "split the rock underlying Judeo-Christian morality." But, the "failure of science to provide a basis for a replacement, underlies much of the tragedy, anxiety, and rootlessness of the present age," precipitating attacks on science.[26] He began a 1970 article by decrying the statements of influential scientists by arguing that "some of these statements, and many articles in the popular press, have tended toward exuberant, Promethean predictions of unlimited control and have led the public to expect the blue-printing of human personalities." Moreover, the "exaggeration of the dangers from genetics will inevitably contribute to an already distorted public view, which increasingly blames science for our problems and ignores its contributions to our welfare." This "irresponsible hyperbole has already influenced the funding of research."[27] A few years later he would explicitly reject the moral project of other elite scientists. He wrote that scientists had accepted a "naive" view that "failed to recognize the fundamental distinction between empirical questions, concerned with the nature of the external world, and normative questions, concerned with moral values."[28]

The theologians and others were successful at getting the public focused upon these new moral challenges from the scientists' newfound abilities. They were so successful that they got the attention of the U.S. government, which eventually established government ethics commissions that would advise the government on what to allow, stripping direct control from the scientists. This was also the beginning of the end for the theologians' involvement in what would come to be known as public bioethical debate. The ultimate consumer of ethical advice regarding scientific experimentation on the human body was now the government, and therefore this ethics had to be in a bureaucratic and calculable form. Debate turned to thinner questions more amenable to regulation, such as safety and the informed consent of research subjects. Theologians were uninterested in such a debate, wanting to talk about the "big questions," such as what it means to be human and debating what the ends or goals of medicine and science should be. A bureaucratic ethics does not want to debate the ends or goals of medicine but wants to set certain goals or ends as undebatable and then ask whether the scientific activity most efficaciously forwards those goals or ends. The profession of bioethics emerged to serve this role.

My point here is that the history of the field of bioethics reveals an elite, exclusively moral conflict between religion and science that has nothing to do with knowledge about the natural world. The bioethics debate was triggered by the moral stance of scientists and physicians of the 1950s and 1960s, despite the ideology of science as a knowledge-gathering enterprise, and the scientists had a morality that conflicted with that of the theologians. In the later years of the debate, with the theologians gone, members of the bioethics profession effectively and implicitly forwarded the moral perspective of scientists. Yet, this debate is not generally considered a "conflict between religion and science," because, I would argue, it does not fit our preconception that such debates will be about knowledge.[29]

Other scholars have pointed out that this attempt by some elite scientists to create a religion of science continues to this day. In historian Peter Harrison's analysis, the new atheists argue that "the biological sciences provide the ultimate guide to life's most profound questions." One new atheist writer insists that "questions 'about meaning, morality, and life's larger purpose' are ultimately questions that science, and not religion, can answer." Science, that writer insists, "will gradually encompass life's deepest questions." Richard Dawkins similarly claims "that whereas theology had once provided the wrong answers to questions about the meaning of life, 'the right answers now come from evolutionary science.'"[30]

Harrison's analysis continues with Harvard biologist E. O. Wilson, who similarly claims that "scientific materialism 'presents the human mind with an alternative mythology that until now has always point for point in zones of conflict, defeated traditional religion.'" Science has finally been able "to provide an alternative account of 'man's place in the universe,' relying upon 'the scientific method.'" Moreover, for Wilson, "it is biology that has become 'foremost in relevance to the central questions of philosophy, aiming to explain the nature of mind and reality and the meaning of life.'"[31]

Transhumanism as a Pseudo-Religion

A critical component of the debate that birthed bioethics was centered on reform eugenics, advanced by scientists who wanted to perfect the human species through genetic engineering. Theologians were skeptical of this effort. The debate about reform eugenics paused for a few decades because it appeared to be scientifically impossible to modify the human genome in any truly substantive way.[32] However, after a few decades' pause, a remarkably similar set of eugenic arguments emerged from the "transhumanists." Transhumanism is another example of science that is not solely about knowledge, but has a moral perspective that can conflict with religion.

Transhumanism is the application of technology such as genetic engineering, robotics, nanotechnology, and computers to surpass human limitations.[33] The central idea is that "the human species can and should transcend itself 'by realizing new possibilities' of and for human nature."[34] This imperative to "improve" ourselves is well expressed by British philosopher John Harris, who writes that "taking control of evolution and our future development to the point, and indeed beyond the point, where we humans will have changed, perhaps into a new and certainly into a better species altogether, is 'nothing short of a clear imperative to make the world a better place.'"[35]

Transhumanism is not a movement in the public, but a movement of elite scientists and philosophers. The scientists are the Silicon Valley "visionaries" who want to change the world through technology. For example, human genome mapping pioneer J. Craig Venter recently announced the formation of a company called Human Longevity to, in the words of one newspaper writer, "cheat aging and death."[36] The cofounder of Human Longevity is Peter Diamandis, who is cofounder and Executive Chairman of Singularity University, a transhumanist educational institution in Silicon Valley.[37]

Transhumanism considers itself to be "the apotheosis of science and technology," and, going further, represents the ultimate form of faith in science—"a secularist project that displaces religion."[38] In the words of one influential proponent: "fundamental changes in our very natures have become both possible and desirable.... [H]umans could become like gods, and in so doing may put conventional religion out of business. Thus it is in the vital interests of Christianity and the other great world faiths to prevent human technological transformation."[39]

Theologians agree that transhumanism is implicitly religious. Theologian Brent Waters considers transhumanism and Christianity to be "contending salvific religions," and he cites the same idea from Martin Luther that Ramsey cited forty years earlier when arguing with an earlier generation of proponents of scientifically reshaping humanity. Transhumanism is:

> not a religion in a formal sense, but as Martin Luther suggests, wherever one places one's confidence is necessarily one's god—or, more broadly, one's object of faith or

ultimate concern. In this respect, transhumanism and Christianity appear to have a number of similarities, particularly with regard to soteriology and eschatology. Transhumanists and Christians agree, for instance, that the finite and mortal human condition is far from ideal. For transhumanists humans have fallen short of achieving their true potential, whereas for Christians humans have not yet become the kinds of creatures God intends them to be. In response both agree that humans require release from their current condition. . . . Both agree that death is the final enemy; transhumanists conquer this foe by achieving the immortality of endless time, whereas Christians are resurrected into eternity, where there is no time.[40]

The existence of transhumanism shows the continuation of the moral project of finding meaning and purpose through science, and that this effort is a competitor with religion, not for knowledge claims about nature, but for morality. Again, in this "recent history" of debates between religion and science, there is no debate about knowledge whatsoever.

Scientists' Hidden Moral Projects in Political Campaigns

Studies of contemporary elite scientists in the public sphere show that they often have a moral agenda and act to forward it—often against religion. Scientists in these campaigns imply that they are simply describing reality in a neutral way, but since these descriptions sound like science, their moral projects largely remain hidden from scholars. However, close studies show that scientists tend to select "neutral descriptions" quite consciously to further a moral agenda.

Public debates about embryonic research are a good example. An analysis of British debates from decades ago shows that the debate was framed as "a conflict between those who wish to enforce unthinking obedience to out-of-date religious beliefs and those who are determined to defend scientists' right to continue their search for truth." Despite this framing, a close academic analysis revealed that the arguments on the two sides "cannot be distinguished in terms of their rationality, their reliance on dogma, or in terms of other features central to the stereotyped contrast between religious and scientific styles of thought." So, in this debate, scientific views portrayed as morally neutral were actually in moral conflict with religious views.[41]

A similar pattern can be seen in recent U.S. debates about embryos. Science studies scholar J. Benjamin Hurlbut shows how in the numerous American bioethics commissions concerning human embryos from the 1970s forward, scientists created scientific descriptions of embryos that implicitly served a particular moral agenda. Hurlbut's best example is the scientists' invention of a new scientific-sounding category of the "pre-embryo" to distinguish it from the "embryo." The "pre-embryo" could still twin, but why this trait matters is obviously moral and not based on facts. More importantly, with "embryo" distinguished from "pre-embryos," research on "pre-embryos" could proceed apace, which is something that the scientific community was interested in doing. Similar efforts were made by scientists to change the terms used in the cloning debate from "cloned embryo" to "therapeutic cloning" (to distinguish from "reproductive cloning"). Later cloning would be relabeled "somatic cell nuclear transfer," which avoids the "cloning" term altogether. Scientists tried to take the same ontological object—the cloned embryo—but create different terms based upon people's intended uses of the object—therapy or reproduction. This is not a description of nature, but a distinction based on people's intentions, with some uses being implicitly moral or immoral.[42]

Hurlbut also examines the political debate in California surrounding Proposition 71, which proposed to have the state of California spend three billion dollars on embryonic stem cell research and explicitly allow the use of cloned embryos to produce stem cells (but not produce babies). It is hard to imagine that any citizen of California would think after this campaign that scientists were merely producing facts about nature. Rather, elite scientists campaigned for political positions that were consistent with their moral agenda.[43]

To start with the obvious, Proposition 71 was centrally about ethics. It implicitly took a position on the moral status of human embryos, which was that they were not as important as potential medical treatments that could come from embryonic stem cell research. Moreover, three billion dollars of state money was three billion that was not spent on schools, roads, and health care that used currently available technology. To say that California should spend three billion dollars on medical research is a moral choice—a moral choice that a majority of the voting citizens of California eventually agreed with.

The campaign to pass Proposition 71, which involved many scientists, was also not about scientific facts. Whereas some people questioned whether cures would come as fast as the scientists implied, nobody claimed that scientists do not know how stem cells work or that the opponents of the proposition had better fact claims about nature. The campaign was, as political campaigns are, about moral choices.

The beginnings of the campaign were meetings with Hollywood couples who had children with Type 1 diabetes, wealthy disease research advocates, public officials, and prominent stem cell scientists. They saw an opportunity in using California's ballot initiative process, and a coalition formed around this project. The campaign suggested that all Californians would benefit from stem cell research because over 70 different diseases and injuries could be cured with stem cells.[44]

Scientists played a central public role because they had the credibility to say that this research would indeed cure disease. Stanford stem cell biologist Irving Weissman said during a TV interview that scientists could make human embryonic stem cell lines that "represented each and every human disease" and that "the chances of disease to be cured by stem cell research are high, but only if we start."

In television ads for the campaign, Nobel laureate Paul Berg described the research as "an important scientific and medical breakthrough." University of California San Francisco diabetes expert Jeff Bluestone said that he was "absolutely confident" that stem cells would cure Type 1 diabetes.[45]

While the scientists were making claims within their area of expertise concerning whether this technology would work, more importantly for this book, many of these scientists portrayed themselves as being in conflict with religion. Many religious organizations opposed Proposition 71, and the motivation for the proposition in the first place was the perception that federal funding for this research had been blocked by religious conservatives' influence on the Republican Party. As an advocate testified in one of the public hearings, it "was the responsibility of the state of California to rectify the failure of the Bush administration to fund embryonic stem cell research," which was the result of "an administration that has ignored science and all its potential in favor of politics and religious extremism."[46]

The scientists did not challenge religion for making false claims about nature, but instead invoked past supposed conflict between religion and science over nature to say why religious *morality* was also wrong. As we would expect from earlier pages of this book, Galileo was the favored symbol for the scientists. Consider a special issue of the *Stanford Medical Magazine*. Hurlbut concludes that "the image and the majority of the articles ... characterized the political battle as a struggle between the antimodern, antidemocratic forces of religion and the enlightened, secular democratic forces of science." The Dean of the Stanford Medical School wrote of the conflict that "it's as if we have entered a time warp, and are spectators at the Inquisition's reading of charges against Galileo for his view of the solar system."[47]

In a 2002 hearing on stem cell research, the president of an advocacy organization for California's biomedical industry said that "much of the opposition is rooted in a set of particular religious worldviews." Moreover, "historically religion has not been the handmaiden of science and scientific progress ... Now, on the left is someone you all know—Galileo. On the right is Pope Paul the Fifth, who's not much remembered, except in his role in the Inquisition and the containment, if you will, of Galileo's astronomical ideas." Similarly, Stanford's Nobel laureate Paul Berg gave a talk titled "Stem Cells: Shades of Galileo."[48]

What is striking in all of the references to Galileo is that scientists are not just using Galileo to justify their role as the preeminent observers of nature, as I described in Chapter 2, but in this case to say that their morality is superior to religious morality. In sum, embryonic stem cell research has probably been the most recent, highly publicized clash between religious and scientific elites, and it was over morality, not knowledge.

ELITE PUBLIC DEBATES ABOUT DARWINISM HAVE BEEN ABOUT MORALITY NOT KNOWLEDGE

It is important to renarrate the debate about Darwin from my perspective because this debate is thought of as conclusive evidence for the systemic knowledge conflict perspective. The debate about Darwin is also the most prominent debate between *contemporary* religion and science for the public.[49]

Again, I am not the first to note the moral nature of debates about Darwin. For example, historian Peter Harrison notes that "what religiously motivated anti-evolutionists fear is not the 'science' as such, but the secularist package of values concealed in what they perceive to be the Trojan horse of evolutionary theory."[50] Rather, the moral narrative is usually submerged beneath a surface-level knowledge conflict narrative, and I want to highlight the moral.

For scientific elites this debate is about knowledge—they say we should look at the fossil record to look where humans came from, whereas conservative Protestants supposedly look to their Bibles to see where humans came from. There are of course conservative Protestants who *do* look to their Bibles for a knowledge claim about the origins of humans, and most would probably say they do so if asked. My point is not that they do not state a belief in knowledge conflict, but rather that if it were not for the moral conflict over Darwin they would not bother to raise the knowledge conflict. The moral conflict is the controlling force here, and the knowledge conflict is subsidiary to it. Moreover, as these debates have progressed over time, they reveal religious activists both making fewer religiously based fact claims and their growing acceptance of the epistemology of science. What is left for the religion side of the debate is a concern with the moral.

While such varied positions as Young Earth Creationism, Old Earth Creationism, Day-Age Creationism, Gap Creationism, Progressive Creationism, and Intelligent Design can be more or less treated as "creationist," it is their qualities as moral criticisms of Darwinism that most tightly bind them together, both historically and sociologically speaking. The concern of creationists in each of their historic incarnations is that when you teach evolution, you are implicitly teaching a certain philosophy at the same time, and that this philosophy undermines some forms of morality.

At the same time, Darwinism has often been the grounds for making moral claims by scientists. It is not that religious challenges erroneously mix morality and science because challengers don't understand science. Rather, challengers understand full well that scientists are also making moral claims, and are acting to counter these claims—and thus we have moral conflict. This contrasts sharply with the self-image of scientists in which they pursue knowledge in a value-free manner.

The Young Earth Creationist Scopes Trial Era

I will highlight these points by reviewing the history of debates about Darwin, broken into three eras. After the publication of *The Origin of Species* in 1859, both supporters and critics recognized that Darwinism had moral implications, a concern that became even more prominent following the publication of the *Descent of Man* in 1871. Scholar of Victorian literature Gowan Dawson concludes that "it was regularly avowed that the growing licentiousness of modern culture . . . actually gave warning of the repulsive direction in which society was being taken by the increasingly influential doctrines of Darwinism." One of the most problematic components of Darwin's theory for Victorian moral sensibilities was that the 1871 book noted "that the 'whole process of . . . the reproduction of the species, is strikingly the same in all mammals,' even down to 'the act of courtship by the male,' who, whether baboon or human, responded similarly to the smell and appearance of the opposite sex." This led to the "disquieting" implication of "rooting human sexuality in animal behavior."[51] While philosophers might question the simple move from "is" to "ought," it is clear that for many contemporaries, Darwinism implied some moral challenges, especially when articulated in Herbert Spencer's terms as "survival of the fittest."

In America, concerns over moral implications of Darwinism led to legal restrictions on the teaching of evolution in public schools.[52] Biology textbooks of the time, such as the popular *A Civic Biology* by George William Hunter, often contained only a limited amount of material on evolution. But even that limited amount discussed moral problems. *A Civic Biology*, for example, suggested that "if the stock of domesticated animals can be improved, it is not unfair to ask if the health and vigor of the future generations of men and women on the earth might not be improved by applying to them the law of selection."[53] That is, the book promoted eugenics.[54]

In May 1925, in order to test the constitutionality of an anti-evolution law, the American Civil Liberties Union provoked the State of Tennessee into prosecuting high school science teacher John Scopes for teaching the evolution lessons from *A Civic Biology* in a public school classroom. Creationists saw an opportunity to demonstrate that Darwinism implied an unacceptable and dangerous moral position that should not be publicly considered at all, much less taught to schoolchildren.[55] The defender of the creationist view was populist former Democratic Party presidential candidate William Jennings Bryan. According to Ron Numbers' canonical analysis of creationism, for Bryan:

> World War I . . . exposed the darkest side of human nature and shattered his illusions about the future of Christian society. Obviously something had gone awry, and Bryan soon traced the source of the trouble to the paralyzing influence of Darwinism on the conscience. By substituting the law of the jungle for the teachings of Christ,

it threatened the principles he valued most: democracy and Christianity. Two books in particular confirmed his suspicion. The first . . . recounted firsthand conversations with German officers that revealed the role of Darwin's biology in the German decision to declare war. The second . . . purported to demonstrate the historical and philosophical links between Darwinism and German militarism.[56]

According to historian Mark Noll, Bryan's "strident opposition to evolution arose not so much from a threat to traditional interpretations of Genesis 1 but because evolution threatened human dignity. A godless theory of evolution . . . would, if generally adopted, destroy all sense of responsibility and menace the morals of the world." Moreover, Bryan "saw clearly that the greatest problem with evolution was not the practice of science but the metaphysical naturalism and consequent social Darwinism that scientific evolution was often called upon to justify."[57]

In the late paleontologist Steven J. Gould's turn-of-the-twenty-first-century assessment, when Bryan "said that Darwinism had been widely portrayed as a defense of war, domination, and domestic exploitation, he was right."[58] According to historian Edward Larson, "many Americans associated Darwinian natural selection, as it applied to people, with a survival-of-the-fittest mentality that justified laissez-faire capitalism, imperialism, and militarism." Reflecting his decades in politics defending the common man, Bryan would in 1904 dismiss Darwinism as "the merciless law by which the strong crowd out and kill off the weak." Larson concludes that "everywhere the public debate over eugenics colored people's thinking about the theory of human evolution."[59] It appears that the most famous opponent of Darwinism was not primarily motivated by the debate about facts.

Indeed, it has been argued that the law that John Scopes violated, signed by the Tennessee governor in 1925, was not even motivated by the evolution issue, but the evolution issue became a totemic symbol of the larger issue of the declining rural life in the state. The content of high school biology of the time is summed up with the title of the book Scopes was accused of using: *Civic Biology*. "*Civic Biology*, with its focus on such issues as quarantine, alcohol, food safety, and the improvement of human society (including a substantial section on eugenics), was geared toward America's growing cities," writes historian Adam Shapiro. Indeed, the new curriculum began in New York City. He concludes that "many rural residents saw the expansion of public education in Tennessee as an attempt to change their culture and to instill foreign values. Civic biology taught students to prepare for a life away from their traditional upbringing. Consequently, parents took exception to the presence of biology as well as its content. The fact that the books taught the historical development of species was a small concern. The overall discipline of civic biology and the presence of new schools intended to bring social progress were much more objectionable."[60]

The Scopes case drew immense attention as a clash over questions of religion and morality.[61] Though technically Bryan won the case, creationists failed to win public support for their moral concerns. In popular culture, the creationists emerged from the Scopes trial as ignorant bumpkins, while evolution supporters came across as proponents of reason and science. These impressions were solidified by the 1960 Academy Award-nominated film depicting the Scopes trial named *Inherit the Wind*.[62]

But while it seemed that Darwinism had triumphed in the popular imagination, the empirical fact is that the teaching of evolution in public high schools, and the inclusion of Darwin in biology textbooks, actually declined after the Scopes era, be it due to the trial itself or the anti-evolution movement. Textbook publishers voluntarily self-censored their materials in order to avoid offending dominant sentiments.[63] For all of the flash of the Scopes trial, there was little interest in, and much public resistance to, expanding the teaching of evolution in public schools.

Without Darwinism moving into the sphere of public morality through the education system, creationists kept to themselves and their own organizations after Scopes. Creationists still worried about the moral claims of Darwinism, but by and large kept their arguments within the creationist community rather than public debate.[64]

Continuing across this era was the eugenics movement, a scientific effort that tried to implement a particular moral vision. In the 19th century Francis Galton, a half-cousin of Darwin, drew heavily on Darwin's theories to promote eugenics, the systematic intervention into human reproduction for the purpose of improving "racial hygiene."[65] Of concern to many proponents of eugenics was the idea that society could succumb to degeneration, making it less fit for survival and therefore doomed to extinction. Yet many were confident that Darwinism provided the answer. As John Haycraft said in his lectures to the Royal College of Physicians in 1895: "We can improve our race by adopting the one and only adequate expedient, that of carrying on the race through our best and most worthy strains. We can be as certain of our result as the gardener who hoes away the weeds and plants good seed, and who knows that he can produce the plants he wants by his care in the selection of the seed."[66]

Early American eugenics drew on Spencer, Darwin, and Galton to justify programs of forced sterilization for "mental defectives," "moral degenerates," and other "undesirables" to prevent the inheritance of their bad traits to later generations. The Eugenics Record Office, founded in 1910 at the Cold Spring Harbor Laboratory, promoted forced sterilization as good public policy.[67] By 1930, half of the states in the U.S. had some sort of eugenic sterilization law on the books. In Arizona, inmates of the State Hospital for the Insane could be sterilized if they were the "probable potential parent of socially inadequate offspring," and in Kansas any inmate of the state, including prisoners, could be sterilized if "procreation by him would be likely to result in defective or feeble-minded children with criminal tendencies."[68] Often, however, "degenerate" meant nonwhite or immigrant. By 1924, the U.S. Congress passed the Immigration Reform Act, setting quotas for immigrants according to their seeming fitness and levels of "social inadequacy." Immigration levels did not recover until the late 1980s.[69]

Of course, the most severe example of eugenics was the systematic sterilization and extermination of those deemed degenerate by the Nazi regime, particularly embodied by the 1933 Law for the Prevention of Genetically Diseased Offspring. The Nazis "regularly quoted American geneticists who expressed support for their sterilization policies . . . [and] frequently invoked the large-scale California experience with sterilization," writes historian Diane Paul.[70] It is clear that Nazi policies drew on ideas about racial hygiene and degeneracy, and it is clear that many American scientists admired such firm policies. Of course, the use of Darwin's ideas to legitimate prejudices reached its apotheosis in the Holocaust where, in Kevles' words, "a river of blood would eventually run from the [German] sterilization law of 1933 to Auschwitz and Buchenwald."[71] Of course, the point is not that Darwin would have approved, but rather that these immoral acts were being justified by others by referencing Darwin's ideas.

Creation Science Era

With the launch of Sputnik in 1957, the American government turned to funding science education in a concerted and systematic way. The Biological Sciences Curriculum Study brought together, perhaps for the first time, practicing scientists and practicing teachers to create a biology curriculum to be used in the nation's public schools.[72] The Biological Sciences Curriculum Study program made Darwinism, and evolution more generally, the cornerstone of biology education in America.

In response to the increase in teaching of Darwinism in public schools, creationists mounted challenges to Biological Sciences Curriculum Study textbooks on many different grounds, including indecency of images depicting reproductive organs, violation of remaining state anti-evolution laws, and violation of the First Amendment.[73] The tactics varied in their approaches, but the common concern remained that Darwinism had dangerous moral implications and should not be taught in schools.

One of the strongest challenges came from "creation science," where creationists dismissed Darwinism based on scientific claims stemming from the Bible. Creation science proponents agreed that students should learn science, but not that they should learn Darwinism. In 1961, Whitcomb and Morris published *The Genesis Flood,* an account of geology and human origins based on Biblical explanations of the world-girdling Noachic flood.

For Whitcomb and Morris, the claim to being engaged in science was as much about the need to replace Darwinian morality with a God- and human-centered morality as it was about floods and geology. In *The Genesis Flood,* they wrote:

> The morality of evolution, which assumes that progress and achievement and "good" come about through such action as benefits the individual himself or the group of which he is a part, to the detriment of others, is most obviously anti-Christian. The very essence of Christianity is unselfish sacrifice on behalf of others, motivated by the great sacrifice of Christ himself, dying in atonement for the sins of the whole world![74]

These sentiments were echoed by local activists, such as one group that distributed a flyer with a pictorial diagram of the "evolution tree" of "evil fruits" growing from the root of Darwinism. These "evil fruits" include (but are not limited to) communism, racism, terrorism, abortion, socialism, crime, and inflation. The accompanying text concludes "What is the best way to counteract the evil fruit of evolution? Opposing these things one-by-one is good, but it does not deal with the underlying cause.... A more effective approach is to chop the tree off at its base by scientifically discrediting evolution."[75]

In 1968, the decision in *Epperson v. Arkansas* rendered anti-evolution laws unconstitutional. In 1974 Morris produced *Scientific Creationism,* a guide to teaching creation science without explicit reference to biblical authority or even religious language.[76] Without the advantage of anti-evolution laws, creationists promoted the idea of "equal time" and "balanced treatment" for creation science and Darwinian science, and even obtained legal protection for such treatment in Arkansas and Louisiana.[77]

In 1982, however, *McLean v. Arkansas* marked the beginning of the end for creation science in public science classes. The *McLean* decision struck down the Arkansas law on the basis that creation science violated the American Constitution's First Amendment prohibition on the establishment of religion. The judge acknowledged that creation science was in part a reaction to the introduction of the Biological Sciences Curriculum Study curriculum, even citing the moral concerns driving the challenge in the official opinion: "Creationists view evolution as a source of society's ills [and that] it has served effectively as the pseudo-scientific basis of atheism, agnosticism, socialism, fascism, and numerous other false and dangerous philosophies over the past century."[78]

Yet the judge focused his legal decision on knowledge issues, itemizing the ways in which creation science did not accord with scientific method or practice, and emphasizing that creation science was not, in his opinion, science at all. While this was not strictly necessary for rendering an opinion on the religious grounds for creation science, it nonetheless reinforced the perception in the public sphere of systemic knowledge conflict. From *McLean* forward, the success of creationist challenges would be measured based on whether or not creationist theories were included in "science" as defined by judges in landmark legal cases, rather than the extent to which moral concerns resonated with a broader public. In 1987, *Edwards v. Aguillard* came before the U.S. Supreme Court, and—largely based on the reasoning about the establishment of religion in *McLean*—the court rendered a decision to strike down Louisiana's Creationism Act, the last remaining "equal time" law in the nation.

The centrality of morality to conservative Protestant anti-evolution movements up through the creation science era is summarized by anthropologist Christopher Toumey, who wrote that "creationism is a moral theory that the idea of evolution is intimately involved in immorality, as cause or effect or both." It is "much more than a narrow doctrine extrapolated from a handful of biblical verses. It represents a broad cultural discontent, featuring fear of anarchy, revulsion for abortion, disdain for promiscuity, and endless other issues, with evolution integrated into those fears."[79]

The Intelligent Design Era

McLean and *Edwards* instituted a legal regime wherein any hint of religious motivations could invalidate an attempt to promote an alternative to Darwinism. In response, advocates reworked an existing creation science textbook to remove all references to creationism and replace them with the term "intelligent design" (ID). They published the resulting text in 1989 as *Of Pandas and People*.[80] The term "ID" refers to the idea that the world we observe is so complex that it could not have arisen without intelligent guidance, an idea that traces its roots back to Isaac Newton and William Paley.[81] Notably, however, ID does not necessarily require specific claims about God or a particular religious belief system.

The most visible and active proponents of ID are fellows of the Discovery Institute, and their strategy for promoting ID is revealed in the "Wedge Document," a text originally intended for internal use, but copied and widely circulated by opponents seeking to discredit ID. The Wedge Document cites as motivation for ID the serious moral concerns implied by the materialist conception of reality promoted by Darwinism, which:

> eventually infected virtually every area of our culture, from politics and economics to literature and art . . . materialists denied the existence of objective moral standards, claiming that environment dictates our behavior and beliefs. Such moral relativism was uncritically adopted by much of the social sciences. . . . Materialists also undermined personal responsibility by asserting that human thoughts and behaviors are dictated by our biology and environment . . . In the materialist scheme of things, everyone is a victim and no one can be held accountable for his or her actions.[82]

As with creation science, ID proponents seek equal time for their position in public school science classes. Unlike creation science advocates, ID proponents take special care to minimize the possibility that ID will be seen as religious. So far, this strategy has met with limited success. In 2004, a school board in Dover, Pennsylvania voted to require a statement about ID as part of the public school curriculum. Shortly thereafter, a group of parents filed suit against the district, and the resulting decision, in *Kitzmiller v. Dover*, once again struck down a creationist challenge based on the First Amendment Establishment Clause.

ID proponents have once again taken up the idea of "equal time" and "teaching the controversy," but in the public rather than the legal arena. A documentary film titled *Expelled: No Intelligence Allowed* claims that alternatives to Darwinism have been suppressed, and that Darwinism is of grave moral concern. An accompanying text for the documentary claims that "In a Darwinian framework, human beings are no better than any other animal and ultimately may be treated as animals by those who consider themselves to be greater, more human, enlightened or evolved . . . Hitler and the Nazis followed Darwinian eugenics to an extreme, carrying 'survival of the fittest' to the radical conclusion of exterminating 'unfit' and 'inferior' races like the Jews and Gypsies, and 'weak' members of society like the handicapped."[83]

Unsurprisingly, reaction to ID from defenders of science in popular and academic venues has focused on ID's religious origins, as this is now the most effective legal way to prevent ID from inclusion in public school curricula.[84] However, the central claim at the heart of ID remains consistent with Bryan, Whitcomb, and many other creationists since Darwin. For creationist challengers past and present, Darwinism implies a morality that devalues human life, causes unneeded conflict and competition, and pushes society in an actively harmful direction. Religion and science debates about Darwin are largely moral.

CONCLUSION

In the previous two chapters I have shown how those who write about the relationship between religion and science presume a systemic knowledge conflict between religion and science. In this chapter I have examined contemporary social science definitions of religion, secularization theory and the sociology of science. These should in principle be at least somewhat based on contemporary American society, and these do not portray religion and science as in systemic knowledge conflict.

As I showed in the last chapter, historical studies of conflict between elite representatives of religion and science largely show systemic knowledge conflict. In this chapter I examined the recent history of the past fifty years or so—debates that evolved into modern bioethics, transhumanism, and scientists' political activism. All show moral and not knowledge conflict. Finally, I re-narrated the history of conflict over Darwin. This debate is particularly significant because it is really the only religion and science conflict today that is conceivably about knowledge claims. I show that this debate has always been largely moral.

In Chapter 6, I will present my own data analyses concerning the contemporary public. In this chapter, by showing that even contemporary elites—who are prone to seeing science and religion as structures of knowledge—do not see religion and science as arguing about knowledge, I have bolstered my interpretation in that later chapter. Before starting that analysis, I turn in the next chapter to existing research on the general public, which also should make us skeptical that ordinary religious people are in systemic knowledge conflict with science and suggests it is likely that they are instead in moral conflict with science.

5

Existing Research on the Public

In Chapters 2 and 3, we saw that the vast majority of academics assume that the relationship, and any conflict, between religion and science is based on systemic knowledge. In this view, both science and religion are hierarchically organized systems of justifying concrete truth claims about nature. These systems are logically coherent, so that if you believe in the scientific method to determine how electrons move, you should not also be able to believe that God caused the emergence of humans. In the last chapter I also focused on elites, but looked at recent history, which may be different from the elite debates from more than fifty years ago. We see that among these elites, the debate is more about morality than it is about knowledge.

In this chapter I turn to the public and review existing research, research that would be largely unknown to scholars in the religion and science debate because it is spread across disparate fields. This research suggests, consistent with the last chapter, that it is not plausible that the religious public is in systemic knowledge conflict with science. Propositional belief conflict and moral conflict is likely. This existing research allows me to lay the groundwork for my own data analyses in the next chapter.

Now that I am turning to the public, I begin by offering more detail about the diversity of religion in the U.S. I start by showing that if you look at the official teachings of religions in the U.S., there is only one tradition where the religious public would get support from religious elites for knowledge conflict with science, and that tradition is conservative Protestantism. I then turn to somewhat abstract social science research about the public's use of systemic knowledge, which suggests that the general public would not have such structures. Thus, systemic knowledge conflict is even less likely. I then turn to what we know about the religion actually practiced by the contemporary American public, and how this has changed in the past fifty years. Contemporary American religion is quite different from the idealized conceptions of academics, and has features that also make systemic knowledge conflict unlikely. In the final section, I examine research on what the public thinks about science and scientists. People are likely to think of scientists in moral terms, and the general public is prone to see scientists as at minimum not like themselves, and at maximum immoral people who need to be controlled. These disparate studies all suggest moral and not knowledge conflict.

ONLY CONSERVATIVE PROTESTANT ELITES TEACH A BELIEF SYSTEM THAT COULD HAVE KNOWLEDGE CONFLICT WITH SCIENCE

Most of the larger religious traditions in the U.S. teach that there is not a conflict between their religious belief system and the methodological naturalist version of a scientific belief system. For example, lightning is not due to God's wrath, but due to differential electrical charges in the atmosphere. One way to describe this is that in most traditions the theological synthesizers examined in Chapter 2 have been successful, so religious people in these traditions would be encouraged by elites to not make a supernatural claim about anything that a scientist makes a claim about. Anything about the natural world that is potentially *demonstrable* will have a naturalistic explanation (like the cause of hurricanes), but non-demonstrable claims that no scientist cares about—like the Resurrection—may have a supernatural explanation. But, since the resurrection is not a violation of methodological naturalism, there is no conflict between religion and science.

I generally will not describe the views of religious minorities, because these groups are too small to be observed using the sociological data that I use in later chapters. The exception is Judaism, which I briefly describe, because there is an extensive academic literature on Judaism and science, and because scholars of Christianity use Judaism as a comparison due to Christianity's emergence from Judaism.

To the extent that we can say there are official theologies for American religions, Catholicism, Judaism and mainline Protestantism all have mechanisms for integrating faith with observation and reason. More specifically, their position is that a scientific claim that has come to be thought of as true needs to be incorporated into theological belief. Synthesis is the official stance. It is then unlikely that members of these traditions would have systemic knowledge conflict with science—nor would they have propositional belief conflict with science, as they would be encouraged to think that what scientists claim is true.

Judaism

I begin my tour of American religion with Judaism, which has long held that if science makes one claim and religion another, either could be wrong, and either could be corrected. So, a central feature of Judaism is to account for scientific claims. Historians show that this view goes back farther than my version of history requires, with nineteenth-century Jews seeing themselves as "bystanders" to the debate among Christians in the U.S. For example, in a mid-nineteenth-century authoritative traditionalist Jewish journal a prominent Jewish leader repeatedly asserted that "Judaism, unlike Christianity, was utterly at ease with science." The founder of the Reform Rabbinical School of the Hebrew Union College, and arguably the most influential Reform Jew in 19th century America, wrote that "Christianity, by its nature, is belligerent towards 'philosophy, science, and criticism,' while Judaism, by its nature, is 'in profound peace' with them."[1]

By the twentieth century, this view of science became interwoven with Jewish aspirations to integrate into America. Historian Noah Efron writes that science promised to rattle the complacency of exclusionary elites, dissolve sectarianism, and expand universal education. Jews saw science as making fact and data the basis of social policy, rather than tradition and prejudice. So, resistance to science "was taken as resistance to the complex of changes that many Jews advocated explicitly, and many more saw as needed, if Jews were to thrive in America."[2] To this day, it is extremely difficult to find Jews in the public sphere who are opposed to any scientific claim, with the exception of some Orthodox Jews. The Orthodox comprise only 10 percent of the 2 percent of Americans who are Jewish.[3]

Catholicism

At least officially, Catholicism incorporates scientific discoveries into its theology, often with a time-lag, and modern Catholic leaders have claimed that they have no methodological conflict with science. For example, every pope since Pius XI (1929–1939) has affirmed the autonomy of science. Similarly, contemporary Catholic teaching holds the doctrine of "two truths," that scientific knowledge cannot contradict supernatural knowledge, since both emerge from the same source.[4] As one prominent Catholic intellectual wrote in the late nineteenth century, "truth cannot contradict truth."[5] This has long been supported by Papal statements, including that of Pope Pius XI, who stated in 1936: "Science, which consists in true recognition of fact, is never opposed to the truths of the Christian faith."[6] More than fifty years later, Pope John Paul II wrote, "science can purify religion from error and superstition; religion can purify science from idolatry and false absolutes."[7]

Catholicism also has no tradition of biblical literalism or inerrancy. One reason that Catholics did not get boxed in as Protestants did, as we will see below, is that Church teaching served as a mechanism for an alternative source of religious authority outside of Scripture.[8]

The one instance of what appears on the surface to be a knowledge conflict for Catholicism in the past two hundred years is instructive. In the 1890s and the first decade of the twentieth century, the newly emerging science on the age of the Earth was not problematic because Church teaching—different from the Bible—had sufficient precedent for seeing the days of creation as either allegorical or representative of another length of time. However, a number of Catholics got in trouble for the endorsement of evolution during these two decades before the Church reverted to its more standard stance of endorsing evolution. It is notable that the conflict was influenced by non-scientific issues and reflected concerns about evolutionary theory outside the realm of biology, disagreements over Augustine and Thomas Aquinas, and growing tensions between liberals and conservatives. For example, Darwinism became controversial when it seemed to move beyond science to claims, such as Herbert Spencer's social evolutionism, that religious thought also was subject to "evolution."[9] In other words, at the turn of the twentieth century, the Church was not opposed to the scientific claims of Darwin per se, but opposed to how these claims were used to influence a social theory and theological truth.

Contemporary Catholic leaders are the theologian-synthesizer types examined in the previous chapter. There has been some ambiguity about evolution, with the Church seeming at times to move toward agreeing with intelligent design theory, then moving back to agreement with neo-Darwinism, which has been more typical of twentieth-century Catholicism.[10] Reflecting this somewhat ambiguous history, in February of 2009 a Vatican analyst wrote that the Vatican had just "dealt the final blow to speculation that Pope Benedict XVI might be prepared to endorse the theory of Intelligent Design."[11] As an example of synthesis, consider this statement by Pope John Paul II to a conference held to commemorate the three hundredth anniversary of Newton's *Principia Mathematica*. The Pope wrote:

> If the cosmologies of the ancient Near Eastern world could be purified and assimilated into the first chapters of Genesis, might contemporary cosmology have something to offer to our reflections upon creation? Does an evolutionary perspective bring any light to bear upon theological anthropology, the meaning of the human person as the *imago Dei*, the problem of Christology—and even upon the development of doctrine itself? What, if any, are the eschatological implications of contemporary cosmology, especially in light of the vast future of our universe? Can theological method fruitfully appropriate insights from scientific methodology and the philosophy of science?[12]

So, Catholic elites do not teach either systemic knowledge or propositional belief conflict, but instead defer to science for fact statements about the contemporary natural world. It is then less likely that Catholic members of the public would be in any kind of knowledge conflict with science.

Protestantism

Unlike the differences between greatly distinct traditions like Catholicism and Protestantism, Judaism and Christianity, or Islam and Protestantism, the differences between types of Protestants in America are quite subtle. The major Protestant traditions overlap with each other, and many contemporary Protestants would have a hard time placing themselves in a particular tradition. Moreover, many Protestant denominations have people from more than one Protestant tradition within them. For example, people who would be considered part of the evangelical tradition are found in what are considered to be mainline denominations. Nonetheless, the differences between Protestant traditions are real, and are best visualized as three overlapping bell curves on a two-dimensional space, with "liberalism" and "fundamentalism" as the end points and evangelicalism in between them. Whereas it is difficult to tell people apart in the overlapping areas, if you talk to a liberal Protestant and a fundamentalist, the differences are quite obvious.

In some parts of Protestantism in the modern U.S., a church member could find support from elites in their tradition for a knowledge conflict with science. To understand why Protestants could be in knowledge conflict with science, I must delve into history. The story of the splits within Protestantism, and how current institutionalized views came to be, has been well told by many historians, and these splits often involved science. For my purposes I will skip to the late nineteenth century, when there *was* a systemic knowledge conflict underway between religious and scientific elites for what would be at the pinnacle of the pyramid of a legitimate science. One group of scientists was advocating for a purely secular science that we could call materialist positivism. The other set of scientists, more open to religion, were advocating for Baconian science, which was supported by Scottish Common Sense Realism.[13]

Baconian science had been the dominant science in the first part of the nineteenth century. The primary goal of Baconianism was to accumulate facts through observation and, crucially, avoid speculations about that which was not observable. "Such speculations and preconceptions Baconians condemned roundly with their worst pejorative: 'hypotheses,'" writes sociologist Eva Garroutte.[14] The fine-grained taxonomies could be developed through accumulating facts and patterns observed, eventually inductively resulting in the laws that govern the detailed facts.

One of the attractions of this particular epistemology of science in the mid-nineteenth century was its democratic nature, since it implied that any rational, intelligent person could make a contribution to scientific knowledge. This was the influence of Scottish Common Sense Realism, which appealed in America because it was an antidote to "the scepticism of the modern age," which was itself the result of abstract speculations by philosophers. Historian George Marsden writes that "Common Sense philosophy could thus combat one of the nineteenth-century threats to certainty—Germanic speculations—by appealing to the American faith in the common person." Therefore, in this epistemology, "all normal people were endowed by their Creator with various faculties that produced beliefs on which they must rely." Basically, you could trust in your sense-perceptions.[15] This fit particularly well with American notions of democracy and the wisdom of the ordinary people.

During this era, the Protestant churches "were populist, democratic, and libertarian, and the churches were strongly identified with the common people."[16] The Protestants, who dominated the public sphere, saw the Bible and nature as the two books of God, and believed that: "Nature constituted one set of facts and that the biblical Scriptures constituted another, and that scientists and theologians could apply the very same scientific method to the study of both."[17] The Baconian method of induction was then seen as a "divinely sanctioned mode of reasoning that characterized both true religion and genuine science."[18]

It is important to be clear that conservative Protestant theologians were not reading Bacon or delving into Scottish Common Sense philosophy, but were simply using the dominant definition of science at the time, which was based on these ideas. As Ronald Numbers summarizes in his canonical study, creationists "cobbled their populist epistemology independently of philosophical experts and acquired their definition of science from the obvious place: the dictionary."[19]

"So in the first heyday of evangelicalism in the United States, objective scientific thought was not tinged with the guilt of fostering secularism," writes historian of evangelicalism George Marsden. "Rather it was boldly lauded as the best friend of the Christian faith and of Christian culture generally."[20] The detailed study of God's creation through direct observation would reveal the truth of God's other revelation—the Bible.[21] In summary, this nineteenth century Conservative Protestant version of science was opposed to abstraction, and held that the things worth understanding were not opaque and were as they appeared to be. Therefore, theories, hypotheses, and metaphysical thoughts were unnecessary.[22] Ordinary people could use their common sense to observe nature, build up generalized understandings from these observations, and trust in their observations, and not in theories or models.

According to Marsden, interpreters often have attributed the American emphasis on inerrancy of Scripture to the influence of Common Sense philosophy and Baconianism. While inerrancy was not invented by Baconianism or Scottish Common Sense Realism, it contributed to this hermeneutic approach. God's truth in nature and the Bible were revealed in the same way: Baconianism meant simply looking at the evidence, determining what were facts, and classifying these facts. One could scrupulously generalize from the facts, but a good Baconian avoided speculative hypotheses. Therefore, the interpretation of Scripture involved careful determination of the facts—what the words mean. "Once this was settled the facts revealed in Scripture could be known as surely and as clearly as the facts discovered by the natural scientist" writes Marsden.[23] Historian Mark Noll concurs, writing that the principles of Scottish Enlightenment rationality had become so influential "that it was increasingly easy for evangelicals to treat the Scriptures as a 'scientific' text whose pieces were to be arranged by induction to yield the truth on any issue."[24]

In Marsden's depiction of the approach to Scripture of one prominent theologian of the time we can see echoes of the good Baconian scientist gathering and classifying specimens to inductively generate a law about insects. This theologian, "like many of his contemporaries, treated Scripture quite frankly as a compilation of hard 'facts' that the theologian had only to arrange in systematic order." The conclusion was that "God would do nothing less than reveal the facts of Scripture with an accuracy that would satisfy the most scrupulous modern scientific standards."[25] Like nature being self-evident to common sense, "the Scriptures fairly translated need no explanation."[26]

Protestants in the post-Civil War period were then consistent with the best of science of the day. However, a faction of positivist scientists associated with the modern universities soon developed different ideas, wanting to separate themselves from religious ideas, and by 1910 the isolation of the sciences from religious considerations had become a strict requirement.[27] The positivists were successful in destroying the idea that there was a direct connection between your observations of the world and truth. More importantly, they eliminated the idea that anyone with "common sense" could conduct science, replacing it with what we would today call "expertise." The connection with religion, that the Bible and nature were both to transparently reveal the same truth, was severed—"the old synthesis of evangelical convictions, American ideals, and a common-sense Baconian science faded rapidly away."[28] With the eclipse of the Baconian synthesis, science and Protestant religion were then, at least according to scientists, separate systemic knowledge systems and, in principle, capable of being in conflict.

Contemporary conservative Protestant knowledge conflict with science—at least among elites—has its origins in this transition when, for social reasons, conservative Protestants had to remain committed to the earlier Baconian version of science. Historian Mark Noll narrates this transition through responses to Darwin and through the rise of fundamentalism. Evangelicals had a choice, he argues. They could "follow time-honored Christian practice" of adjusting traditional conclusions to evolution as they had earlier done in response to proposals about the age of the Earth and the nebular hypothesis." Or they could "draw the line against this new challenge," he writes. The latter path was to reject evolution out of hand, because it did not fit with standard interpretations of the Bible.[29]

The challenge was how to square the idea that both the Bible and the best of science were both true. Part of the problem was that the fundamentalists had created a biblical exegesis built upon the best science from an earlier Baconian era—on the idea that "properly scrutinized results of the main culture's scientific enterprises should assist biblical interpretation."

This was the result of "an ominous weakness" in the Common Sense Baconian outlook. In order to obtain interpretive stability in the face of Protestantism's focus on individual interpretation, "theologians leaned the weight of divine Biblical authority squarely against the wall of humanity's current scientific knowledge and assumed that the two would support each other." However, now that science had become autonomous, problems emerged, as it was not clear that the current scientific understandings of nature would be consistent with reverent scientific interpretations of Scripture.[30] Noll considers this move to be a huge error for conservative Protestant theology, because it locked his tradition's theology into nineteenth-century science.

Therefore, "goaded on by the questionable use of science in the larger culture, fundamentalists and their evangelical successors dropped the nineteenth-century conviction that the best theology should understand and incorporate the best science."[31] Synthesis was out, potential for conflict was in. The way forward was American fundamentalism, and fundamentalists remained committed to the old Baconian definitions of science. Marsden writes that "the old balance between scientific rationality and Scripture was shored up. The objective authority of Scripture and its inerrancy were affirmed and accentuated. Science and reason continued to be regarded as confirming Scripture, but Darwinian theories were declared speculative hypotheses and not true science."[32] This foray through the history of American Protestantism's relationship to science explains why contemporary conservative Protestants—to the extent they have been influenced by fundamentalism—could be opposed to at least some propositional beliefs claimed by scientists.

The other path forward during this transition period for science and Protestantism was taken by Protestant liberals, also known as mainline Protestants or modernists, who were the other half of the divide that would define American Protestantism for over one hundred years. In contrast to the conservative approach, they engaged in separating religious truths entirely from dependence on scientific data. Therefore, the Bible's authority did not need to rest on any scientific claims, and religion was authenticated by personal experience.[33]

Disputes over science were just part of the divide between these two traditions of Protestantism, and the conflict over the application of Enlightenment reason to the Bible was probably even more divisive. For example, perhaps a greater divide than whether Protestants could believe Darwin was the question of whether Mary was a "virgin," as the Bible had traditionally been thought to say, or whether she was a "young woman," as some modernist theologians using Enlightenment reason would assert.[34]

Mainline Protestants did not reject all of traditional theology, but remained committed to what they thought of as essential tenets of Christianity. I would say that these tenets were those not threatened by a methodologically naturalistic science—like the idea that there is a God. For example, Roberts points out that late nineteenth-century mainliners had consensus on the idea that humans were made in the image of God, which is an unfalsifiable belief.[35]

But, in general, mainline Protestants "maintained that the progress of scientific investigation required Christians to make significant revisions in their apologetics, doctrine, and biblical interpretation," and that this "has rightly been viewed as one of the defining features of the American liberal Protestant theological tradition."[36] This is the synthesizing approach we examined in Chapter 2.

Mainline Protestant elite thinking eventually evolved into what Barbour would call an independence relationship with science, similar to Gould's notion of non-overlapping magisteria. Scientists were responsible for the "how," and theologians for the "why." This general strategy, which emerged from the divorce from fundamentalist Protestantism, accounts for the fact that there has been no conflict between mainline Protestant elites and science over knowledge. Indeed, you could say that the entire mainline tradition was invented to make religion consistent with modern Enlightenment rationality—including science. To return to the point of this chapter, this means that a mainline Protestant is not going to find support from the elites in their tradition for opposing a concrete scientific claim about the natural world.

This leaves the largest religious group in contemporary America for last—the evangelicals, who I have been lumping together with the fundamentalists under the term conservative Protestants. In the early twentieth century, the divide was between the fundamentalists and the modernists (also called mainline Protestants). But, in the 1940s, within conservative Protestantism, the fundamentalists splintered off a group of relatively more liberal members that would form a compromise movement between what they saw as the rigidity and separationalism of fundamentalism and the wishy-washy compromising of the mainline. This movement is called evangelicalism.[37]

Evangelicalism ended up being a far more successful movement than either fundamentalism or mainline Protestantism because it found the most efficient niche in American culture.[38] It thoroughly embraces the individualism of American culture and its love of technology. It is engaged and not separatist, so people can be exposed to the tradition and potentially join it. But, its views of the relationship between religion and science is ambiguous and still in flux, best described as falling between the orientations of the fundamentalists and the liberals.

A major difference between fundamentalist, evangelical, and mainline elites is in their orientation toward synthesizing science with theological belief. The mark of the fundamentalist is that they are the only one of the three to sometimes simply state that science is wrong. At the other extreme, a mainliner would have long ago abandoned the idea of the Bible as containing accurate fact-claims about the natural world. An evangelical wants to be a synthesizer like the liberals we have examined earlier, and wants to say that our observation and reason through science is also correct, while maintaining that what the Bible says is true. To make the fact-claims of science and the Bible both true often requires high-powered hermeneutic feats that are probably lost on ordinary members.

These hermeneutic efforts are exemplified by views of human origins. Nowadays, being a young-earth creationist—who believes that scientific claims about the age of rocks are totally wrong and the earth is six thousand years old—might be the best operationalization of fundamentalism we have. Evangelicals are those who have found a way to make the Bible and contemporary geology both true, by saying, to take one of the many hermeneutic formulations, that each "day" in Genesis actually means millions of years because the Hebrew word in the original Bible can also mean "time period." So, God still did create the Earth and humans, like Genesis says, just not in a way that contradicts a bottom of the pyramid claim of modern science. Mainliners would not bother with any of this, and simply say that the Genesis writer was from a different era and was struggling to understand the mystery of God, so none of Genesis is meant to be taken literally. While evangelical members of the public are unlikely to get support from leaders for a knowledge conflict, they may well be in knowledge conflict because the fundamentalist approach is influential among the masses and simpler for people's busy lives than learning the more subtle hermeneutics of evangelicalism.

Finally, African American Protestantism is considered by scholars to be a tradition distinct from all of the essentially white traditions I describe above. African American Protestants generally follow a conservative Protestant and not a liberal Protestant biblical hermeneutic. However, African American Protestant elites have been uninvolved with debates about science but have rather focused on more pressing issues for their communities, like civil rights. They have also not had the modernist/fundamentalist theological split that in many ways created the science debate among white Protestants, with the conservative theological position remaining hegemonic.[39] So, while examining attitudes, African American Protestants will appear similar to white conservative Protestants, but it is unlikely that African American Protestants would be centrally concerned with issues of religion and science.

To conclude this section, the elites of Judaism, Catholicism and mainline Protestantism do not teach members to be in knowledge conflict with science, nor do they teach a religious belief system that has incompatibilities with at least the methodological naturalist version of modern science. Protestant fundamentalism is different, and elites would support at least propositional belief conflict with science over a few claims, mostly having to do with human origins. We can imagine, for example, fundamentalist Pastors saying that scientists are wrong about the age of the Earth because the Bible disagrees with the scientists. Whether members would also learn systemic conflict is the open question. I will leave further discussion of this to the empirical chapters. Evangelicals are an unclear case. On the one hand, the leaders would not advocate either type of knowledge conflict with science. On the other hand, their solutions for making their religious belief system consistent with modern science are so subtle that ordinary members probably lack the time to understand it, and may well adopt the more straightforward fundamentalist approach.

THE PUBLIC LACKS SYSTEMIC KNOWLEDGE STRUCTURES

Having addressed which religious traditions would teach its members either systemic knowledge or propositional belief conflict with science, I now turn to what is in many ways the preceding question. Would the public even use systemic knowledge? Contemporary social science research suggests, in general, that it is unlikely that members of the general public are using deductive logical decision-making pyramids, as I described in the Introduction, regardless of whether they are religious or not. Elites do in their areas of focus, but that is because they are rewarded for doing so. Therefore, it is unlikely that religious people see it as inconsistent that they believe a biblical claim about human origins but believe scientists about climate change. A number of disparate social science writings can be brought together to support this claim.

People's Knowledge Systems Have Low Coherence

You could argue that academics have coherent pyramids of logical justification because this is what being an academic is all about, but academics have also assumed that the public also has these structures. The reason for the difference is that the only people who have the motivation and the time to create logically consistent beliefs all the way up to first principles are those who are rewarded for doing so. Academics are so rewarded, with philosophers being an extreme case. Theology is similar, and theologians specialize in what Max Weber called theoretical rationality, rationalizing "the values implicit in doctrines into internally consistent constellations of values."[40] Traditionally, this was also the case with politicians, to the extent that journalists were scouring their every statement looking for inconsistencies. Importantly, if you made an issue important for the man or woman on the street, they would come up with a logically consistent belief system. But, given that scientific beliefs are not important to most people, the difference with elites will remain.

There are many terms for these structures, such as "belief system," "ideology," and "worldview." As one scholar writes about the attitudinal version of these structures, they are "organized in a hierarchical fashion, in which more specific attitudes interact with attitudes toward the more general class of objects in which the specific object is seen to belong."[41] For example, in political decision making, ideologies "assume that causation flows from the abstract to the specific," so that individual preference is "based, in part, on more general principles."[42]

The worldview version of these structures implies the strongest hierarchical influence, with the belief at the top being the one that is so deeply assumed that it is tantamount to your sense of reality, and from which flows your sub-beliefs. This is very similar to the imagery in the religion and science debate, where the pinnacle would be something akin to a statement of faith, such as "truth about the natural world is best obtained through observation and reason." Worldviews have been thought to be so coherent that merely encountering someone who uses a different one—like two people with different religious ideas at the pinnacle—would make one lose faith in one's own worldview.[43]

That elites construct these structures but the public does not has long been known by social scientists. As early as 1964 it was demonstrated that political opinions are not organized by more abstract ideologies. Only those with more education and more political involvement—that is, those with the motivation on this topic—have somewhat more coherent constellations of ideas.[44]

Similarly, and much more recently, sociologist Paul DiMaggio summarized cognitive psychology as concluding that "our heads are full of images, opinions, and information, untagged as to truth value, to which we are inclined to attribute accuracy and plausibility."[45] It therefore does not bother people that much of this information is contradictory. Moreover, it has been shown that people use incompatible ideologies depending on their social context, such as having one form of reasoning in church and another in their workplace.[46]

Other studies show that the highest level elements in worldviews are very weak predictors of more concrete attitudes on social issues at the bottom of the pyramid.[47] This suggests that logical entailment from the most abstract justificatory principle to the concrete claim is at best very weak. Other studies of supposedly mutually exclusive worldviews show that they are more diffuse in practice than the worldview imagery suggests.[48]

The result of these investigations of the last few decades is that sociologists are now counselled to avoid assuming that ordinary people hold these logically deductive pyramid structures. For example, William Sewell Jr. states that "our job as cultural analysts is to discern what the shapes and consistencies of local meanings actually are and to determine how, why, and to what extent they hang together."[49] Similarly, sociologist Ann Swidler has written that scholars should "no longer build into our assumptions and our methods the notion that culture is by definition a 'system'" (like an ideology or a worldview), and instead describe the amount of structure that is observed.[50]

So, while philosophers may say that it is not logical to have a scientific explanation for how flowers move but a nonscientific explanation for the emergence of humans, regular people do not have a problem with this reasoning because they do not reason back to first principles. For regular people, there is no scientific belief that matters enough to their lives to spend the effort on creating a coherent logical structure like an expert would. But, Darwin is very important to religious biologists like Francis Collins, so they definitely spend the time to make their religious and scientific beliefs coherent.

Studies of Religion and Science as Knowledge Systems

For over forty years, nobody has spent more effort describing change in the American public's religious beliefs and practices than sociologist of religion Robert Wuthnow, so this chapter will extensively reference his voluminous work. Wuthnow was early in calling for sociologists to not assume that members of the general public have logically coherent belief structures based in deductive reason. In various essays, Wuthnow applied this vision to religion, and occasionally science, but he did not systematically develop a theory of the relationship between the two.

Wuthnow argued that since people do not use high-level concepts to justify lower-level beliefs, any knowledge clash between religion and science is unlikely. He started by rejecting the idea that ordinary people's religion is based on the logical knowledge pyramids required for systemic knowledge:

> Elaborate philosophical and theological doctrines sometimes supply rational answers that satisfy canons of logic and empirical evidence. Certainly the great creeds and confessions . . . give precise, rational answers to the perplexing questions of human existence and those answers are said to be integrated into larger, internally logical systems. But in daily life the enduring questions of human existence are more likely to be addressed through narratives, proverbs and maxims, and iconic representations rich with experiential connotations. Religious orientations are likely to be structured less by abstract deductive reasoning than by parables that raise questions but leave open precise answers, by personal stories that link experience with wider realities, and by creeds and images that have acquired meaning through long histories of interpretation in human communities.[51]

Since people's religion is not structured through deductive logic from first principles, Wuthnow concludes that science (and philosophy) does not strongly impact the religious beliefs of the general public. That is, if a person learns that science says the Earth is four and a half billion years old, this will not cascade through their other beliefs and wipe them out. Religious orientations will not be immune from "the naturalistic attacks of scientists," but "the influence of science and philosophy will be felt more at the level of story than in terms of rational argument alone."[52] "Story" would be, for my case, his explanation for how people make conclusions about on-the-ground-level beliefs, and I will address this specific possibility in subsequent chapters.

Other sociological studies also throw the existence of systemic knowledge conflict into question. If people really reason with systemic knowledge, and the systemic knowledge of religion and science are incompatible, then learning science should cause people to have less religious belief. By extension, education is thought to orient people to science, so education and religion should be incompatible. However, one study shows that education in general does not lead to the decline of religious belief, and the greatest decline in religiosity among youth occurs among those who do not go to college. The authors cautiously conclude that the greatest cause of a decline in religiosity among youth is a clash between moral expectations in religion and the moral experience of most youth of today.[53]

Similarly, another study shows that taking classes in the natural sciences does not cause a greater decrease in religious belief compared to classes in other fields.[54] Moreover, having more education only leads to stronger belief in evolution for nonbiblical literalists. For biblical literalists, more education does not change one's views.[55] Apparently, learning science does not impact religious belief, suggesting that there is no systemic knowledge conflict between religion and science.

Turning far afield from sociology, psychological research deeply assumes the systemic knowledge conflict model. Psychologists Cristine Legare and Aku Visala have a similar assessment as I do of at least the philosophical and theological literature, saying that these literatures produce theories that "tend to be highly abstract and operate at the level of ideal rationality rather than in the reality of actual believers."[56] They *do* assume that both religion and science are about knowledge— both are an "attempt to explain and influence the working of one's everyday world by discovering the constant principles that underlie the apparent chaos and flux of sensory experience." The authors also presume that people strive for logical coherence, that "the cognitive task of coordinating multiple explanatory frameworks is a general cognitive problem" and that "people in all societies are faced with the task of conceptualizing potentially contradictory explanations for biological phenomena."[57] That is, they are testing the systemic knowledge conflict model.

In my terms, the authors conclude that when people start with on-the-ground beliefs about nature and engage in logical entailment up the pyramid, they do not get very far, and have no problem with holding two seemingly contradictory high-level concepts like "evolution occurred naturally" and "evolution was caused by God." The authors conclude that "the common assumption that natural and supernatural explanations are incompatible is psychologically inaccurate," and that "there is considerable evidence that the same individuals use both natural and supernatural explanations to interpret the very same events and that there are multiple ways in which both kinds of explanations can coexist in individual minds."[58] That is, for the public, the systemic knowledge conflict model is psychologically inaccurate.

Religious Americans Avoid Appearing to Be in Systemic Knowledge Conflict with Science

Wuthnow recently published a study of what he calls "The God Problem," and that problem is how to express your faith and seem reasonable in a secular society at the same time. His study is a bit difficult to integrate into other studies because he does not make claims about what people's motives are, or whether they are truly in conflict with science, but rather is concerned with the arguments they use. For my purposes, I would describe his study as a description of the discourse people use to fulfill the social requirement of providing a scientific account of the world by making sure their propositional belief conflict is not perceived to be a systemic knowledge conflict. That religious people seem to accept this social requirement suggests that *if* there are people in systemic knowledge conflict with science they are not teaching this perspective to others.

Due to the fact that scientific reason is so dominant in the public sphere, Wuthnow concludes that "the very notion of God raises intellectual difficulties. It is not something that can be studied scientifically or proven logically: It conflicts with ordinary ways of thinking about the affairs of daily life." As noted previously, one of Wuthnow's premises is that people do not engage in deductive reason back to first principles. He writes that "we need not assume that thoughtful people are amateur philosophers to see that there is a problem in reconciling God with ordinary life." Therefore, "the typical middle-class American is not so philosophically wedded to naturalism as to deny the possibility of a supernatural reality. And yet the tacit epistemology of everyday life is quite naturalistic. We do not expect demons to speak, tumors to disappear instantly, or pigs to fly. . . . Yet the vast majority of middle-class Americans believe that God exists, pray fairly often, and claim that miracles can happen."[59]

In my metaphor, he is asking how, for ordinary people, conflicting beliefs at the bottom of the religion and science pyramids can be publicly presented as not resulting in systemic conflict. An example of these claims would be that "God heals people's diseases" and "diseases heal only through naturalistic processes." So, how is it that religious people maintain belief in the transcendent without seeming to be insane by implying they do not believe scientists regarding how diseases function?

The answer is that there are a number of discursive devices that at least well-educated people learn in the public sphere. These language devices provide ways to acknowledge the uncertainty about God while also expressing the convictions that religious people hold. For example, how is it possible to claim that you communicate with God through prayer and not appear to be mentally ill? The answer is that religious people use devices of language that express a degree of doubt or ambivalence about prayer and what it accomplishes. For example, in a discursive device Wuthnow calls "schema alignment," people talk about God's actions in a way consistent with common sense ideas about human action. In one study, evangelical college students are more likely to pray for psychological interventions from God than mechanical or physical interventions, which are less culturally plausible. Or, in another example, people are not praying for God's direct healing of someone with cancer, but praying for the doctors to be extra wise in dealing with cancer. Believing that God acts through doctors is a lot more sane than believing that God directly intervenes and removes cancerous cells from the body.[60] It also keeps conflict lower in the pyramids by accepting more of the scientific pyramid.

Similarly, in religious ways of talking about natural disasters, "people who believe in God find ways to think about large-scale catastrophic events that keep God in the picture," while avoiding viewing God as magician, God as an explanation, or God as a comforter. Religious people have "a kind of script or cultural device that makes it possible to believe God exists and is in charge of everything that happens without having to assume that God intervenes specifically and deliberately in particular events." One strategy is to invoke inscrutability—the inability to know God's plans.[61]

Of course there are some religious people who make what Wuthnow calls "weird and spooky" claims about the nature of reality that violate scientific fact claims, such as that God directly and thoroughly healed their paralysis in an instant. Or, more spectacularly, claims such as those of Pat Robertson, who claimed that his prayers steered a hurricane away from Virginia Beach, where his broadcasting business was located. My point, consistent with Wuthnow's data, I believe, is that such people are far and few between—not a large enough population around which to build an entire religion and science debate. By far the dominant move is to make religion compatible with science.

Religious Americans Do Not Think They Are in a Knowledge Conflict with Science

Finally, at one level of abstraction above Wuthnow's study of how people talk about events in the world are studies of whether the public *thinks* religion and science are in conflict over knowledge. One survey found that when asked whether "science and religion are incompatible," 17 percent of the public agreed, 14 percent were undecided, and 69 percent disagreed.[62] While this question does not say what conflict is about, someone holding the systemic knowledge conflict view would not see any compatibilities.

Similarly, sociologists Elaine Howard Ecklund and Christopher Scheitle conducted a survey of the general public's views of religion and science, asking "which of the following BEST represents your view. For me personally, my understanding of science and religion can be described as a relationship of: Conflict . . . I consider myself to be on the side of religion; Conflict . . . I consider myself to be on the side of science; Independence . . . they refer to different aspects of reality; Collaboration . . . each can be used to help support the other."[63]

While this question also does not indicate whether conflict is about knowledge or moral values, the questions that proceed this one in the survey frame any conflict as concerning knowledge conflicts for the respondent. The most basic finding is that it is the respondents with no religious identity who see knowledge conflict, not the religious respondents. In these data, 53 percent of the nonreligious see conflict. Only 30 percent of evangelicals see conflict, whereas 21 percent see independence and 48 percent see collaboration. This relatively low level of seeing conflict for conservative Protestantism is even lower for other Christians, with only 19 percent of mainliners and 19 percent of Catholics seeing conflict.[64] I take this to mean that contemporary religious people do not think that they are in knowledge conflict with science. All in all, the research in this section casts doubt on the likelihood that the religious public is in systemic knowledge conflict with science.

WHAT WE KNOW ABOUT CONTEMPORARY AMERICAN RELIGIOUS PEOPLE

The idea of a knowledge conflict between religion and science is very old, and came into place with a particular notion of what "science" and "religion" are. The nature of science has roughly stayed constant from the twentieth century forward, but I will argue in this section that "religion" has changed in the past fifty years. Sociological research of recent decades suggests that American religions, including conservative Protestantism, are not perceived by their members as being centrally about truth or belief, making conflict over systemic knowledge highly unlikely. And, to segue into my point about moral conflict, this recent research also suggests that American religion—and particularly conservative Protestantism—is more about social relationships and morality than belief or knowledge. Like the recent history examined in the last chapter, research suggests that this is a post-1960s change in American culture, so it is not surprising that many academics in the religion and science debate would not even be aware of it, given that many of them were adults by this point in American history.

The Collapse of Truth

You cannot be in systemic knowledge conflict unless you believe something to be true, or what would there be to be in conflict over? The idea at the top of the pyramid in my analogy has no justification—there are no locations higher in the pyramid. That is, "God acts in the world" is a statement of faith, but so is "knowledge should be ascertained via observation and reason." Logical deduction of belief only works if you deeply assume your top statement is true.

But, the contemporary world discourages the public from thinking they know what is true. Sociologists of religion may recognize hints of Peter Berger in this argument, who famously described modernity as a situation in which communities with incompatible notions of ultimate truth or ultimate reality come to interact with each other. He conceived of Catholicism, for example, as ultimately based upon a certain perception of reality, about truths that were so unquestioned, you were not even aware that you believed in them. Science was another worldview with a distinct conception of truth, from which flowed various beliefs. These were just the way the world "is," as everybody in the communities that held them knew and could not even question. Muslims had a different version of truth, as did Buddhists, and so did the scientific secular worldview.

For Berger, the problem with modernity was the increasing ease of interaction between people with disparate truths. First the wheel, then the train, the airplane, the telephone, television, and then the internet—all make it possible to become aware that there are other people who have ultimate assumptions about truth and reality that differ from yours. Critically, encountering someone who has a different ultimate assumed truth makes you wonder if you should so deeply assume your own truth. This lack of certitude about ultimate truth was, for Berger, the tragedy of modernity.[65]

This meant that since religions were idea systems based upon notions of ultimate truth, the lack of certitude would result in secularization. While Berger may have been wrong about immanent secularization, I think that his view of the decline of certainty in belief in truth—in the top of any pyramid—was accurate. Religion does exist in the U.S., even at nearly the same level of participation as a century before, but in my opinion members of religions have less certitude about truth. Berger's only error, in my mind, was to assume you need absolute certitude to keep going to church. Observing this lesser level of truth, Chris Smith has labeled this as a shift from Berger's "Sacred Canopy" to "Sacred Umbrellas."[66]

Wuthnow concurs, arguing that the public has "a kind of tentativeness, even cynicism, about truth," that most people think both science and religion are true, and have no problem with the supposed inconsistency. One reason for cynicism about truth is the normative emphasis in American culture on tolerance of opposing viewpoints. We can imagine someone saying, "If you want to say that the Earth is six thousand years old, that is fine, and I'll just say that the Earth is billions of years old. We are all entitled to our view." Partly, this is civility. But, Wuthnow points out that in the contemporary world, "a person has difficulty holding fast to a conviction because it is no longer possible to know what is true."[67]

As an example of this loss of certitude about truth, for fifteen years or so I regularly taught an undergraduate class in the sociology of religion, where I taught

Berger's ideas. In earlier years, I tried to use examples from Christianity or science to find students who assumed some facts to be unquestionably true, such as "Jesus rose from the dead," or "the Earth goes around the Sun." The students never quite understood what I meant by an absolute assumption of truth, and I came to realize that this was because they were not absolutely certain about any of their own religious or scientific beliefs. After a few years I found examples of absolute truth that they *were* absolutely certain about—which were physical properties of reality that they themselves had experienced, not simply a truth that some authoritative figure told them. My new question for the students was: "How many of you are absolutely certain I cannot jump through this wall without making a hole in it?" Finally, I had found a truth that contemporary students, religious and secular, believed in. I could then explain that Berger's theory is premised on religious beliefs having the same status as beliefs about my inability to jump through walls.

In sum, systemic knowledge conflict between religion and science requires people to believe strongly in the truth at the apex of their knowledge pyramid. If people even have such pyramids, which above I suggest they do not, in this section I suggest that their confidence in the truth at the top would not be strong enough to lead them to conflict with competing knowledge claims. You would have to have very high certitude about the earth being six thousand years old to see the claim of a billions-of-years-old earth to be a threat to your entire knowledge structure. Yes, such people do exist, but again, there are not enough of them on which to build a theory of religion and science.

The Collapse of Religious Doctrine

In recent decades, sociologists of religion have also noted the related phenomena of the collapse of doctrine in American religion. Doctrine is "a set of ideas or beliefs that are taught or believed to be true."[68] In the assumed systemic knowledge conflict, scientific facts disrupt religious doctrine. One of my favorite examples of science impacting doctrine is an early twentieth-century British elite debate between scientists and theologians. One of the concerns of the theologians was that if Darwin was right, there was then no Adam, and then the doctrine of the Fall of humanity[69] and original sin was moot, and thus most of Christian doctrine—the belief structure—would have to be re-done:

> Since the late nineteenth century, liberal Anglicans had accepted the general idea of evolution on the assumption that the progressive development of life could be interpreted as the unfolding of a divine plan. But while this position was compatible with a general theism, it was not widely appreciated that to accept the human race as improved animals was to undermine the foundations upon which the traditional notion of the Fall and the need for redemption were based. Putting it bluntly, even

if evolution was conceived as the unfolding of God's plan, the element of progress made nonsense out of the idea of original sin (since there could be no Fall from an earlier state of grace), and if there was no original sin, one would have to ask what the point of the Atonement would be within the new theology. It would be easy enough to see Christ as a messenger from God pointing the way to future spiritual development, but what was the point of His death on the Cross if there was no need for redemption?[70]

This is the standard concern among elites, that logically believing in one piece of knowledge leads to needing to change another piece of knowledge. These doctrinal claims such as the Fall are midway up the pyramid in my metaphor, and the fact claim of Darwinism is only a problem because the theologian sees that this is inconsistent with the fact claim that God created humans. The knowledge conflict—what motivates the angst and actual human action—is that believing the wrong fact destroys Christian doctrine.

This conflict makes sense for theologians. But, what if contemporary Christians do not know or care about doctrine? In this particular example, they may see that there are two contradictory fact claims about where humans come from, but not be bothered by it, because it does not have any implications for anything—if you do not believe in Christian doctrine. Perhaps they do not know about the doctrine of the Fall.

In a chapter titled "The Strange Disappearance of Doctrine from Conservative Protestantism," social scientist Alan Wolfe says of fundamentalists: "doctrinaire they may be but interested in doctrine they are not," due to their belief that the words of the Bible alone are all you need. Evangelicals too have a "lack of confidence in doctrine," and are then "sometimes hard pressed to explain exactly what, doctrinally speaking, their faith is." Wolfe concludes that "these are people who believe, often passionately, in God, even if they cannot tell others all that much about the God in which they believe."[71]

Studies of "new paradigm" or "seeker" conservative Protestant churches show something similar. These churches are those that eschew all symbols and trappings of traditional American religion—no steeples, no organs, no formal dress. Rather, churches like this try to make themselves look more like office parks, prefer informal dress, and definitely have no pipe organs. One study of these churches concludes that although the churches in this growing segment of conservative Protestantism "are insistent on the belief in Christ, they disavow dogma. . . . The emphasis is on the individual's relationship with God rather than on holding the correct theological doctrine." In a telling quote that reveals what is important, one pastor in this tradition said "there are a lot of people who have their theology down but are not in love with Jesus," while another said "purity of heart is more important than purity of doctrine." The author of the study concludes that for these churches, "Christianity is not primarily a matter of cognitive assent; it is an attitude and a relationship between the individual and God." The people in these churches "express their emphasis on personal conviction over doctrine."[72]

Survey data also suggests this shift. In a 1999 survey, when asked to choose between church doctrine and personal experience as the best way to understand God, about 66 percent of young adults aged 21–39 picked personal experience and about 25 percent picked doctrine. Among those over age 65, about 50 percent picked experience and 40 percent picked doctrine.[73] While the older respondents could be different because they are in a different stage of life, given its consistency with other data, the fact that younger people are rejecting doctrine seems more likely to reflect a change in American culture.

In my terms, doctrine *is* the religious systemic knowledge structure. If contemporary conservative Protestants are unconcerned with doctrine, they do not have a religious systemic knowledge structure, or at best have a very loose one, and thus cannot be in systemic knowledge conflict with science. However, conservative Protestants picking beliefs from the Bible without regard to doctrine *could* lead to propositional belief conflict with science.

The Rise of the Bricoleur

Perhaps there was a time in American history—say, the 1950s—when ordinary people's religious beliefs were more likely to be organized like a hierarchical pyramid. But, if so, that has changed. Religious knowledge in recent history is much more fragmentary. If contemporary religious people do not have doctrine or a religious belief structure, what do they have?

According to Wuthnow, since the 1950s there has been a shift from "dwelling" to "seeking" conceptions of the sacred. He writes that "people have been losing faith in a metaphysic that can make them feel at home in the universe and that they increasingly negotiate among competing glimpses of the sacred, seeking partial knowledge and practical wisdom."[74] The "seeking" conception then is "partial" and "practical," not so concerned with whether disparate ideas taken from different places are all logically consistent with each other. A "dwelling religion" is more cohesive and based on tradition, and a "seeking religion" involves "picking and choosing what they consider personally meaningful rather than feeling a need to accept entire traditions or universal truths."[75]

The growth of this amorphous, less organized seeking conception of the sacred is best exemplified by belief in angels. According to Wuthnow, encounters with angels are "relatively fluid, personalized, ephemeral, and amorphous, all of which fits with the complex, homeless world in which spirituality is currently sought." There is no well-organized theology of angels: they are the sort of fragmentary sacred experience of the seeking variety. Wuthnow also does not think that belief in angels and other seeking conceptions of the sacred is the basis of a new hierarchical belief structure—a "profound epistemological transformation in Western thought." Rather, "such conclusions are drawn by elites," where spirituality "often generates thinking that does challenge Cartesian philosophy or Freudian psychology."[76]

For ordinary citizens, a seeking religion with little to no structure in its knowledge fits with the limited time most of the public has. Beliefs in angels and other supernatural phenomena prominent in the new seeking notion of the sacred can be reconciled with the scientific knowledge that also characterizes American culture because "most people live from day to day, focusing on the realities of daily life, rather than thinking about scientific images of the universe."[77] That is, as I have previously noted, most people do not have the time to create hierarchical knowledge structures.

Other sociologists of religion describe contemporary religion similarly. "Sheila," the now infamous interviewee in the canonical 1985 study of American culture titled "Habits of the Heart," would be one of Wuthnow's seekers, and represented a strain of contemporary religious belief scholars now call "Sheilaism." She treated religious beliefs like a smorgasbord of ideas to pick from, with the principle that moved her fork to the steam pan being "that which makes me feel good."[78] At this point I will also just gesture to the massive literature on the rise of religious individualism, which is essentially documenting the same change in American religion.[79]

The underlying cause of this change, and thus the change in the relationship between religion and science, is the structure of American society. The "dwelling" religion idea is less plausible in a society where people experience their social lives as compilations of changing events. People do not have one job from college graduation to retirement, but rather multiple jobs across multiple industries. There is not one family to reside in, but rather your original family, your step parents, your step siblings and step step siblings, as well as various living situations outside of the "traditional" family. People do not live in one neighborhood their whole lives but in a series of neighborhoods in different cities and states. The change is even reflected in how people obtain information: an old fashioned book is very "dwelling," clicking through links quickly on the internet is very "seeking." In a world perceived as endless freedom and choice—of fifty types of cereal and two hundred TV channels—people are not going to believe in an inherited knowledge structure when they can believe in something they construct through their own idiosyncratic choices.

In a 2007 summary of myriad data sources, with a focus on younger adults, Wuthnow concludes that those aged twenty-one to forty-five are "a generation of tinkerers" who put "together a life from whatever skills, ideas, and resources that are readily at hand." They are more likely to be a bricoleur (handyman), producing a bricolage—"a construction improvised from multiple sources." Thus, in the contemporary world, and particularly for the younger generation, "we piece together our thoughts about religion and our interests in spirituality from the materials at hand." And, critically for my point, a bricolage is not the airtight logical structure that the academics use: "ordinary people are not religious professionals who approach spirituality the way an engineer might construct a building. They are amateurs who make do with what they can. . . . Bricolage implies the joining together of seemingly inconsistent, disparate components."[80] To continue the metaphor, the constructed machine does not have to make sense, it just has to work.

Wuthnow uses a man in his late twenties as an example. He started his journey by thinking "I believe in Christianity, but that's all I've ever known, so how can I know it's the truth if I don't look around and see what else is out there?" He continues to try to "develop a satisfactory faith of his own" by "piecing together ideas from any source that comes his way," including ideas from a Muslim friend, a book about the Buddha, New Age ideas, Orthodox Judaism, and music.[81]

Again, if Americans are seekers, bricoleurs, or religious individualists, taking pieces from different religious traditions without regard for how they would be embedded in a larger logical structure, it is hard to imagine that they have the logical structures about religion and science that elites assume they have.

Conservative Protestantism Increasingly Focused on Individualistic Therapy

The immediately preceding sections described how contemporary religious Americans do not have hierarchical, logically organized belief structures. They have belief, but this belief is not organized like elites would assume. This is still consistent with the idea of propositional belief conflict in that we can imagine conservative Protestants disagreeing about the age of the Earth, but this religious belief would not be related to other scientific or religious beliefs. Contemporary American religion does not include systemic knowledge, but does it even focus on *any* beliefs about the natural world?

People think of conservative Protestantism as the most doctrinaire of the Christian traditions, and to the extent there has been any conflict about beliefs with science by elites, it is primarily with conservative Protestants. However, a number of studies show that if conservative Protestantism was ever about truth claims, it is increasingly an instrument of individualistic therapy and fulfillment. That is, conservative Protestantism is increasingly about people's social relationships and, more specifically, helping people with their problems. Jesus has been transformed from the messenger of God's truth into a friend who helps you in your time of need.

In a strongly worded critique, Alan Wolfe's study of the transformation of American religion in the late twentieth century concludes that conservative Protestantism has joined the culture of narcissism. This religion is no longer about worshiping a transcendent God, but has transformed "already individualistic worship styles into ones even more capable of helping believers with the mundane practicalities of modern life." As many a contemporary critic has noted, gone are the days of Jonathan Edwards talking about how you are barely perched above the fiery pit of hell. Today, Jesus is your friend, here to solve your social problems.

Wolfe describes a prayer group at one Baptist church where the group does not offer prayers of adoration or devotion, but prayers about the health and healing of members, financial difficulties, real estate, and issues facing the church. The group keeps a large tablet that serves as "God's scorecard" where prayers God has acted upon are put in the "praise" column and those not acted upon yet are put in the "petition" column. Wolfe concludes that "the concerns that so many believers express in prayer suggest that, in their minds, God helps those who focus on themselves." In fact, a survey shows that this is a broadly accepted idea. Eighty percent of Americans believe that Benjamin Franklin's aphorism "God helps those that help themselves" actually comes from the Bible.[82]

Similarly, a sociological review of what is known about the growing number of American megachurches, which are largely conservative Protestant, states that these churches are based in "the therapeutic personalism that marks Baby-Boomer religiosity," with the "seeker" sub-variety of church emphasizing "the personalistic aspects of faith—a believer's personal relationship with Jesus and the ways in which faith can help individuals address numerous domestic or personal issues." One of the explanations for the rise of these churches is that Americans have come "to expect religion to be a tool in the individual's quest to develop the self."[83]

This narcissistic approach to religion has apparently reached epidemic proportions among the young, where religion is almost exclusively about social and moral relationships. In an extensive study of American teenagers, Christian Smith concludes that if you generalize across the religions of American youth, their beliefs are best described as "moralistic therapeutic deism." The principles of this new dominant form of religion include: "A god exists who created and ordered the world and watches over human life on earth;" "God wants people to be good, nice, and fair to each other, as taught in the Bible and by most world religions;" "The central goal of life is to be happy and to feel good about oneself;" "God does not need to be particularly involved in one's life except when God is needed to resolve a problem;" and "good people go to heaven when they die."[84]

Religion in the modern age is thus about being moral to each other, about God helping you feel good about yourself, and about God solving your problems. Smith concludes that in this view of religion, God is "something like a combination Divine Butler and Cosmic Therapist: he's always on call, takes care of any problems that arise, professionally helps his people to feel better about themselves, and does not become too personally involved in the process."[85]

Therapeutic religion reaches its peak in a conservative Protestant movement called the Prosperity Gospel. While roundly condemned by evangelical elites who see Prosperity preachers as heretical charlatans, it is the logical extension of the aforementioned trends in conservative Protestantism. The movement is based on the idea, at its most crass, that if you give the pastor ten dollars, God will somehow give you one hundred dollars.

More generally, the central message of the Prosperity Gospel is that God and religion exist for your happiness. In her extensive study of the origins of the American Prosperity Gospel movement, Kate Bowler defines it as "a wildly popular Christian message of spiritual, physical, and financial mastery." She sees some of the unifying themes of the Prosperity Gospel as faith, wealth, and health. Faith is "an activator" that "unleashes spiritual forces and turns the spoken word into reality," and proper faith is demonstrated by a person's wealth and health.[86]

The "hard" version of the Prosperity Gospel makes a mechanistic connection between your action and the good outcome. This is the "give me ten dollars and God will give you one hundred dollars" variety. This "hard" version is nowhere near as prevalent now, at least in the U.S., as is "soft prosperity," embodied in phrases like "God is a good God!" and "Expect a Miracle!" and "Something good is going to happen to you!"[87] Bowler describes megachurch pastor Joel Osteen sitting down on the TV talk show *The View* and providing a "confidence that God provides the tools to reach into the heavenlies and pull out a blessing: a promotion, weight loss, a lovely home, a happy marriage or top-flight schools for their kids."[88] Bowler sees this movement as the culmination of the trends I have been discussing in this chapter, writing that the soft version "rose to popularity in the 1990s with the turn toward therapeutic religion and the desire for language of sweet certainty. It was the perfect theological language for an experiential and consumptive generation who longed for a God who not only showed up but whose blessings could be measured."[89]

Some of the most famous conservative Protestant pastors fit into this mold. Joel Osteen has a thirty-eight-thousand-member congregation and is the author of self-help bestsellers such as "I declare! 31 Promises to Speak Over Your Life." His television show is ubiquitous. Nielsen Media has determined him to be America's most-watched inspirational figure, with a weekly audience of seven million. T. D. Jakes was described by *Time* magazine as "one of America's most influential new religious leaders" with a thirty-thousand-member church, media conglomerate, and more than two dozen books on emotional healing. Creflo Dollar is the pastor of a thirty-thousand-member congregation in Atlanta.[90]

While you would be hard pressed to find an evangelical theologian who agrees with this movement, it seems to be very influential among the conservative

Protestant public. While a recent poll found that only 17 percent of Christians identified themselves as part of the prosperity gospel movement, this underestimates the more generalized acceptance of these ideas. In the same poll, 31 percent believed that "God increases the riches of those who give." Two-thirds agreed that "God wants people to prosper." Another survey showed that 43 percent of Christians agreed that the faithful receive health and wealth.[91]

Needless to say, this is not the only version of Christianity that is possible. A nice counterpart for our thinking is an older "gospel" movement, the *social* gospel movement. Found among mainline and liberal Protestants in the early twentieth century, the point of this movement was to create the Kingdom of God on earth by eradicating social evils like poverty that befell *others*.[92] Religion was not supposed to make *you* happy, but you had a religious obligation to make *others* happier.

I refer you to Bowler's fascinating book for more details about the Prosperity Gospel. Suffice it to say that adherents of the Prosperity Gospel probably "know" that as evangelical Protestants they are supposed to believe that evolution is incorrect. But, this seems like it would be a very minor aspect of their faith. Front and center is a concern about social relationships—most notably, for this movement, how they themselves are doing socially compared to everyone else in the world. Again, this is not a religion dedicated to fact claims about nature, but to social and moral relationships, making knowledge conflict unlikely.

It is only because the religion and science debate started so long ago, when a different version of conservative Protestantism was in place, that we think that a conflict between religion and science for the public would be about fact claims about the natural world. If we restart the debate today, as I am advocating, we would instead be looking at the moral values of science and religion to see how and when they clash.

THE PUBLIC IS LIKELY TO THINK SCIENCE AND SCIENTISTS ARE CONCERNED WITH MORALITY

We should remind ourselves of what would be required for the religious public to be in systemic knowledge conflict with science. On the one hand, they would need to think of their religious belief system as a cohesive knowledge structure where a scientific claim like human evolution would threaten a religious belief such as the Resurrection. So far in this chapter, I have shown a plethora of disparate studies that collectively suggest that if American religion was once a coherent structure of belief that could be threatened by a scientific fact claim, that is no longer the case.

For moral conflict, religious people would need to think of religion as producing moral claims. I think that it is uncontroversial that this is indeed the case. However, they would also need to see science as producing moral claims. While this is not what we find in the elite debate, and is contrary to scientists' self-perceptions, existing research across the social sciences and humanities suggests that the public is likely to see science and scientists in moral terms.

Let us then start with what is obvious when we move our gaze from elites to the public. Where does the public learn about science? Not from science teachers, at least after they finish twelfth grade. Communications scholars conclude that after formal science education ends, the media is the most available and sometimes the only source of information about scientific discoveries and scientists.[93] This media—such as TV, movies, and the news—describes science as deeply concerned with morality, so it is no surprise that religious people would interpret scientists as engaging in moral action.

For example, a study of the discursive frames found in media stories about science-related policy debates included categories of: social progress (improving or endangering the quality of life); economic development; morality and ethics; scientific and technical uncertainty; public accountability/governance; and "Pandora's box/Frankenstein's monster/runaway science." Of these categories, only scientific and technical uncertainty could be described as concerning scientific knowledge per se.[94] The remainder are largely about social relationships or morality.

Depictions of Scientists in Popular Culture

I suspect that most people's view of scientists comes from popular culture, not newspapers. As of this writing, the BBC drama *Orphan Black* is in its third season, having won numerous awards. The premise is that in the 1980s, a group of scientists in the U.K. decided that the time was right to clone humans—illegally. The motivation of the scientists was to use our human abilities to direct our own human evolution. The cloned embryos were placed in a large number of surrogates, born and grew up apart—but, each clone with a spy monitoring them to gather data for the scientists. Control of the human species was not the only motive of scientists, but written into the DNA of each of the clones, using code, is a patent statement. Not only would the species be perfected, but the perfection would be profitable.

The underlying theme of much of the show is the consequences of trying to control the nature of human life. That of course sounds like the eugenics movement, and those who are aware of the history of the eugenics movement are given sly references as the plot of the show develops. For starters, one of the sinister scientists' name is Aldous. This is a vaguely British name, but surely this is a reference to Aldous Huxley, author of the dystopian classic *Brave New World*. In fact, as clever bloggers with too much time on their hands have noted, if you look carefully in the beginning scene of the pilot episode, the name of the train station where the plot first develops is "Huxley Station."[95] Later we find that the scientific institute dedicated to creating the clones was called the "Cold River Institute." In the real world, the Eugenics Record Office in Cold Spring Harbor, New York was the base of the American eugenics movement of the early twentieth century. Much later we discover the inspiration for the cloning was a 19th century British eugenicist.

Part of the popularity of the show is undoubtedly that the same actress plays, as of this writing, seven different adult cloned women, each with different mannerisms, surface-level appearance, and accent. But the message of the show is not far under the surface. While perhaps the original scientists who created the seven female clones were just interested in what would happen, the team of scientists who took over and have been following the women are simply sinister, soulless, and have no problem killing people to protect their experiment. At minimum, scientists are portrayed as amoral and at maximum they are portrayed as wanting to flaunt the morality of the public in Promethean schemes for control of nature. The show does not show any knowledge conflict—no one questions the science of human cloning—only moral conflict.

The original *Star Trek* series is another great example of how the morality of scientists is portrayed as being at odds with public morality. The science officer for the Enterprise was Mr. Spock, a Vulcan who tried to enact the perfect emotionless rationality of his species. It makes complete sense given the tropes of American culture that he was the science officer and not the doctor, who was portrayed as having the expertise, values, and mannerisms of a small-town family practitioner transported to space. A repeated theme in the show was that Spock's radical utilitarianism, depicted as "rational" and thus scientific, was kept in check by Captain Kirk's Kantianism. "The needs of the many outweigh the needs of the few," Spock would proclaim when urging that someone be allowed to die to save others, whereas the emotional Kirk would risk the many to save the individual, which is depicted as the "human" response. Kirk channels his inner Kant when he turns Spock's catchphrase on its head saying "because the needs of the one outweigh the needs of the many," thus representing the "human" vs. the Vulcan (i.e., scientific) response. Science, logic, and rationality are thus put at odds with human values.

The scientist as utilitarian works for *Star Trek* because it has a kernel of truth to it. If we go back to the 1950s, medical research scientists were conducting experiments on prisoners and orphans without their knowledge. For example, the Tuskegee syphilis study was based on not treating poor African American men who had developed the disease to see what would happen to them. All of this was justified with the premise that medical knowledge that would benefit everyone needed to be developed. Then, a social movement in the 1960s now called "bioethics" began to argue that individuals cannot be sacrificed for the greater good, rejecting the morality of many scientists at the time. People would have to give their informed consent to be experimented upon—they would have to agree to sacrifice themselves for the greater good. The degree of public outrage that occurred when the public found out about the Tuskegee experiment, as well as experiments on orphans and so on, is indicative of how the scientists' morality differed from the public's morality, and entire institutions of research ethics were invented to rein in the questionable morals of the scientists. Indeed, the system of ethics that is now used to govern human experimentation is described by academics as "the public's morality."[96]

Star Trek and *Orphan Black* work because their portrayals of scientists are so deeply entrenched in American culture. For the public, the most famous scientist is probably not Francis Collins, or even inventor of the polio vaccine Jonas Salk, but Dr. Frankenstein. While the original 1818 novel had a different meaning, the movie version which most people know does not question whether Frankenstein knows his science, or whether he was making correct fact claims about the natural world. Rather, Dr. Frankenstein is famous for circumventing public morality to do what he wanted to do. As one scholar writes, "in the Hollywood tale, the fate of the Frankenstein monster becomes a moral lesson illustrating the punishment for ambitious scientists who seek to usurp the place of God by creating life."[97]

The scientist who does what they want regardless of what the public thinks is a vision that continues to this day. For example, in the 1993 movie *Jurassic Park*, scientists figure out how to clone dinosaurs and bring them back to life, resulting in negative consequences, suggesting that scientists should not really be led by their own moral compass.

Frankenstein and Jurassic Park are not unique stories in this regard. One study of 990 horror movies from 1931 to 1984 found that "science is historically the most frequent type of monstrous threat in horror films."[98] Another analysis of 222 movies is even more clear that scientists are depicted as amoral or immoral people who cannot be trusted. The title of the study is telling: "Of Power Maniacs and Unethical Geniuses." Science is portrayed as alarming because it concerns the modification of the human body and the violation of human nature. Scientists are portrayed as pursuing new knowledge in secret without social controls.[99]

Besides a reiteration of the finding that scientists are portrayed as having a moral agenda, and a negative one at that, this study is important because it also summarizes what morals the scientists are violating. Movies are not made about scientists measuring quarks or describing molecules. Rather, the immoral scientists are intervening in humanity itself—in our human nature and in our bodies. The author of the study of the Frankenstein movies writes that "more than a moral lesson, the celluloid Frankenstein story is a powerful metaphor for addressing the ways in which American society responds to the rapid pace of discoveries in biology and medicine, discoveries that challenge traditional understandings of what it means to be human."[100]

As I will describe in Chapter 7, declining trust by religious conservatives in the scientists who run scientific institutions in the U.S. coincided with a shift in scientific interest from the physical world (e.g., physics, nuclear power) to the human body (e.g., human genetic engineering). "The human" is religious territory, and scientists are not only moving into that area in recent decades, but our popular culture is teaching the public that the morals of the scientists are particularly untrustworthy in this area.

It is even worse for scientists. In the study of 222 films, many of the scientists are portrayed as the "mad scientist" who trespasses ethical boundaries to gain forbidden knowledge or fame. However, even the scientists coded as "good" or "benevolent" should not be trusted, because they are naive, meaning well but seeing their discoveries put to some unethical use.[101] Cultural historian Christopher Frayling reaches similar conclusions, writing that in popular films "the mad scientists (the fictional ones) have outnumbered the saintly scientists (the real life ones) by a very wide margin indeed."[102]

According to one review of this literature on science and popular culture, the overall picture is "a cinematic history expressing deep-rooted fears of science and scientific research in the twentieth century."[103] Frayling concludes that studies show "that the dystopias outnumber the utopias by a factor of about a hundred to one ... the cinema has spent much of its history telling audiences that science and technology, actually or potentially, are likely to be very bad for them."[104]

These depictions of scientists are not only found in television and movies. Western literature also teaches the public that science is primarily a moral or social enterprise, stocked with scientists whose morality is in contradiction to the morality of the public. In her sweeping analysis of scientists in Western fiction from the Middle Ages to the late twentieth century, Roslynn Haynes finds that "scientists as depicted in literature have, with few exceptions, been rated as "low" to "very low" on the moral scale. The early Faustian stereotype of the enchanter, versed in the black arts and most probably in league with the devil, has spawned a series of equally unattractive offspring: megalomaniacs bent on world destruction; absent-minded professors shuffling in slippers and odd socks while disasters befall their beautiful daughter in the next room; inhuman researchers who think only in facts and numbers and are unable to communicate on any other level." Haynes finds six archetypes of scientists that are reworked over the centuries, the majority of which "represent scientists in negative terms, as producing long-term liabilities for society."[105]

These teachings from popular culture about the behavior and motivations of scientists appear to be already known by very young children. Scholars have been studying the images of scientists held by adolescents for over fifty years by having them draw pictures of scientists. The classic study from 1958 determined that children viewed the scientist as an elderly or middle-aged man with glasses, beard, and a white coat in a laboratory surrounded by equipment. More importantly, a summary of more recent studies concludes that in addition to these physical traits, the stereotypical scientist is viewed as a genius "who may be antisocial, crazed, or even evil."[106]

These data are supported by some of the experiences of scientists tasked with improving their image. A scientist leading a project on the impact of the media on children's attitudes about science tells of visiting elementary schools with scientists, and how the children do not believe they are actually scientists. The reasons are that they are "too normal," and "too good-looking." More strikingly, some children say "I did not think he was real because he seemed to care about us."[107]

There is not an extensive social science research literature on what the public thinks about the morality of scientists. One exception is a set of recent psychology experiments where the subtitle of the paper is a good summary: "Scientists are associated with violations of morality." Using a number of controlled experiments about the sort of person who would engage in extremely deviant acts, they find that scientists were perceived by Americans as more likely than others to engage in serial murder, incest, and necrobestiality. This finding is even more striking given that the experimental surveys were administered to samples from the population that are, in the authors' own estimation, more similar to scientists than other Americans. The sample is far less religious, far more liberal, and more educated than the general public. If replicated with a nationally representative sample, the results would presumably depict scientists even more negatively.[108]

For my purposes, it is not only important that scientists in popular culture are depicted as people who are morally at odds with the rest of society. The more general point is that scientists are not depicted as sticking to conducting investigations about the natural world that society has asked them to do. Rather, scientists are portrayed, both positively and negatively, as people who act morally with a particular agenda, for good or bad. It is hard to imagine that any average citizen views science as just a morally neutral investigation of the natural world. Rather, they probably perceive scientists as a group promoting moral and social interests.

If Not Immoral, At Least Not Like Us

The scientist as madman portrays a particular morality of scientists. What is worse for scientists is that, even if portrayed as good or neutral, they are perceived as not like "ordinary" people. If scientists are not like you and me, as foreign, it is hard to imagine that scientists can be trusted to have the same values as you or me.

Consider one last TV show, *The Big Bang Theory*. This American comedy is about a group of young scientists at the paragon of American science institutions—the California Institute of Technology. The show and its actors have won multiple awards, such as the Emmy Award and the People's Choice Award. It is in its ninth season, with between twenty and twenty-five episodes per season and about twenty million people watching each episode in the U.S. About 6 percent of the population of the U.S. is watching each original episode, and its global reach is further. Earlier seasons are now in syndication, suggesting that even more people are watching.[109] In terms of what "an elite scientist is like"—the type that a citizen would read about in the newspaper—I have no doubt that *The Big Bang Theory* is far more influential than any other non-TV cultural work or movie in shaping the public's views.

The show works with stereotypes of the nerd and the mad scientist.[110] The show largely lacks the "scientists as evil" trope described above, with a sympathetic view of the mad scientist, but fully reinforces the view that scientists are not like you and me. The basic comedic premise of the show is to play off of all of the available tropes in American culture about how scientists are unlike the rest of us. "The rest of us" is played by a waitress from Nebraska who moves into the apartment across the hall from the two primary scientific characters in the show, and we see through her eyes how odd the scientists are compared to everyday people.

The star of the show is Sheldon Cooper, a brilliant theoretical physicist who started college at age eleven, studying string theory and quantum mechanics. He lacks the ability to understand social situations or others' feelings and continuously notes that he is smarter than everyone else. Sheldon's friend is another physicist, Leonard Hofsdtater, who plays the one scientist in the group who approaches a normal understanding of social relationships—which provides a continuous comedic well. Another physicist is Raj Koothrappali, who, at least in the earlier seasons, is so awkward that he cannot speak to a woman unless he drinks a lot of alcohol. The final member of the group is Howard Wolowitz, who is not quite the failure with women that Koothrappali is, but is nonetheless wildly inappropriate. The group of friends pass their time at the comic book store and watch a lot of science fiction movies. The basic message one gets from the show—never explicitly said, but not needing to be—is that elite scientists are not like you and me. Since they are not like you and me, it seems unlikely that the public will assume they share the public's values.

Social science research also finds that the public views scientists as not like the general public. The psychology study referenced a few paragraphs ago found that "scientists are perceived as significantly more nerdy, robot-like, goal-oriented, and emotionless than regular persons and atheists."[111] Similarly, the National Science Foundation conducted surveys in 1983 and 2001 that in part measured the public's images of scientists. We only need to look at the questions they asked to see how scientists are thought of as "not like us." The survey asked for evaluation of the statements: "scientists have few other interests besides their work," "scientists don't get as much fun out of life as other people do," scientists "are apt to be odd and peculiar people," scientists "are not likely to be religious people," and "scientific work is dangerous."[112] The conclusion is that scientists are not considered to be "like us."

CONCLUSION

In Chapters 2 and 3 we saw that the systemic knowledge conflict view dominates academic thought. Academics either explicitly extrapolate this view to the public, or by not being explicit that they are only talking about elites, imply that this is what ordinary religious people would think. In Chapter 4 I showed a range of recent elite debates that throw the systemic knowledge conflict perspective into doubt, even for elites. In this chapter I summarized disparate existing research on the public that suggests that while we may find some instances of propositional belief conflict between religion and science, we are unlikely to find systemic knowledge conflict. Research has shown that the only people who have hierarchically structured belief systems controlled by logical constraint are those who spend the time to construct them, and the vast majority of regular citizens do not have the incentive to do so. Therefore, people are not "logical," as the systemic knowledge perspective implies.

If we look at recent studies of American religious people, we see that they are not, if they ever were, concerned with systems of belief, but rather see religious belief as episodic, taking beliefs as they need them from various cultural sources. Moreover, conservative Protestantism has turned, probably in the past fifty years, toward being quite concerned with therapeutic individualism. If religion is, for the average person, "about" solving their problems, then even if they claim a fact that is opposed by science, it will not matter enough to them to actually act upon it.

For the religious public to engage in systemic knowledge conflict with science, they need to think of their religion as making fact claims about nature—and scientists as doing the same. Whereas people probably know that scientists try to discover fact claims about nature, it is extremely unlikely that they view this pursuit as morally neutral. Given how science and scientists are portrayed in the popular culture, and the public sphere more generally, it is most likely that they see that fact gathering as having a moral agenda that is different from their own. Religion and science are primed to conflict—over social and moral issues, not knowledge.

6

Empirical Tests of Knowledge and Belief Conflict for the Religious Public

In Chapters 2 and 3 I showed that the academic religion and science debate presumes systemic knowledge conflict and that science and religion are logically coherent intellectual structures of justificatory belief about nature. If this were the case, conservative Protestants would be opposed to a fact-claim made by scientists (such as humans evolving from other primates) because they hold a different higher-level justificatory belief than scientists do, such as "Facts can be determined through Biblical exegesis." Critically, a conservative Protestant would be inclined to not believe in any scientific claim, since scientific facts were derived using the wrong higher-level belief.

A second position that is *not* advocated for or described by academics in the religion and science debates, but that is suggested by contemporary studies of American religion, is propositional belief conflict—that some religious people *do* oppose particular fact-claims of science (like humans evolving from other primates), but *not* because this fact was generated through a scientific way of knowing. They may just have been taught differently and believe religious authority and not scientific authority in this one instance. For elites, systemic knowledge conflict is plausible and propositional belief conflict is implausible, as elites are encouraged to create systemic knowledge structures. This is likely to be the reverse for the religious public. That is, it is likely that there is no systemic knowledge conflict, but there is possibly some propositional belief conflict. In this Chapter, I put this thesis about the public to the test.

In the previous two chapters I relied upon other scholarship to suggest the plausibility of my interpretation of the relationship between religion and science. This was necessary because data to precisely test my claims does not exist. I would argue that this is because the academics who produce such data largely assume the systemic knowledge conflict when they gather data. In this and the next chapter I conduct indirect tests from available data that allow us to infer the existence of the relationships I posit. In the second half of this chapter, I try to explain the patterns I find.

SURVEY TESTS OF KNOWLEDGE CONFLICT

I ultimately want to make empirical claims about the U.S. public, and the best way to make a generalizable claim about the U.S. population is to use a nationally representative survey. My first survey analyses use the General Social Survey (GSS), a high-quality nationally representative survey paid for by the National Science Foundation that has been fielded since the early 1970s. The basic logic of survey analysis is to see if one type of person (e.g., an evangelical) is more likely than another (e.g., a nonreligious person) to have a particular view, be engaged in a particular practice, or have a particular identity. The raw averages in response to a survey are usually not very relevant, because the percentage agreeing is so dependent upon question wording. For example, the percent of the population who are Young Earth Creationists is very dependent on how that question is asked. The more analytic tradition is to compare two groups of people who have been asked the same question. That is, we could show that 60 percent of evangelicals were identified as Young Earth Creationists using our question, but only 35 percent of the nonreligious. This is the standard for scholarly analysis of surveys.

The power of being able to make nationally representative claims with a survey comes at a steep price—the thinness of how concepts are measured. For example, while scholars have written one-hundred-and-fifty-thousand-word books about what "creationism" means, a survey might be limited to ten words to describe the phenomenon. Surveys are ideally used in conjunction with more rich data, and that is why I have been building my case using the more expansive, yet typically nonrepresentative data from others' research.

The first question I examine using survey data is the most basic: do religious people disagree with all scientific claims about nature? If so, then the strongest version of the systemic knowledge conflict perspective is correct. The first step is then to measure the religion of the respondent because, as we saw in the previous chapter, different religions have different relationships to science.

With the survey I can determine whether a respondent is a frequent church attender with an identity as a literalist conservative Protestant, nonliteralist conservative Protestant, conservative Catholic, nonconservative Catholic, Black Protestant, or Mainline Protestant. The literalist/nonliteralist distinction is meant to distinguish between those who are most likely to be taught religious fact-claims that conflict with scientific fact-claims, and who would, if the systemic knowledge conflict is truly operative, be most likely to be taught an alternative epistemology.

The attendance threshold for each of these religious identities is designed to identify respondents who actually participate in the discourse of the religion, not those who simply have an identity from their youth. For statistical reasons, groups of less than 4 or 5 percent of the entire sample cannot really be separately analyzed. Therefore, all of the religious minorities who do not fit into one of the categories above are put into one group that is not separately analyzed, due to its heterogeneity, but necessary to include in statistical calculations to make the correct comparisons.

But, *compared to whom* would committed literalist conservative Protestants be more likely to be opposed to scientific claims? Social science research either explicitly or implicitly makes comparisons, so what we need is a comparison group. For example, if the question is whether conservative Protestants avoid exposure to science to avoid knowledge conflict, we have to account for the fact that most Americans avoid exposure to science. The test, in this particular example, is whether a religious group is avoiding science more than those who are not exposed to the religious teaching.

The comparison should be to the nonreligious, because the debate is implicitly framed as the religious having a different view than those who are not religious, who are then, implicitly, scientific. This is not about belief in God per se, as belief in God is compatible with all but the most extreme versions of metaphysical naturalism held by scientific atheists. And, most Americans believe in God, so atheists are not the proper comparison group. Rather, the nonreligious comparison group should be people who are not exposed to religious teachings (even if they residually believe in God). In my first survey analysis, this nonreligious group is best represented by the 54 percent of the public who do not participate in religion. In that analysis, survey non-participation means claiming to attend services "several times a year" or less.[1]

Therefore, the systemic knowledge conflict thesis would predict that: Compared to the non-participants in religion, participating literalist conservative Protestants will tend to avoid being exposed to all science, presumably because their tradition has an alterative epistemology of biblical exegesis for all scientific claims. If there is propositional belief conflict, then we would see members of a religious tradition participate in science as much as anyone else, but not believe in the few claims that conflict with a religiously derived fact-claim (like human evolution).

To measure belief in religiously derived facts about the world, I create a category I call "contested facts," where science and a religion make contrary claims. Respondents were asked a series of fact questions and evaluated as to the extent they knew the scientifically correct answers. These included two "facts" that are actually contested by many conservative Protestants: whether the universe began with a huge explosion; and whether human beings, as we know them today, developed from earlier species of animals. The answers to these two questions were combined into a numeric scale that ranged from getting both "wrong" to getting both "right." Or, in the more neutral language I am trying to use, the scale measures belief in the conservative Protestant versions of facts on one end and scientific versions on the other.

I have a number of ways to measure a respondent's exposure to science. First, exposure is indicated by knowledge of uncontested scientific facts, which are those for which there is no known counter-claim in Christianity, and such knowledge would come from engagement with science. Responses to nine uncontested scientific fact questions were added together to form an overall measure of the extent to which the respondent knows established scientific facts. These fact questions included whether: 1) the center of the Earth is very hot; 2) all radioactivity is man-made; 3) the father's gene decides whether the baby is a boy or a girl; 4) lasers work by focusing sound waves; 5) electrons are smaller than atoms; 6) antibiotics kill viruses as well as bacteria; 7) the continents on which we live have been moving their locations for millions of years and will continue to move in the future;[2] 8) the Earth goes around the Sun; and 9) how long it takes for the Earth to go around the sun.[3]

The survey also asked a number of questions about the scientific method, such as understanding experimental design and odds. These were combined into an overall measure of the extent to which the respondent understands the methods of science. Similarly, if a respondent is avoiding science because it violates their religiously-derived knowledge, they will not obtain scientific knowledge, and will claim less scientific knowledge. The survey also asked how informed the respondent was about "science and technology," "global warming," and "the North and South poles." These questions were combined to create an overall measure of claimed scientific knowledge.

Not pursuing scientific knowledge is also measured by how many college-level science classes the respondent has taken, and whether they hold an undergraduate degree in a natural science or engineering.[4] I also measure whether the respondent is a full-time worker who has an occupation that requires knowledge of science.[5] These are all measures of acceptance of scientific claims, and with these measures we can see if people in religious traditions that have conflicting propositional belief claims (e.g., conservative Protestantism) are actually in systemic knowledge conflict by rejecting the rest of science.

I use types of regression analysis to determine if there is a relationship between participation in particular religions and knowledge of and exposure to science. I also control for demographic identities that can co-vary with religion and science. These controls are important because, for example, if I see a relationship between religious participation and less exposure to science, it could actually be that what I am actually seeing is the hidden effect of gender. Women are more religious, and perhaps they have less exposure to science, so what seems to be a relationship between religion and science may actually be about gender. To avoid these problems, I use statistical controls for variables that may vary with religion and may also predict pursuit of scientific knowledge, including education, age, family income, gender, African American ethnicity, Hispanic ethnicity, southern residence, and rural residence.

With the setup in place, we are now ready to run some tests. The first is of propositional belief conflict—are there religious groups where the members do not agree with some of the claims of scientists? For this I see if members of religious groups "know" fewer of the contested scientific facts about the origins of the universe and of humans—after statistically controlling for all of the other reasons they might not know the scientifically correct answer, such as their level of education. We can then assume that they get these questions "wrong," because they disagree with the scientists, not because they do not know what scientists' claim.

To see the formal statistical results, see either the technical published papers or the tables in the online appendix, both of which are referenced in the endnotes. Since regression results are not intuitively understandable, to understand the magnitude of these differences, Table 1 reports the predicted probabilities for hypothetical ideal-type respondents to the survey.[6] For example, the first entry in the first line lists the average number of religiously contested scientific "facts" that a literalist, high-attending conservative Protestant knows, after controlling for reasons they would not know these facts. This sort of "average" hypothetical respondent is also set to be as close to an average respondent in the survey as is possible, in that she is a Caucasian woman who lives outside the south in a nonrural area, with the average age, income, and education of the respondents included in that particular analysis. In each line, the critical comparison is between a religious group and the nonreligious category in the final column.

For example, the average nonreligious respondent knows on average nearly one of the two contested facts (.97), which does suggest limited knowledge of science in the public in general. But, a literalist conservative Protestant with the same level of education, income and age, and the same race, gender and region of residence, only knows the scientific version of .28 facts. That is, literalist conservative Protestants are much less likely to know these facts. (At least one "*" in the table means that the difference between that number and the one in the final column is not simply due to chance—technically called statistical significance. If there is no "*" it means that the difference is so small it could be the result of chance in the selection of the survey population.)

We find nonliteralists, mainline Protestants, and black Protestants to be somewhat more likely, followed by Catholics. Again, since I have controlled for being in a position to know what science claims about these facts, I interpret not knowing as

TABLE 1. Expected values and predicted probabilities: General Social Survey

Measure	Literalist Conservative Protestant	Non-literalist Conservative Protestant	Mainline	Traditional Catholic	Non-traditional Catholic	Black Protestant	Non-religious
# of contested facts	0.28***	0.44***	0.56***	0.71**	0.94	0.52***	0.97
Knowledge of methods	17.86	18.07	18.86*	17.54	17.64	17.30	18.09
# of uncontested facts	5.19	5.35	5.69*	5.05	4.72	4.63	5.13
Claimed scientific knowledge	6.70	7.39*	6.82	6.70	5.97*	6.45	6.83
# of college-level science classes	1.04	1.57*	1.59	1.10	1.38	1.24	1.10
Probability of majoring in science	.16	.28	.15	.11	.12	.18	.18
Probability of having a scientific occupation	.014	.012	.014	.014	.005	.010	.017

Note: With controls. *** = $p < .001$, ** = $p < .01$, * = $p < .05$ (two-tailed) for comparison of religious group to the non-religious in a regression model.

disagreement. Therefore, every religious group but the nonconservative Catholics disagree with the scientific "facts" compared to the nonreligious. That is, members of most Christian groups, liberal and conservative, are in propositional belief conflict with science over these few contested facts. This is contrary to what we would expect from the official teachings in the more liberal groups, and I will offer explanations for this discrepancy later in this chapter.

I am primarily interested in the assumption of systemic knowledge conflict, where believing a religious fact-claim about evolution, for example, would lead to not believing other scientific fact claims for which there is no conflicting religious version, like global warming. If there is systemic knowledge conflict, then members of those religious groups that have propositional conflict with science—and conservative Protestants in particular—should avoid exposure to all of science.

The rest of Table 1 shows that there is no religious group whose members are more likely to avoid noncontested parts of science compared to the nonreligious. The second line in Table 1 shows that the only difference between participants in religious traditions and the nonreligious in knowledge of scientific methods is that mainline Protestants know slightly *more* science than do nonparticipants in religion. Again, this means that, as I control for the level of education of the respondent, literalist conservative Protestants with college educations—and thus with equal chance of exposure to science—are equally likely to know the scientific method as the nonreligious with college educations.

The systemic knowledge conflict thesis would also predict that conservative Protestants would hear religious fact claims that conflict with scientific claims, conclude that the scientific way of knowing is opposed to the Biblical way of knowing, and therefore avoid science knowledge and thus know fewer science facts. However, Line 3 in Table 1 shows that there is no religious group that knows less, and that mainline Protestants know *more* established scientific facts than those who are not religiously active.

Similarly, the fourth row is for the measure of claiming to know more scientific knowledge. The scale of this measure is not intuitive, but it ranges from zero to twelve, with higher numbers meaning more knowledge. This analysis shows that the only difference with the nonreligious is that nonliteralist conservative Protestants claim to know *more* scientific knowledge than do the nonreligious. (Nontraditionalist Catholics claim less knowledge than do the nonreligious, which is an outlier finding in these analyses.)

If conservative Protestants are avoiding all science, they should have taken fewer college-level science classes, be less likely to have majored in science and engineering, and be less likely to have a scientific occupation. The fifth, sixth, and seventh lines show that the only difference between any of the religious groups and the nonparticipants in religion is that nonliteralist conservative Protestants have taken *more* science classes. The final line in Table 1 shows that there is no religious group that is more or less likely to have a scientific occupation than are the nonreligious once we control for factors like education, gender, and age. Overall, this analysis shows that systemic knowledge conflict does not exist for the religious public, including for conservative Protestants.

So far I have shown that there is no *religious tradition* whose members are in systemic knowledge conflict with science. Despite believing in some nonscientific claims, they are equally likely as the nonreligious to participate in the rest of science. I generally find it useful to compare members of social institutions like religious traditions because we can at least imagine the communication processes like training systems, educational materials, communication channels, and statements of belief that lead to these particular views. But, another tradition in sociology would focus on an individual's beliefs separate from institutions. In this sociological tradition, the test of the systemic knowledge conflict thesis would be whether the *individuals* who are in propositional belief conflict with science (by not believing the scientific version of the contested fact claims) are those who are in systemic knowledge conflict, and thus avoid any science. I conducted additional analyses using these different assumptions and reached the same conclusions as the previous analysis.[7]

A Socially Urgent Issue: Scientific Claims about Global Warming

In the first few pages of this book I gave examples of how participants in the public sphere who want to combat global warming were making the false assumption that religious conservatives would deny scientific claims about anthropogenic climate change because they do not believe science in general. This, I claimed, was distorting public debate. This is then a great issue to specifically examine for systemic knowledge conflict.

This is also a good test of systemic knowledge conflict for conservative Protestants because there is not an explicit propositional belief claim in this tradition that contradicts scientific statements about global warming. The Bible does not depict God as saying, "And in later years I will cause global warming." Rather, the few conservative Protestants in the public sphere who contradict scientific claims about global warming using religion appeal to somewhat more abstract higher-level theological beliefs midway up the pyramid about how nature works, such as "God is in control."

Opposition to climate change research is being promoted by ideological conservatives and Republican party activists.[8] Moreover, a study has recently shown that ideological conservatives are less trusting in science, and conservative Protestants are more likely to be both Republicans and political conservatives, both of which are associated with skepticism about climate change.[9] Therefore, it is important to determine whether it is religious belief itself, or the political orientation of the majority of evangelicals that is associated with not believing scientists' fact-claims about global warming, by controlling for these political measures.

A question in the survey I used above asked: "The first issue is global warming. Global warming means a trend toward warmer temperatures throughout the world, with more extreme weather in many places and changes in food production that could affect our way of life. Some people believe that the burning of gasoline and other fossil fuels causes global warming. Others say that global warming has purely natural causes. . . . How well do the following groups understand the causes of global warming? Environmental Scientists." Respondents who believe in the scientific consensus in knowledge about global warming, that global warming is caused by humans, will think scientists understand the causes of global warming. I use the same religion and demographic measures as in previous analyses, and as before, start with comparing members of different religious traditions, followed by comparing those who are in propositional belief conflict with science with those who are not.[10]

The first line of Table 2 shows the predicted probability of a member of each of the religious groups thinking that scientists understand global warming "well" or "very well" without control variables. The probability that a nonreligious respondent will say scientists understand it well or very well is .68, but the probability of a literalist conservative Protestants saying the same is only .55. (A probability of 1.0 means it is a certainty.) This is a small but statistically significant difference. No other religious tradition is different in this view from the nonreligious. That is, analyzing the simple bivariate relationship between religious tradition and believing scientists' fact-claims about global warming shows that literalist conservative Protestants *are* less likely to believe scientific facts compared to the nonreligious.

However, is this opposition due to the respondent's religion or due to characteristics that people in this religious tradition also tend to have, like political conservatism? In the second line of the table I account for the influence of political ideology and political party identification, and the relationship between literalist conservative Protestantism and believing scientific fact-claims about global warming disappears. With these controls in place, the probability of a literalist conservative Protestant thinking that scientists understand global warming well or very well is .73, while the probability for the non-religious is .74.[11] This small difference is not statistically significant. Therefore, the conservative Protestant effect in the earlier model is not the result of religious belief, but the result of conservative Protestants being more enmeshed in politically conservative and Republican party discourse.

As before, I re-ran this test by not focusing on religious groups, but on individuals who are or are not in propositional belief conflict with science. That is, are the individuals who do not believe science about human origins the same people who do not believe scientists about global warming? This analysis (not shown) reveals

TABLE 2. Expected values and predicted probabilities: General Social Survey

Measure	Literalist Conservative Protestant	Non-literalist Conservative Protestant	Mainline	Traditional Catholic	Non-traditional Catholic	Black Protestant	Non-religious
Probability respondent agrees scientists understand global warming well/very well (without controls)	.546*	.629	.707	.718	.674	.662	.681
Probability respondent agrees scientists understand global warming well/very well (with controls)	.731	.755	.752	.814	.717	.766	.742
Probability happy if daughter becomes a scientist	.793	.868	.697	.784	.951*	a	.735

Note: With controls. *** = p < .001, ** = p < .01, * = p < .05 (two-tailed) for comparison of religious group to the non-religious in a regression model. a = category combined with non-literalist conservative Protestant category.

that they are not—believing those religious "facts" is not associated with believing scientists one way or the other about global warming.[12]

This concrete case of scientific claims about global warming reinforces the conclusion that there is no systemic knowledge conflict between any religious group and science. If there were, conservative Protestants would not be willing to accept any scientific claim based upon scientific ways of knowing and would instead appeal to high-level religious ideas to make fact claims about nature. People who do not believe in evolution or the Big Bang would do the same. That not believing scientists on global warming is largely an effect of political ideology—which itself may be a proxy for embeddedness in particular information flows like Fox News—suggests what the motivations of elite conservative Protestant opponents of global warming science may actually be.[13]

Do You Want Your Child to Be a Scientist?

When social scientists want to cut to the quick of a respondent's social aversions, they ask what they would want for their children. For example, to measure bias against members of a religion, social scientists often ask respondents if they approve of their children marrying a person from that religion.[14] In 2012, the GSS asked about wanting your child to be a scientist, and if conservative Protestants were in systemic knowledge conflict with science, they would presumably not want their children to be scientists. However, it is also the case that if they were in total moral conflict with science, they would not want their children to be scientists either. Therefore, the survey question does not allow us to distinguish between knowledge and moral conflict, but allows us to rule out both extreme situations—that conservative Protestants are opposed to *all* science because of knowledge *or* moral reasons. Put differently, do conservative Protestants think you can be a "good" scientist?

The question asked "If you had a daughter, how would you feel if she wanted to be a scientist—would you feel happy, unhappy, or would you not care one way or the other?" The raw responses tell us most of what we need to know about conflict over science in the U.S. Of the 517 people who were asked the question, only four selected "unhappy," while five did not know or did not answer. That is, seven-tenths of 1 percent of Americans object to their daughter being a scientist. They asked another question that began "If you had a son . . ." One fewer respondent objected to the son being a scientist, for a grand total of three. Essentially nobody is utterly opposed to their child becoming a scientist, so actual opposition will not be found among any religious group. While scientists may be seen as Dr. Frankensteins in waiting, people believe there are either parts of science or individuals in science who are good.

We can look for a milder effect we could call unease at the prospect of their child becoming a scientist by comparing those who said they would be "happy" their daughter became a scientist to those who said they would "not care." We should be cautious that this may be measuring a propensity of some religious groups to be less concerned with the occupational choices of their children than a concern about the occupation of science in particular. That said, I analyzed the question about the hypothetical daughter using the same statistical model as above.[15]

The final line in Table 2 shows that the probability that a nonreligious respondent will say they are happy if their daughter becomes a scientist, compared to not caring, is .735. The probability for a literalist conservative Protestant is .793—actually a little *higher* than the nonreligious, but not a statistically significant difference.[16] The only statistically significant difference is that nontraditional Catholics are *more* likely to be happy if their daughter becomes a scientist than would be the non-religious. Therefore, conservative Protestants are not opposed to science writ large on the grounds of either knowledge *or* morality, but think there are at least parts of science, or individuals in science, that are consistent with conservative Protestant beliefs and values.

In contrast with the academic science and religion debate, for the public it does not appear that there are any systemic knowledge conflicts between religion and science, including with members of the conservative Protestant tradition. What we appear to be left with is what I am calling propositional conflict—conservative Protestants just believe religious versions of facts of the world that they have been taught, and these seem to be unrelated to any other aspects of science.

TOWARD AN EXPLANATION OF WIDESPREAD PROPOSITIONAL BELIEF CONFLICT

The systemic knowledge conflict perspective provided an easy answer to any conflict between religion and science—the conflict was over entire ways of knowing about the natural world. Now that it has been demonstrated that the systemic knowledge perspective is unlikely, we are adrift without an explanation for the remaining propositional belief conflict that we do see. I see this as opening up a new family of empirical examinations of religion and belief about the natural world that is not constrained by old stereotypes. In this final section I speculate about what conflict about beliefs about the natural world could be about if it is not about systemic knowledge. I look forward to the future scholarship in this area.

Explaining Catholic and Mainline Protestant Propositional Belief Conflict

While Catholic and mainline Protestants are much less likely to believe conservative Protestant religious claims about human origins than do conservative Protestants, they *do* believe these claims more than the nonreligious do, and more than their leaders or the established theology in their traditions would. This is a bit mysterious. For the mainline Protestants, one explanation is that the mainline laity are much more conservative than their clergy (and the evangelical laity much more liberal than their clergy). Another possible explanation is that it is difficult to tell the difference between a mainline Protestant and an evangelical in a survey, and the highest attending mainline Protestants (who I focus upon) are the most like evangelicals. So, my results could simply be a measurement issue. I also suspect, but cannot prove, that while a mainline Protestant may believe in the Big Bang and human origins as depicted by scientists, they also want to give a response not available in the survey, such as "There is more to it than that." Their view may actually be that the Big Bang occurred, but was caused by God, and not seeing the fullness of what they want to express, they select "No."[17]

The finding for conservative Catholics is similarly surprising. These are the Catholics who should be more attentive to Church teaching, and their answers to these survey questions makes them "bad" Catholics, in that they are contradicting Church teaching. It is possible that while the liberal Catholics just believe what scientists say, in their survey responses the conservative Catholics want to make what they think of as the conservative religious statement. Due to the prominence of the conservative Protestant claims in the public sphere, and being unaware of actual Catholic teaching on this subject, they think that the conservative Protestant belief is the proper "religious" or "Christian" response. Again, it is also possible that they select the nonscientific response about human origins, as if to say "There is more to it than that." Future research with instruments that properly distinguish between the possible types of conflict will hopefully help explain why mainline Protestants and Catholics are in this propositional belief conflict with science.

Conservative Protestants Are Using 19th Century Baconian Science

For conservative Protestants the question is why they disagree with scientists about these particular fact claims, given that they mostly agree with scientists. One possible explanation is that conservative Protestants are locked into a mid-nineteenth-century version of science that was inspired by Bacon. Returning to my pyramid metaphor, a nineteenth-century Baconian science pyramid of knowledge claims would look very similar to a contemporary science pyramid at the bottom. The two would reach the same conclusions about the majority of fact claims. But, the pyramids would be different starting halfway up, because the principles by which the lower-level knowledge is generated would ultimately be different. Midway up the nineteenth-century version would be the principle that fact claims need to be observable, and that you cannot generate a fact claim via abstractions. Since the Big Bang and human evolution are abstractions that cannot be observed, they are not properly scientific questions, but are religious questions.

But, observable scientific facts, like a warming earth, would be scientific, and thus scientists' claims should be believed. This would distinguish the scientific claims that are and are not believed.

There is some evidence that at least the elites in contemporary conservative Protestantism are still Baconian, and therefore a scientific claim is only believed if it can be demonstrated through your own senses. This contemporary Baconianism is most evident in debates between what we might call elite fundamentalist literalists and elite fundamentalist superliteralists. The latter are the tiny group of geocentrists who reject modern astronomy to say that since the Bible says that the sun moves around the earth, the sun moves around the earth. Geocentrists are reviled as extremists by the group most people think of as the poster child for epistemological extremism—the creationists who want to defend the young earth and literal Genesis accounts of creation. But, what is useful for my purposes is that the creationists have had to account to the geocentrists why they believe in science in some instances but not others, thus revealing their principles of selecting one scientific claim over another.

In the words of one creationist: "Many evolutionists claim that disbelief in evolution is like disbelief that the earth goes round the sun. The obvious flaw is that the latter is repeatable and observable while the former is not." This means that "the historical sciences, including evolution, are less legitimate than the experimental sciences because they purport to explain unwitnessed and unrepeatable events." Other nongeocentrist creationists state that the geocentrists fail "to take into account a distinction between observations and the *conclusions based on observations.*" As two scholars of creationism note, creationists have long stressed the distinction between "'origins science,' in which the primary authority is given to Scripture, in contrast to 'operation science,' in which the assured results of current observations and experiments are allowed to influence the interpretation of Scripture."[18]

Elites attempt to teach this Baconian approach to knowledge to fundamentalist Protestant children. The textbook *Of Pandas and People: The Central Question of Biological Origins* is most famous for teaching an intelligent design perspective on human origins, which has led to the book being a centerpiece in ID court cases. Less remarked upon is the fact that the book also has a "note to teachers" in the back which outlines a proper stance toward developing knowledge about nature. The authors of this section of the textbook want to explain the "scientific method," and make a distinction between the "inductive sciences"—certainly a Baconian term—and the "historical sciences."[19] The "inductive" are also "nomological," which means "relating to or denoting certain principles, such as laws of nature, that are neither logically necessary nor theoretically explicable, but are simply taken as true."[20] "Simply taken as true" is the nineteenth-century Baconian and Scottish Common Sense Realist idea of the transparent truth of observed facts.

The inductive sciences concern "how the natural world generally operates"—it does not ask how it came to be this way.

On the other hand, "the historical sciences seek to understand how things came to be." In this historical science, "the goal is not to find new laws or regularities but to reconstruct past conditions and events." Critically, "postulating intelligent intervention is completely inappropriate in the inductive sciences, the same is not true in the historical sciences." In the inductive sciences, "the whole point is to discover how the natural world normally operates on its own," no matter how it was created in the first place.[21] That is, for how the world currently works, fundamentalist kids should use mainstream science. But, as for how things came to be, that is not observable and would be speculation.

All of the theories in the historical sciences pertain to "the unobservable past," including the Big Bang and Darwinism, which postulate "unobservable objects and events." This is straight Baconianism—the observable is science, the unobservable is not science.[22] The message here is clear—being a good conservative Protestant scientist means using a justificatory science that is ultimately based upon direct observation.

So, this Baconian approach to knowledge continues among the contemporary conservative Protestant elite, who try to teach it to their members. I doubt many ordinary members learn it, as scientific epistemology is not a common sermon topic, and only a small percentage of conservative Protestant children would attend schools that use books like *Of Pandas and People*. I suspect these kids remember as much of high school science as do secular high school students, which is not much.

For the average conservative Protestant, I think it is more plausible that Baconianism has survived since the nineteenth century by incubating in conservative Protestant biblical hermeneutics, which are definitely learned by the ordinary members. Discussion of how to read the Bible is indisputably a central part of being a conservative Protestant. As described in Chapter 5, a Baconian approach to nature supported a Baconian approach to the Bible, which is that its meaning is on the surface, open to examination like a set of collected plants, with no high theory required to interpret it. Contemporary conservative Protestants are taught that true knowledge of the Bible is uncomplicated, transparent, and available via a common sense reading, so they may think that other knowledge—like knowledge of nature—is similarly uncomplicated, transparent, and available via common sense.

If they continually learn this approach to truth in general, then conservative Protestants will believe scientific claims that can be immediately observed (such as the average temperature of the Earth) and not claims based on "theories" like climate models and "speculations" about prehuman primates who roamed millions of years ago. Even if conservative Protestants never teach their children how to interpret nature through science, they may be teaching a general approach to truth claims through biblical hermeneutics.

Defending Literalist Theological Claims . . . from Liberal Protestantism

Another possible explanation for conservative Protestant propositional belief conflict with science over human origins will be obvious to those who know American religious history, once I describe this history using my terminology. If you ask conservative Protestants about human origins, you will often hear the claim that they are defending the truth of the literally read Bible. They would say that if Genesis is not literally true, then the Resurrection is not literally true and the virgin birth is not literally true and so on. A recent ethnography of evangelical high schools confirms that opposition to evolution is primarily about defending the Bible.[23]

Therefore, belief in the conservative Protestant version of human origins is only incidentally a scientific conflict—what they are actually defending is a list of literalist theological claims about the Bible. But, no scientist cares about the Resurrection, the virgin birth, or most of the literalist claims being defended against the liberals. Belief in the conservative Protestant account of human origins is then not a conflict with science per se, but is rather a battle with their archenemies the liberal Protestants, using scientific claims as a weapon. It is liberal Protestants who also care about claims like the Resurrection and the virgin birth, and the proper nightmare for any good fundamentalist is their child becoming a liberal Protestant. It was of course this conflict between fundamentalists and liberals—not fundamentalists and scientists—that shaped American religious history and these religions' approach to knowledge.

So, in this explanation, the reason there is not systemic conflict, but there is propositional belief conflict about human origins, is that they are not really concerned with whether these are knowledge claims about *the natural world* at all. Rather, they are concerned with defending other sets of nondemonstrable theological belief claims. Therefore, it is possible that conservative Protestants do not think of a six-thousand-year-old Earth or a literal Adam and Eve as scientific claims. They are instead but a few of the many theological statements that must be held to be literally true in order to defend the Bible from liberal Protestantism and secularism (often thought to be the same thing).

Status Politics or Identity Formation for Conservative Protestants

A fairly old social science tradition holds that "status politics" are political movements concerned with the status of a particular group in society, not necessarily an attempt to gain anything concrete. Some groups are losing prestige in society, and they promote their values as a way of demonstrating that they are still important.[24]

In a classic study of American temperance movements, Joseph Gusfield demonstrated that middle-class, small-town Protestants felt their status was declining compared to urban Catholic immigrants, and used temperance to demonstrate the importance of their values. Gusfield demonstrated that it was a symbolic politics because temperance advocates were not very interested in actually stopping people from drinking alcohol, just in establishing a constitutional amendment as a symbol.[25]

We could construct a status politics explanation of why conservative Protestants have not given up on their nonscientific beliefs about human origins, while the liberal Protestants have. It is central to conservative Protestant identity to see themselves as embattled group, whether this is true or not.[26] It is then not so much that they want to show that Darwin was factually wrong so much as the want to show the importance of the creationist idea that has become symbolic of their religious group. If they can get the public schools to give equal time to creationism, they establish that their religious group still has status in society. Adopting this symbol does not require accepting any larger knowledge structure, because all that is needed is a symbol that has come to represent the group.[27] This identity explanation is consistent with the survey findings above that show that belief in creationism is not connected to any other aspect of science.

When interviewing conservative Protestants about anything, it is common to be given what are essentially identity-based reasons for beliefs rather than reasons based upon higher-level beliefs. For example, when interviewing conservative Protestants about reproductive genetic technologies, I was often told by respondents that they are opposed to abortion "because I am Christian" and not because "human life begins at conception" or any other higher-level principle.

In the aforementioned ethnography of evangelical high schools, Jeffrey Guhin reaches a similar conclusion about evolution, seeing rejection of evolution as a defense of biblical literalism, which is itself a form of identity boundary-drawing. For evangelicals, the "symbolic boundary" with the secular United States is necessary to differentiate themselves. These boundaries are important for convincing people to be a member of any group, in particular those in which membership comes at a social cost.[28] If this insight is generalizable beyond Guhin's particular cases, it would suggest that not only would a religious fact-claim not need to be connected to any broader system of knowledge, but that a religious fact-claim that conflicts with a scientific claim is actually more useful for demarcating the border of the group, because science can stand in for secular society.

Moral Opposition to Science by Conservative Protestants

It is difficult to test these possible reasons as data are not available. However, I think that the final possibility is the most plausible, which is that conservative

Protestants select religious facts to disagree with scientific facts that have the strongest moral ramifications. That is, not only does moral conflict exist independent of any knowledge concerns, many religious people want to say that evolution is morally incorrect. They then do the next best thing in the context of a survey question—they say it is not true.

I would argue that this is what is occurring with the entire Intelligent Design movement. They seem to be primarily motivated by a concern that Darwinism is teaching that morality is random. They then want to overthrow Darwinism by showing that human evolution was at the hand of a designer. What appears to be about knowledge is actually driven by morality—an explanation I begin to address in the next chapter.

CONCLUSION

In this chapter I looked for systemic knowledge conflict. This would matter for the lives of citizens, as disbelief in human origins would lead one to not believe chemistry, physics, or any other field requiring the scientific method, and would result in disengagement from society. I did not find it. There does not seem to be any religious group, including conservative Protestantism, that takes the actual *action* of conflict of avoiding science writ large by not taking science classes, learning about science, having a scientific occupation, and so on. I did find that the members of most Christian traditions are in propositional belief conflict with science over fact-claims about the world. These fact-claims are few, and do not matter to the everyday lives of the vast majority of Americans.

Having dislodged the systemic knowledge conflict thesis, I engaged in some informed speculation about why propositional belief conflict would exist. First, I considered why mainline Protestants and Catholics would not follow the elites in their tradition and agree with scientists about all claims that scientists make. Second, I speculated about why, if not driven by systemic knowledge constraints, a conservative Protestant would not believe scientists' accounts of human origins. One possible reason is that they could still be Baconians. Another reason is that conservative Protestants defend nonscientific ideas not because they are in conflict with scientists, but because they are in conflict with evangelicals and liberal Protestants over Biblical exegesis. Propositional belief claims that differ from the scientific consensus could also be serving as an identity symbol in creating a collective identity against liberal Protestants and the broader society. A final possible explanation is that conservative Protestants oppose scientific facts not because of how they were generated, but because of their moral implications. I think that what we otherwise know about American society and religion suggests that this is the true conflict with science. I turn to these explanations in the next chapter.

7

Empirical Tests of Moral Conflict for the Religious Public

In the previous chapter I concluded that there is no evidence for systemic knowledge conflict but that there is evidence for propositional knowledge conflict. Existing academic research on American religion, as well as existing research on what the public thinks about science and scientists, suggests that a more likely conflict is over morality, not knowledge. In this chapter I turn to new evidence for moral conflict between religion and science among the U.S. public. Due to the dominance of the idea of systemic knowledge conflict among academics, including the sociologists who design nationally accessible surveys, data concerning moral conflict are extremely limited, so most of the data I will use are indirect. What is needed to reach more confident conclusions are new survey questions, along with new qualitative research, that focus on moral conflict. My hope is that the results are suggestive enough that future scholars take up this topic.

The analyses in the previous chapter ruled out the idea of irreconcilable and complete conflict over knowledge *and* morality. The analysis of whether the respondent wants their daughter to be a scientist is the most persuasive—if a respondent believed that all of science was irredeemably immoral, they would not want their daughter to be a scientist. However, this was not the case, and what we have is partial moral conflict. Those religious groups who have moral conflict with science either think that there are some types of science that do not have this conflict and/or that no type of science is inherently corrupt, because a person with good morals, such as their daughter, can remain a good person within science.

Religious people are in moral conflict over multiple aspects of modern science. The first is over which institution will be looked to to set the meaning and purpose of society. The second is more specific—that religious people are opposed to the implicit moral teachings of some scientific claims. The third is not about fact claims about scientific research per se, but about the technology that such research produces.

FAITH IN SCIENCE VS. FAITH IN RELIGION

Science is more than simply facts. It can also be a source of societal hope—a way to save our society from its troubles, in the same way that societies have looked to other saviors, like religion. That is, people can have "faith" in science, with faith being defined as a "firm belief in something for which there is no proof."[1] There is a lot of proof offered that molecules are made of atoms but very little proof that science will solve the world's problems. To believe that science will solve the world's problems, people have to rely upon faith in science as an institution, and there are competing institutions that they could have faith in.

Religious elites have upon occasion engaged in this conflict when they see scientists claiming that science can set the values and aims of society. As discussed in Chapter 4, the origins of the field of bioethics are in theologians' reactions to scientists trying to determine societal values. For example, inventor of in vitro fertilization Robert Edwards claimed that "moral laws must be based on what man knows about himself, and that this knowledge inevitably comes largely from science."[2] This is the type of view opposed by theologian Paul Ramsey, also described in Chapter 4, who claimed that scientists of the 1960s were not engaged in "an exact science as such, but a religious view of where and how ultimate human significance is to be found."[3]

The extent to which a population has such a faith in science obviously has important ramifications. For example, if people have faith in science to provide a source of direction that humans should aspire to, then scientists would be looked to to set societal goals. Survey analyses suggest that religious people are in the greatest moral conflict with science when science is portrayed as something to have faith in.

The GSS Survey I used in the last chapter has a question that can be interpreted as measuring the degree to which the respondent has faith in science as providing meaning and direction for society.[4] The survey contains a block of questions with five-point responses, ranging from "strongly agree" to "strongly disagree," prefaced by the statement: "How much do you agree or disagree with each of these statements?" The first statement is "we believe too often in science, and not enough in feelings and faith."[5] This is a measure of faith in science's ability to provide meaning and direction for society.[6]

To examine whether religious citizens are less likely to have this type of faith in science, I defined religious groups as I did in the analyses in the last chapter.[7] Analogously to the previous analyses, if members of a religious group are more likely to say that we should believe in feelings and faith than the nonreligious, I interpret that to mean that the religious group is in this particular type of moral conflict with science.

The first line in Table 3 shows the probability of a respondent from a group agreeing or strongly agreeing that "we believe too often in science, and not enough in feelings and faith." The general pattern in the results is clear. Controlling for demographic variables, every religious group has less faith in science producing meaning than do the nonreligious. It is conservative Protestants who have the least amount of faith in science compared to the nonreligious, with an enormous difference between the literalist conservative Protestants and the nonreligious. The odds of a nonreligious person agreeing is 32 percent, but for a literalist conservative Protestant it is 62 percent. In general, the religious respondents, compared to the non-religious respondents, do not want science to set meaning in society, which is a high-level moral conflict.

As a comparison, we can examine religious faith in science's ability to solve concrete problems in the world through technology. The survey also asked the respondent to evaluate whether "modern science will solve our environmental problems with little change to our way of life." Solving environmental problems would be consistent with the morality of all of the religions I can measure in this survey, so this question is measuring faith in technologies without religious valence, but not faith in science's ability to set meaning.

In the second row of Table 3, we see that it is only African American Protestants who have less of this type of faith in science. I can only speculate that African Americans have a different experience with environmental problems than do other Americans. But, more critically for my claims, the other religious groups are not different from the nonreligious to the extent that they have faith that modern science will solve this concrete technological problem. In sum, religious Americans, and conservative Protestants in particular, are very likely to think society puts too much faith in science and not enough in religion. They are in conflict over setting the meaning for society. This interpretation is supported by comparing this result to faith in solving a concrete problem like pollution, where most religious groups and the nonreligious have the same amount of faith.

OPPOSITION TO THE MORAL STANCE OF SCIENTISTS

The second type of moral conflict is more specific, and is that religious people are opposed to the implicit moral teachings of some scientific claims. These moral teachings can be intended by scientists, such as when they use science to justify a moral position, or they can be unintended. As an example of the unintended, conservative Protestants have long claimed that people exposed to evolutionary ideas are going to make certain moral connections regardless of what scientists

TABLE 3. Expected values and predicted probabilities: General Social Survey

Measure	Literalist Conservative Protestant	Non-literalist Conservative Protestant	Mainline	Traditional Catholic	Non-traditional Catholic	Black Protestant	Non-religious
Probability agree that we believe too much in science, not enough in feelings and faith	.621***	.505***	.495**	.489***	a	.651***	.326
Probability agree that modern science will solve our environmental problems	.576	.614	.480	.435	a	.320*	.493
Probability want scientists to have "a great deal of influence" on debates about global warming	.376**	.302***	.595	.408	.486	.793*	.561
Probability want scientists to have "a great deal of influence" on debates about embryonic stem cell research	.271*	.175***	.415	.418	.515	.424	.444
Probability want scientists to have "a great deal of influence" on debates about genetically modified food	.445	.465	.367	.497	.390	.521	.501

Note: With controls. *** = p < .001, ** = p < .01, * = p < .05 (two-tailed) for comparison of religious group to the non-religious in a regression model. a = traditional and non-traditional Catholics cannot be distinguished, so the traditional Catholic entry represents all Catholics.

may intend. One claim is that if high school students learn that humans evolved due in part to random events, they will conclude that morality is random, even if a scientist never says anything about morality.

Similarly, religious elites have long been concerned that certain biomedical technologies implicitly teach the public that humans are defined by their biology, not by being made in the image of God. They believe that if we learn we are biological beings we will treat each other slightly worse than we would if we consider ourselves to be made in the image of God. I show elsewhere that members of the public who think that humans are defined by biology do indeed advocate treating people in a way that is more similar to the way we treat objects.[8] Below I will conduct a number of survey analyses that suggest that conservative Protestants see this type of moral conflict with science.

Opposition to Scientists' Influence in Public Debates

If there *is* this type of moral conflict, members of religious groups will not want scientists to be influential in public debates about moral issues, independent of their view of scientists' ability to generate true knowledge. I can test this with survey data, continuing the analysis of the GSS data. To evaluate opposition to scientists' influence on moral debates in the public sphere, I use three questions that asked how much influence should: environmental scientists "have in deciding what to do about global warming"; "medical researchers" have on "government funding for stem cell research"; and "medical researchers" have in deciding whether to "restrict the sale of genetically modified foods.[9] "I will generalize and call these three groups of professionals "scientists."

The first two of these issues are currently framed in the U.S. public sphere as moral debates. At first glance the global warming debate concerns whether it is occurring at the hands of humans. But, the reason that scientific claims about climate change are contested is that conservatives do not want to have to change our society's behavior. They do not want to drive smaller cars, make smaller houses, avoid airplanes, stop mining coal and so on in order to mitigate global warming. At its extreme, climate change deniers see scientific claims as part of a "hoax" or even a conspiracy to install liberal values regarding consumption, as revealed by the "Climategate" incident, in which conservatives claimed scientists were manipulating data.[10] Climate change is at its heart a moral debate. What we should do about stem cell research is connected with the abortion issue, and its morality is constantly debated.

There is almost no moral debate on the final issue, genetically modified food, in the U.S. (although there is such a debate in Europe.) Rather, the moral issue is settled—if it is determined to be safe, then it is acceptable. The survey question itself poses the issue as one of evaluating risk, not morality, which makes the question about scientific influence over a public debate about facts and knowledge. This final question then serves as an effective comparison because it asks about scientific influence on a question not currently framed as implicating morality.

If conservative Protestants are opposed to scientific influence in first two debates, but not the third, this suggests that conservative Protestants are not opposed to scientists' influence on all debates. They are only opposed to influence on moral debates. This is consistent with seeing scientists as a group they are often in moral conflict with, and that they then have an interest in keeping out of these moral debates. They would have no problem with scientists' participation in the public sphere if it is not framed as moral, but about knowledge—limited to making technical assessments (e.g., whether genetically modified food is safe).

The analyses control for the same variables as in previous GSS models. They also control for the extent the respondent thinks scientists understand global warming or stem cells and the respondent's understanding of the methods of science, which should account for any effect of not wanting scientists to be influential because the respondent disagrees with the science per se. I also use two measures of wanting other professional groups to be influential in the debate to control for not wanting anyone to be influential in a public debate.[11]

The third and fourth lines in Table 3 show that the literalist and nonliteralist conservative Protestants are more opposed than are the nonreligious to the influence of scientists on public moral debates over global warming and stem cells.[12] For example, nonliteralist conservative Protestants are only about half as likely as the nonreligious to want scientific influence in these debates.

Importantly, the final line in Table 3 shows that for genetically modified food, no religious group is different than the nonreligious in wanting scientists to influence these debates. This means that there is not an opposition to scientific influence in the public sphere in general—to, for example, giving advice on knowledge issues. There is only a religious opposition to scientists influencing public debates about moral issues.

I later repeated the same analysis for wanting scientists to be influential in debates about global warming but while also controlling for political identification and political ideology, which allows us to separate out any religious effect from a political effect.[13] In that analysis (not shown), the most powerful predictors of *not* wanting scientists to be involved in the public debate are not believing that scientists understand climate change, not wanting the influence of politicians, and identifying as a Republican.[14] This suggests a generally political explanation for not wanting scientific influence on this one issue.

However, even after controlling for these political variables, literalist conservative Protestants are still less likely to want scientists involved in this debate. This difference between literalist conservative Protestants and the nonreligious is not large. However, it is striking that there is a difference at all. While global warming is moral, it is not an issue that has particularly religious valence in the same way that embryonic life does. The small religion difference here is indicative of the fact that these conservative Protestants do not want scientists involved in *any* moral issue, not just the ones where the morality of conservative Protestantism and science are thought to differ.

Is the Scientific Community Self-Interested?

In 1942 sociologist Robert Merton described the four "norms of science:" universalism, communism, disinterestedness, and organized skepticism.[15] Universalism means that truth claims are subject to impersonal evaluation, regardless of who the scientist making the claim is. Communism means the findings of science belong to the community. Disinterestedness means that scientists do not make personal gain from their work. Organized skepticism means not making conclusions until data are at hand, and that all claims are subject to empirical and logical critique. In a later critique of the "norms of science," sociologist Michael Mulkay described a longer list that included additional norms that had been created by scholars standing on Merton's shoulders: "rationality, emotional neutrality, universalism, individualism, disinterestedness, impartiality, communality, humility, and organized skepticism."[16] Merton and those in his intellectual lineage took these norms to be how scientists actually operated.

If this is what scientists are like, then it is hard to see how science and scientists could have a moral agenda. However, by the late 1960s, critics were pointing out that these norms are actually not in force among scientists, and Mulkay concluded that the Mertonian norms were not norms, but rather an ideology. Scientists only describe themselves in this way to justify "their claim for a special political status." Moreover, this "biased image of science ... supports their collective interests [and] amounts to the utilization of an occupational ideology."[17] This depiction of scientists is more consistent with scientists having a collective moral agenda.

I lack a measure of whether the public perceives scientists to be observing each of these norms. However, a series of GSS survey questions did ask respondents if they thought scientists were acting in their own self-interest. Respondents were asked "when making policy recommendations about global warming, on a scale of 1 to 5, to what extent do you think the following groups would support what is best for the country as a whole versus what serves their own narrow interests?" Best for country is "1" and narrow interests is "5." They were asked similar questions about stem cell research and genetically modified foods. For each technology respondents were asked about the self-interestedness of scientists plus two other groups.[18]

These questions effectively measure the extent to which scientists are perceived as working in the nation's interest or their own collective interest. Believing that scientists have a distinct agenda from the rest of society is a prerequisite for thinking that scientists have a distinct morality that should be opposed in the public sphere. Therefore, if members of a religious group are more likely than members of the nonreligious group to think that scientists are not acting in the nation's interest, I consider that evidence for moral conflict of that religious group with science.

The evaluations of the self-interestedness of scientists for global warming and stem cell research were combined into an overall "self-interestedness" measure.[19] For technical reasons, the responses to the question about genetically modified foods had to be analyzed separately.[20] I needed to find a way to account for the fact that conservative Protestants are more likely than others to think that *any* group is self-interested—or, more theologically, that everyone is sinful. I therefore control in the statistical models for thinking other groups that the survey asked about were self-interested, to see if respondents think that scientists are *particularly* self-interested.[21]

As in previous analyses, the regression models also control for demographics. The analytic question is, as before, are particular religious groups likely to think that scientists are self-interested when they enter the public sphere, even after controlling for the extent to which the respondent thinks that all groups are self-interested? The results shown in the first row of Table 4 suggest that both literalist and nonliteralist conservative Protestants are much more likely than the nonparticipants in religion to say that scientists are working for their own and not the country's interests.[22] No other religious groups are different from the nonreligious.

On the other hand, the second row shows that there are no differences between religious groups and the nonreligious on thinking scientists are self-interested on genetically modified food. This is consistent with the earlier findings about wanting scientists to be influential in the public sphere. That is, on the two issues that are constructed as moral issues in the U.S.—global warming and embryonic stem cell research—conservative Protestants think that scientists are forwarding their own and not the public's interests. But, this is not the case for the one issue that is constructed as being about knowledge—genetically modified foods.

Similarly, in 2012, the GSS asked about the level of agreement with the statement "Scientific researchers are dedicated people who work for the good of humanity."[23] This produces an image of disinterested scientists forwarding the consensual morality. The analysis shows that the probability that a nonreligious respondent will *not* strongly agree that scientists work for the good of humanity is high, at .769. There is clearly generalized skepticism about scientists among the entire public. The probability for a literalist conservative Protestant is even higher, at .869. (see the third row of Table 4.) That is, despite only 443 people being asked this question, making it less likely that any difference would be statistically significant, literalist conservative Protestants were more likely than the nonreligious to disagree that scientists work for the good of humanity. In sum, these survey analyses suggest that conservative Protestants are more likely than the nonreligious to think that scientists are working in their own self-interest. While this is not morality per se, it suggests that conservative Protestants do not think scientists are neutral investigators of nature.

MORAL CONFLICT OVER TECHNOLOGY

The third type of moral conflict is not a moral objection to scientific research per se, but rather to the technology that scientific research allows. Technology is "the application of scientific knowledge for practical purposes," so medicine and engineering are technologies.[24] While it could be argued that science is distinct from technology, I doubt the general public sees a distinction between, for example, scientists and medical researchers or scientists and engineers.

Technology has even more direct moral implications because it is applied to the social world. And there is a moral critique of almost every technology we can imagine: automobiles, airplanes, television, the internet, nuclear energy, and on and on. However, most technologies do not have a particularly religious valence, and Western religions do not have a problem with technology per se.

But, there are some technologies that do have implications for religious beliefs and morals. While the computer is religiously neutral, the Christian religion at least is in general centrally concerned with the human body—particularly reproduction and sexuality.[25] Therefore, technologies that concern the body, life, and death are those most likely to have moral implications for Christians. Technologies that concern human embryos and the hastening of death, as well as human genetic engineering, reproductive genetic technologies, pregnancy, childbirth, organ transplantation, and human enhancement are all examples that are probably seen by religious people as having moral implications. We are all familiar with public debates about these technologies and that religious people are often front and center in these debates.

Below I conduct quantitative and qualitative analyses that show that religious people are not opposed to technology itself, nor are they opposed to manipulating the human body. For example, they do not think that manipulating the human body is "playing God." Rather, they think, to use the phrase of the late Paul Ramsey, that we should "play God as God plays God" with nature and the human.[26] The question is moral—what is the appropriate version of playing God?

Moreover, opposition to a technology by religious people is never about knowledge. For example, if you look at the papal documents that argue for the sanctity of human embryos, and thus that abortion, most reproductive genetic technologies, and embryonic stem cell research are all morally wrong, these documents accept and use the latest scientific research on embryos.[27] It was embryology, after all, that taught the institutional church about what exactly happened at fertilization. The Catholic Church just reaches a different moral conclusion from the scientific facts than most scientists do.[28]

In another example, in an earlier book I engaged in an in-depth interview study of 180 largely religious Americans to discern their views of reproductive genetic technologies such as pre-implantation genetic diagnosis, human genetic engineering, and cloning. In general, these religious citizens were more opposed to these technologies than were the nonreligious people. In the analysis of all of those interview transcripts, I do not remember an instance of a respondent, including the fundamentalists, challenging the scientific claims behind any of these technologies. It was just accepted that the science was accurate. They did have a moral analysis of those facts that often conflicted with the moral analyses given by the proponents of these technologies.[29]

Growing Moral Conflict Between Conservative Protestantism and Technology Applied to the Body

It is quite easy to show that conservative Protestants and conservative Catholics are more opposed than are the nonreligious to many technologies that involve the human body, like embryonic stem cell research. It is a greater empirical challenge to show that they see their opposition to embryonic stem cell research to be part of a moral conflict with scientists. Below, I infer this moral conflict through an evaluation of changes in the level of confidence in scientists from 1984, when the available data begins, to 2010.[30] Over this time period, scientific innovation shifted to the human body—at the same time that religious conservatives were also shifting attention to the human body. Thus, moral conflict.

In the 1950s and 1960s, conservative Protestants were involved with anticommunism, and in the late 1970s, they joined conservative Catholics in the religious right movement. While the original motivation of the religious right was to defend its schools from what it saw as government interference, it later began to take positions on issues like abortion, homosexuality, and sexual ethics, later turning to euthanasia and embryonic stem cell research.[31] These questions of the body, and particularly reproduction and female sexuality, have always been central to the Christian tradition.[32] They had just had not previously been as central a part of public debate.

The public face of science was changing at the same time, making it more likely that conservative Protestants would see science as a competitor in moral debates about the body. The scientific issues in the public sphere from the 1950s through the 1970s were nuclear energy, pollution, weapons, and the genetic modification of micro-organisms. These were not generally thought of as "religious." However, by the 1970s, science began to debate issues having to do with the human body such as abortion, birth control, human genetic engineering, organ transplantation, the definition of death, euthanasia, mind control and, later, embryonic stem cell research and cloning. These could be seen as part of the moral agenda of scientists, but these were traditionally more "religious" issues. By the mid-1970s theologians and scientists were solidly engaged in clashes over the morality of these technologies in the emergent public bioethical debate.[33]

Therefore, a growing moral conflict with science could have resulted from this change in the social priorities of both conservative Protestants and scientists, as both groups began to make often conflicting moral claims about the human body in the public sphere. If so, it should also be the case that conservative Protestants have become increasingly opposed to the moral influence of scientists since 1984.[34]

I focus on the respondents' response to the question: "I am going to name some institutions in this country. As far as the people running these institutions are concerned, would you say you have a great deal of confidence, only some confidence, or hardly any confidence at all in them? Scientific community." This question is not framed as asking the respondent for an evaluation of the legitimacy of the methods of science. The wording and context of the question clearly indicate that it is read as the view of the social influence of science as an institution in the public sphere.[35] When asked for their level of confidence in the scientific community, 43 percent of the respondents replied "a great deal," fifty percent replied "only some," and seven percent replied "hardly any." I conducted analysis by comparing those who said "a great deal" to those who said "only some" or "hardly any."

As with the analyses above, I controlled for the demographic qualities and political orientation of the respondent and used regression models to see what characteristics of a respondent predict responses to this "confidence in scientists" question.[36] As you might imagine, one of the strongest predictors of confidence in science is confidence in any institutions about which the GSS asked. People who do not trust one set of elites usually do not trust any elites. That is not especially interesting but is important to account for in any analysis, given that conservative Protestants may be inclined not to trust elites in general.

More important to my interpretation is to show that people do not lack faith in the leaders of science simply because they think that the methods of science are wrong or that science does not generate accurate truth claims. That would be knowledge conflict. To ensure that I am not measuring knowledge conflict, we can see if those who have avoided science (as I measured in the analyses described in Chapter 6) have less confidence in scientific elites. I looked to see whether people who knew more uncontested scientific facts, claimed more knowledge about science, knew more scientific methodology, had taken more college level science classes, or had a scientific occupation had more confidence in the leaders of scientific institutions. None of these factors have any influence on what the public thinks about scientific leaders, so their confidence in institutional science is not about true or false knowledge.

A stronger test is whether those people who believed in the conservative Protestant claims about human origins had less confidence in scientific elites.

This would mean that the lack of confidence was about a knowledge conflict over human origins. I used the same measure introduced in Chapter 6 that measures belief in this contested knowledge. Here again there is no difference in confidence in scientists between those who agree more with the scientific versions of human origins versus those who agree less with the scientific version of human origins. Confidence in scientific institutions in the U.S. appears to have nothing to do with knowledge claims at all. While I make this point in service of larger claims below, it is itself further evidence for a lack of systemic knowledge conflict in the contemporary U.S.

Further analysis shows that, consistent with the general narrative of this book, confidence in science for the entire public—not just the religious—is at least partly based on morality. There were few appropriate survey questions available, but I was able to use the question from the previous analyses in this chapter, where the respondents were asked whether they wanted scientists to be influential in debates about embryonic stem cell research.[37]

Even after controlling for all of the knowledge measures and demographics, there is a quite large difference in confidence in the scientists between those who are opposed to scientists' influence on stem cell research and those who are supportive of this influence. The analysis, not otherwise shown, reveals that similarly situated respondents who want little to no influence of scientists in debates about stem cell research have a one in four chance of saying they have confidence in the scientists running the institution of science. Those who want a great deal of influence of scientists on stem cells have a one in two chance. Confidence seems quite highly structured by how much the respondents want scientists to be involved with moral debates in the public sphere, so I will treat this confidence measure as a proxy for moral conflict.

I continued the analysis to see if the lack of confidence in elite scientists was influenced by religion, even after controlling for variables indicating exposure to science. It is. The last row in Table 4 shows that a literalist conservative Protestant has only a fourteen in one hundred chance of having confidence in scientists, whereas the nonreligious have a thirty-eight in one hundred chance. There are no other differences by religion. Moreover, additional analyses show that if someone is opposed to scientific influence on embryonic stem cell research *and* is a literalist conservative Protestant, they have even less confidence in elite scientists.[38]

In sum, for the entire public, confidence in the scientists who run American science institutions appears to be driven by moral evaluation of the scientists, not by opposition to the knowledge claims made by science. This is particularly true for conservative Protestants. Has this moral evaluation of scientific elites changed over time? If so, we can infer what the moral conflict may be about.

If we look over time, we see that the level of confidence by most religious groups has remained constant over time. For example, mainline Protestants were slightly

TABLE 4. Expected values and predicted probabilities: General Social Survey

Measure	Literalist Conservative Protestant	Non-literalist Conservative Protestant	Mainline	Traditional Catholic	Non-traditional Catholic	Black Protestant	Non-religious
Extent agree scientists serve their own narrow interests on global warming and stem cells	4.27***	3.87***	3.33	3.10	3.34	3.74	2.85
Extent agree scientists serve their own narrow interests on genetically modified food	2.29	1.87	1.87	1.99	1.82	2.52	2.06
Probability of not strongly agreeing that scientists work for the good of humanity	.869*	.852	.841	.728	.764	.831	.769
Probability of having confidence in scientists	.141*	.333	.382	.395	a	.315	.382

Note: With controls. *** = p < .001, ** = p < .01, * = p < .05 (two-tailed) for comparison of religious group to the non-religious in a regression model. a = traditional and non-traditional Catholics cannot be distinguished, so the traditional Catholic entry represents all Catholics.

less confident in scientists in 1984 then were the nonreligious, and they are equally less confident in 2010. The one difference is for literalist conservative Protestants, who have become even less confident over time.[39] In 1984, the difference in odds between literalist conservative Protestants and the nonreligious was only .10, but by 2010 the gap had about doubled.

We can then ask what has changed socially or morally for science and/or conservative Protestantism between 1984 and 2010 to cause this increased level of conflict. Here I run out of available survey questions, and it is my hope that if social scientists become more attuned to moral conflict, they will begin to incorporate questions into future surveys. But, I believe the answer is, as described above, that during this time period both science and religion moved from concern with the physical world toward concern with the human body, which has long been a moral focus of Christianity.

Religious Views of Engineering the Human Species

I finish this chapter by trying to more precisely describe religious Americans' view of technology, so that we can see possible present and future moral conflict with science. I focus on one of the technologies with a great deal of potential religious implications—genetic modification of the human species.

I lack data on the views of the scientific community concerning genetic modification or, more importantly, what the religious public thinks the view of the scientific community is. I examine in-depth interview data with religious Americans that allow us to imagine what points of consensus and conflict would come into being if the scientific community is seen as taking various positions in the years ahead. The most obvious conflict would be if the scientific community is seen to be on the side of "improving" the human species, as it was in the eugenics movement. However, we need to see that there would be many points of consensus that may surprise many. I will make the following points about the moral views of religious Americans.

First, far from being opposed to applying technology to the human body, religious Americans see technology as a source of hope and an engine of human progress. However, religious people have ethical concerns about the end goal of this progress. They would be opposed to the use of this technology for creating an improved human species beyond what it is "supposed" to be. For the religious, the goal for these technologies should be to restore the nonsuffering human, not create a super-human.

Second, common wisdom is that religious people are opposed to modifying the human genome to improve the species, because God created humans as they should be. I will argue that this is not correct, and that the majority of religious people are not opposed to genetically modifying the human species per se. They do not view the current human genome as somehow sacred and not to be "tampered with." That is not where any moral conflict lies.

Third, in actuality, religious people think we have an obligation to use technology to transform the world and even the human body. The difference with much of the scientific ethical thought on this issue is that the religious believe we should not use our own vision to make the blueprint for the future, but should instead determine what God would want us to do. This subtle difference could result in future conflict if technological abilities improve.

I conducted an inductive discourse analysis of responses from an in-depth interview study that focused on what religious people in the U.S. think about reproductive genetic technology.[40] The interviews began with a series of hypothetical scenarios about couples who are planning on having children, and I asked the respondent what advice they would give the couple. The first scenario was about a couple who had found that they are both carriers for cystic fibrosis. "What should they do?" the respondent was asked. In the next scenario, the woman is already pregnant, and they are offered amniocentesis possibly followed by abortion. "Should they do this?" the respondents were asked. In the next scenario, a couple is offered pre-implantation genetic diagnosis to avoid cystic fibrosis.[41] Another couple are offered pre-implantation genetic diagnosis for early onset Alzheimer's disease, and another for deafness, and yet another are offered pre-implantation genetic diagnosis to avoid having an obese child. Finally, a hypothetical couple is offered pre-implantation genetic diagnosis to obtain the smartest child possible. Another scenario involves sex selection, and another sperm sorting to determine the gender of the baby. The scenarios then turn to germline human genetic engineering to engineer traits such as cystic fibrosis, obesity, and intelligence in an embryo that eventually becomes a child—and thus that trait would be found in all of that child's descendants. A final scenario asks about reproductive cloning. Questions then turn to what the respondent thinks the effect of these technologies will be on society, some questions about religion, and finally how the respondent thinks our society should have a debate about reproductive genetic technologies.[42]

The questions I primarily focus upon here were near the very end of the interview after an hour or more of conversation about religion and reproductive genetics. The typical conversation by that point has been, at least for the religious respondents, interwoven with religious discourse, and due to the priming early in the interview, many responded with religious reasons for and against the use of these reproductive genetic technologies.

The first of the questions I examine occurred at the very end of the interview. It was different than the previous questions, in that the interviewer handed the interviewee a card that had ten words listed in a column on it, and the interviewee was asked, "When you think about all the issues that we have talked about today, which one of these words best summarizes your feelings. Or, you can pick a word that is not on the list. Or, you can talk about more than one if you want." When the respondent would pick a word, they were asked, "Why that word?" It is in their reasons for picking that word that we can determine their moral vision for these technologies. The words on the card were humility, worry, fear, hopefulness, happiness, hopelessness, anger, helplessness, reverence, and awe. The other responses I focus upon in this analysis come from us asking, "Should the ability to change the genes of the human species be reserved for God?" This is designed to get to the question of who should modify and/or provide the design for future humans.

Let me start with the data generated from the word selection exercise, which helps me address my first point, that religious people in the U.S. generally see reproductive genetic technologies through a lens of hope. The question comes after extended discussions of technologies, some of which nearly all respondents are opposed to. For example, almost nobody was in favor of human cloning, with most people finding it repellent. The vast majority of respondents had some technologies and applications that they approved of, and some that they did not. Overall, what was the conclusion about reproductive genetics? Were they hopeful, and thus tended to ignore the "threat" of technologies like cloning and creating super-intelligent babies? Or, did they focus upon the negative, and see human bodily modification through genetics as a foreboding picture of our future?

I deductively coded the responses by the word selected, and then inductively coded the reasons given for selecting that word. There were certainly people who fit the stereotyped depiction of religious people seeing *dread*, with some selecting "worry," "fear," "worry and fear," "anger and fear," and "hopelessness." A few suggested their own word to summarize their thoughts about reproductive genetic technologies—"concern." The response of one of the Catholic respondents was typical. His word was "worry," and when asked why, he said "I would hate to see society come to the place where we can manufacture a human being the way we want it to be. That would be very worrisome to me."

Similarly, a mainline Protestant who approved of the individual use of many of the technologies talked through the other possibilities on the card. "Well, not 'happiness' or 'anger,'" he said. "I think probably 'fear' and 'worry' more than the 'hopefulness' reference and 'awe,' which probably reflects my cynicism more than anything else. But—I mean it could potentially be a very good thing, but human history being what it is, you know, when we meddle in these things, we tend to end up doing more harm than good. So, I think 'fear' and 'worry.'"

However, these negative visions of the future of genetic modifications of humans were not the dominant response. The majority of words selected by conservative Protestants, mainline Protestants, and Catholics could be categorized as either "all good" or "good and bad." Mainliners were the most positive, with almost all selecting "all good" words or "good and bad" words. Conservative Protestants were a bit less positive, followed by Catholics.

By far, the "all good" word most chosen by respondents was "hopefulness," and nearly everyone said the reason they selected that word was that we would soon be able to relieve the suffering of disease by using reproductive genetic technologies. As one mainline Protestant respondent put it:

> I think hopefulness would be the selection that I would make. I get to thinking about it and think that we can contribute significantly through the development of these technologies to reduce human suffering. I can't imagine anyone not being hopeful about that. It's not going to be easy. It's going to be very complicated. We need to exercise humility in the process, but I don't find it hopeless or helpless. I'm hopeful.

Earlier, she was asked about a scenario in which a doctor could "fix the genes in a fertilized egg to remove the chance that any baby would have cystic fibrosis," so that "not only would this child be free of this gene, but so would the child's children, the child's grandchildren, and so on." She responded that she would be supportive of the use of this technology to change "the lineage," in her words, because "I think it's a great technique, if that exists, and I think it would be wonderful to eliminate cystic fibrosis from our world, and that will take some time to do, I'm sure."

A fundamentalist Protestant said he picked "hopefulness" because "I think we're on the verge of some good things for people for our society and hopefully we'll be able to handle these new technologies with wisdom. And if we're wise in what we do, we only improve society. If we're not wise, they're very dangerous. So I guess I'm hopeful that we'll be wise in the way we can handle them."

Earlier, in a discussion about using germline genetic engineering to remove cystic fibrosis from the family line, he was not concerned about the technology itself, only that it did not involve killing embryos or fetuses—a common response for conservative Protestants. "Sure, if that technology is available, certainly," they should use it, he said. When asked, "Do you have any concerns about this technology at all?" he said no, as long as "it's not done by replacing a gene with fetuses, that stem cell stuff." We can see the boundaries of his moral conflict with science.

A Catholic man said the choice of words was easy, and his choice was "hopefulness." The reason was "because we have within our grasp, like no other time in history the chance to eradicate so much human suffering. We're on the cusp of a great era of discovery and . . . hopefully my children will live to see it. . . . I remember getting . . . polio shots and you know polio and small pox has been eradicated. Amazing things have . . . happened in my lifetime and my kids are going to see remarkable things."

Perhaps more interesting was the very common impulse to select a positive and negative word to indicate the good and the bad. The positive was always a word that they chose to represent the hope of the relief of suffering through genetic technology. The negative was a word to represent either fear of misuse (typically radical enhancements) or of forgetting that we humans are not God. The most common words selected together were "hopefulness" and "worry." One respondent stated, "Actually, two things kind of pop out. The hopefulness because I think that a lot of good could come from being able to control some really major medical problems and worry . . . a little worry about just how far the scientific community would maybe want to go with the technology that they are developing or that they have."

Similarly, a mainline Protestant stated that "I would put hopefulness in there and I think I have to add worry." Hopefulness was selected because of "the good things that can happen with the technology that you have described," and worry was selected because "the technology could be . . . misused for frivolous reasons." She was typical in her support for revising the human species to eliminate disease, but not for changes that she thought were not disease-based. She was in favor of germline genetic engineering for cystic fibrosis, as long as there were no "unforeseen consequences." The interviewer then began "what about for ..." and she interrupted with "for blue eyes . . . no!"

Religious respondents often also selected terms of reverence and awe, signifying caution, that we are interfering, perhaps with good reason, in something that is far above our human perspective. Similarly, it was common for respondents to select "hopefulness and humility," with "humility" a reminder that we are not God. As one conservative Protestant put it, he selected humility "because it helps—you know, helps me realize that I'm not God. I'm not able to make perfectly correct decisions." He was hopeful, "because I think that this is a technology [that] will help people."

A smaller group of people selected "hopefulness" and "awe," with hopefulness for the prospect of curing disease, and "awe" meaning "at awe of our awesome technological abilities." A fundamentalist Protestant said he picked these words because:

> I believe of course there is, you know, as we progress along as a society, there are things to be hopeful for that diseases will be eradicated and that people will live comfortable lives. You know, and an ultimate hopefulness of someday getting to Heaven and sitting face-to-face with the Creator. It is kind of awesome to think that we have this technology to be able to do some of these things, but I believe of course that credit should be given where credit is due. It's not necessarily us that are actually doing this. We're the clay in the potter's hands, even those that may not necessarily be someone who believes in Christ, because God certainly has the capability and power to do that. So I would say probably hopefulness and awe. Some of these more negative feelings, you know, I just don't see that. I for one, I'm certainly not worried or fearful.

Roughly equal numbers of religious people in each religious tradition selected "all good," "good and bad," and "dread" terms. There was a slight tendency for mainliners to be more "glass is half full and Catholics to be more "glass is half empty." For the "all good" category, these were people who, despite being opposed to some aspects of reproductive genetic technology, had an overall exclusively positive, hopeful vision for genetic intervention going forward.

Religious people in this study are not anti-science or anti-technology. By and large they do not see the human genome as sacred and thus inviolable. They believe in what they perceive as the relief of suffering, most notably through "medical" interventions. However, religious people in the U.S. seem to entirely lack a eugenic vision, where we intervene in the human genome to "improve" the species. Rather, the present-day healthy "walking-around" sort of human is the ideal, and the goal is to get everyone to that "normal" state. However, their positive vision going forward is largely tempered by a caution at what humans might do wrong. When future scholars closely examine any moral conflict between religion and science, I expect that they will find these subtle points of convergence.

Subtle differences between religion and science should also be expected to emerge. To the extent that scientists are more sympathetic with the idea of "improving" humans according to our own human definitions of quality, we can expect moral conflict. In contrast, one could imagine religious people in the U.S. in favor of creating a Humanity 2.0, as long as the blueprint was made by God. Again, the difference in these moral visions is *not* in their view of scientists' knowledge or abilities. *Nor* is the difference in their view of whether humans should change nature. On this they would agree. The difference is that the religious would try to get the moral principles behind any change from the "objective" source of God's will. The scientists would look to contemporary human values where, if the current culture values super-intelligence, than that is what Humanity 2.0 should have.

I turn to my second point, which is that the religious are not opposed to modification per se, and my third, which is that humans are to enact this modification, not God. Religious respondents believe in modifying the current human, but want to constrain changes to those that would please God. Of course, an academic analyst could say that these people should recognize that what is thought to be "pleasing to God" is also a matter of social consensus, ultimately no different than simply polling a society. However, this is not how religious people see it.

The limitations on human improvement in the Western religious vision can be found in the elite theological discourse, where there is a strong dichotomy between God and humans. Humans are not God, but were created by God, along with all of "nature." A long-running part of Christian theology concerns what actions in the physical world are then the responsibility of humans, and which are to remain the province of God. This is represented by the theological debate concerning whether we humans are simply a created creature of God or co-creators with God.[43]

With a technology like the genetic engineering of humans, if we are purely creatures, God is entirely responsible for our human bodily form, and we are not to interfere. To take this to its logical conclusion, we should not heal diseases humans are born with, because God created them. However, if we are co-creators with God, we participate in fulfilling God's desires for the human bodily form. In this vision, God wants us to heal disease and relieve the suffering of an imperfect world and an imperfect human.

In the interviews, well after all of the questions about what people should do in the face of various genetic conditions, the respondent was asked: "Do you think that the ability to change the genes of the human species should be reserved for God?" The responses here point directly to the respondent's notion of whether we are co-creators with God and whether something like human genetic modifications should be something "left to God." We can also see what is left to God and what is left to humans and, to anticipate the conclusion, it is God's job to come up with the plan, and it is humanity's job to implement it.

A minority of religious people do say that yes, the ability to change the genes of the human species should be left to God, and these are typically the people who are opposed to all applications of all technologies. It is hard to imagine that they do not believe in the human modification of God's creation, because presumably they all believe in medicine, mechanized agriculture, and so on. I suspect that it is the intervention into the design of the human species that is particularly problematic for this group. I also suspect that this response is not an objection to technology itself, but rather that they can think of no morally acceptable application for the technology, so they oppose it by saying humans should not have the authority to do it.

It is hard to tell what these outright opponents were thinking, because they rarely gave their reasons, and just implied that it was obvious from their previous comments. The few who really articulated their reasons sound like the stereotypes of religious people as theological Luddites. The common wisdom would be that religious people would say that we "should not play God" with technologies, and one Pentecostal respondent seemed to agree, saying "yes," we should leave it to God, "because He created us . . . I don't think someone should change you just because they want you to be a certain way. . . . If God wants you to be better, then He will make you better. . . . No, I think it's up to God to do it, not to wait for scientists to put you out in a lab and you're sort of like a guinea pig or something. So I think it's up to Him. I mean, we're here. He made us a certain way for a reason."

However, the strong majority of religious respondents said "no," the ability to change the genes of the human species should *not* be left to God. There were three major reasons: that God works through humans; that we should transform the human if limited to good, God-given purposes; and that we have God-given free will to do both good and bad.

The first reason is well articulated by one Catholic respondent, who put it quite succinctly, stating that "He created the people and He helps people to create technology to change these things. I don't think it should be just God. . . . No, I think He's out there saying, you know, 'I hope you find a cure for cancer' or whatever." A mainline Protestant said that "We are God's hands on earth. So it's up to us to use it, not—God's not going to do it. [Normally], He's going to have us do it. So, it's our responsibility to use those techniques." Similarly, an evangelical responded that:

> it goes back to the sense that God has given us these abilities and this intelligence to create penicillin to wipe out, not wipe out, but to be able to fight bacterial diseases, to create drugs that combat cancer and other disease. It gives me medicine to take for my thyroid to make it work right, and I think that is all good stuff. I think there can be good stuff coming out of genetics and genetic technology. But there is always the flip side of how that technology is going to be used. I mean, we create all these drugs, and we also create dangerous viruses that can be used as weapons. That is the flip side of everything. God has given us the ability, so . . . I don't believe you can say, "Okay, God alone can do this," but on the other hand I believe you have to be willing to look at things as not just as a "What can I do?" but "What should I do? What is the right thing to do?"

The second common response is that genetic transformation should not be reserved for God, as long as we are doing God's will, which is obviously related to the first reason. A mainline Protestant respondent said that:

> If it's something like medical science would determine that if they removed a gene and prevent someone from being born with the disease or could prevent disease from occurring in that child, yeah, I think that's great. Again, I look at that as medical science that knowledge . . . a God-given knowledge. It's not creating life . . . it's improving the quality of life. It's human life, but I think that's as far as I can go. But altering genes to make a superhuman being or, you know, making someone . . . making a life, cloning, cloning a life to be something that wouldn't otherwise be naturally, I don't think that's within our purpose as human beings. I don't think it's our right.

An evangelical responded that "some of this genetic engineering is good and some of it's bad, but overall, I think He's given us the intelligence that I think our soul and our spirit—if the soul and the spirit's not lighted up with God, then that's where you get into trouble." We have to be doing it "from the right perspective . . . and from God's perspective." Finally, a mainline Protestant said that:

> It goes back again to, what are you going to do with it? Like, that's the big question in all of this. It's not so much that should you or shouldn't you do it. It's like once you learn how to do it, the genie is out of the bottle, right? You're never going to put him back in. What are you going to do with it, now that you're able to do this? Are you going to do things good for society and for humankind or use it for trivial things like picking kids' eye color. That's the question.

The third reason is not so much that God's plan should be in control, but that we humans are on our own to select good and evil. We have free will. There is still good, and the respondent seems to know what it is, but this choice is part of the human condition. God is not a micro-manager. As one Catholic man said, "We're always going to be able to do miraculous things. We're always going to be able to go to the moon . . . It's what we do with it and how we use it is where we stay connected to God. I think we're capable of dickering with just about anything we want to. That's just our nature, because we're that smart or that intelligent and we can. We have that free will."

Similarly, a conservative Protestant woman told us that "my belief is that the Lord has these things at our disposal or at our use, if needed, if necessary, and we make the choice of how we want to move with that. Do we want to use it—do we not want to use it? Why do we want to use it? I don't think it's an issue of are we going to upset God if we do it. Are we going to upset Him if we don't do it? No. I think these are the different options we have. What are we going to choose and what are we doing in making our choice?"

Yes, there are some religious people who are opposed to developing some technologies at all. I suspect that this is because they can think of no moral use for the technology, like a pacifist who could see no moral use for a weapon. Most religious people instead view scientific technologies like most people view guns. It is not that they should not exist, it all depends upon what they are used for and who controls them. Most religious people think reproductive genetic technologies are great—as long as they are used to further God's wishes, such as the elimination of disease. They are concerned that these technologies will be used for other purposes, like creating blue-eyed, blond-haired "perfect" children.

This is the sort of subtle moral conflict that to some extent already exists among religious and scientific elites and could become more pervasive among the religious public if genetic modification technologies continue to improve. Again, none of this is about knowledge, as the religious people are willing to conclude that scientists have their facts right about genetics and reproduction. What would be in conflict are subtle moral differences, such as scientists and the religious having different notions of what a disease is, with the scientists relying upon contemporary conceptions of disease and the religious on their interpretation of religious views. These subtle disagreements are fruitful territory for future scholars to examine.

CONCLUSION

In this chapter, I demarcated three types of moral conflict between religion and science, and used what social science data exists to try to evaluate such conflict. The first is conflict over whether science or religion will set the meaning and purpose of humanity. That is, at its most abstract, should we have faith in religion or faith in science? Evidence shows that religious Americans in general are in this type of conflict with science, and that conservative Protestants are even more strongly so.

A second type of moral conflict is over the moral teachings of scientists. Scientists typically do not think that they are promoting a particular morality, but in Chapter 5 we saw a wide range of evidence suggesting that the public will view scientists through a moral lens. That is what we also see in this chapter, with the evidence suggesting that conservative Protestants do not want scientists to be influential in moral debates in the public sphere, which suggests conflict. Moreover, conservative Protestants do not think of scientists as selflessly working on society's behalf, suggesting that they could also see scientists having moral interests.

A third type of moral conflict is over the technology that science empowers. Analysis shows that the most conservative of Protestants are increasingly in moral conflict with science over time, which I interpret to be a reflection of both religion and science becoming more concerned about technologies of the human body. Finally, I engage in fine-grained analysis of interviews with religious Americans of their views of reproductive genetic technologies. These show that religious Americans are not opposed to technology per se, but may be in subtle moral conflict with scientists now and in the future over these technologies. In the same way that Brooke's historical "complexity" thesis of the relationship between religion and science disrupted simple claims of universal knowledge conflict, the qualitative data reviewed in this chapter show that the moral relationship between religion and science is also a complex mix of consensus and conflict that depends on many situational factors.

8

Conclusion

It has long been claimed that one source of conflict between science and society is the religious citizens who are inevitably in conflict with science. They are so, the narrative continues, because they are opposed to scientific claims, since religion has a different way of knowing facts about the world. The common conception is that religion ultimately determines truths about the natural world through supernatural revelation and science ultimately determines truth through observation and reason. This is what I have termed the systemic knowledge conflict between religion and science. Since all on-the-ground beliefs about nature are derived from high-level abstract ideas of how belief is generated, religion and science should not agree about any beliefs about the world. Therefore, if a citizen believes the conservative Protestant and nonscientific claim that the Earth is six thousand years old, then they cannot believe scientists' claims about the origins of global warming. In the first pages of this book I showed how this exact systemic knowledge conflict claim is common in the public sphere.

The reason this systemic knowledge conflict view is common, as I argued in Chapters 2 and 3, is that most academics, and especially those who focus on the "religion and science debate," assume it is so, and broadcast these views to the public. Scientists, theologians, historians, and particularly social scientists have all long made this assumption, with the origins of this view for social science reaching back to the birth of social science in the Enlightenment. One general reason academics assume that any relationship between religion and science will be based on systemic knowledge is that academics are rewarded for using hierarchical logically deductive systems of justification. The problem for contemporary public debate is then that these academic debaters do not acknowledge that their conclusions about the relationship between religion and science may not apply to the general public, who use a different form of reason.

THE DOMINANCE OF THE SYSTEMIC KNOWLEDGE PERSPECTIVE

A final example will show that the public is indeed being taught that the systemic knowledge conflict is in force for both elites and the public. This extrapolation from elites to the public is typically a sin of omission, not commission, primarily occurring by using the words "religion" or "Christianity" without a modifier. As the first sentence on the dust jacket of the influential edited volume *When Science and Christianity Meet* states, "Have science and Christianity been locked in mortal combat for the past 2000 years?"[1]. Is "Christianity" in this case the members or the elites? By not specifying whether a text is talking about the elite or the public, and by not theorizing the link in general, the public is being taught that knowledge conflict is what the public also holds. We end up with Huffington Post articles using these assumptions and thus misinforming readers about the religious public.

Of course, the public does not read books like the aforementioned edited volume. I have no doubt that such writing trickles down through college education and other elite information venues. Empirically demonstrating that trickle-down would be extremely difficult, but I do not think that this claim is controversial. I will use as an exemplar a Google search that any high school student may make if interested in "religion and science."[2] Such a search reveals what would be learned by an uninformed person, and they would learn that the public is in systemic knowledge conflict over science and religion.

In a Google search for "religion and science," the first link seen is an advertisement for a documentary called *Closer to Truth?* that interviews academics about "humanity's deepest questions." Apparently these documentaries are shown on PBS, but this advertisement encourages you to watch an interview series titled *Are Science & Religion at War?* Our first indicator of the content is that these interviews are all with academics. This links to another series of interviews titled *Do Science & Religion Conflict?* Here we see content from atheists and science/religion synthesizers such as Daniel Dennett and Francis Collins. These are all participants in the elite struggles about systemic knowledge conflict, and there is no interviewee qualified to talk about what the public believes. One is left with the impression that members of religions believe this because these elites do.

The next link is seemingly a paid link from the National Academies of Sciences, Engineering, and Medicine. Titled "The compatibility of science and religion," it begins, "Science is not the only way of knowing and understanding. But science is a way of knowing that differs from other ways in its dependence on empirical evidence and testable explanations."[3] While it is not explicit from this page whether religion is about knowledge, it is clear that science is only about knowledge. This page implies that any conflict in the public is similarly structured when it claims that "Today, many religious denominations accept" evolution. Given that denominations are filled with ordinary citizens, we see that the one issue discussed for these citizens is the knowledge claim about evolution. On this page, science and religion are in knowledge conflict, primarily over evolution, which seems to stand in for all "compatibilities," and this same conflict is implied to be held by the public.

The third link is to the place where most people would probably start, which is Wikipedia. The entry is called "Relationship between religion and science," essentially what the book you are presently reading is about. The first sentence says this relationship has long been studied, with the second saying that some people characterize the relationship as conflict, harmony, or of little interaction. The third sentence reveals the assumption of the entire extremely long page: "Science and religion generally pursue knowledge of the universe using different methodologies." This is clearly systemic knowledge conflict, since methodologies for generating knowledge are near the top of both pyramids. Now that both science and religion have been defined as institutions dedicated to producing fact claims about the natural world, the page continues with innumerable details about these fact claims. The next sentences talk about how "Science acknowledges reason, empiricism, and evidence, while religions include revelation, faith, and sacredness." We are introduced to Galileo, Dawkins, Weinberg, and Sagan. We read about non-overlapping magisteria. The public makes an appearance in a way that makes it clear that the religious public is also only concerned about fact claims: "Public acceptance of scientific facts may be influenced by religion; many in the United States reject the idea of evolution by natural selection, especially regarding human beings."

Many of the scientist-theologian synthesizers are discussed, such as Polkinghorne, Barbour, and Arthur Peacocke. Various scientists and atheists are introduced to talk about knowledge claims, with Neil deGrasse Tyson saying that the two institutions rely upon "irreconcilable approaches to knowing," and Victor Stenger saying that the conflict is based upon "approaches to knowing." It runs through more scientists and talks about the dialogue movement populated by the theologian-scientists. The elite views from different religious traditions are discussed.

The public appears again in a discussion of American creationist movements, which are at least outwardly about fact-claims. Creation science, for example, "began in the 1960s as a fundamentalist Christian effort in the United States to prove biblical inerrancy and falsify the scientific evidence for evolution." Since the only suggestion of the religious public's view is fundamentalist views of evolution, the impression is given that the religious public is engaged in a fact conflict with science. Getting much closer to the public is a section on "Studies on Scientists' Beliefs" that summarizes the research on the religiosity of scientists.

The final 550 out of over 10,000 words are about the "public perceptions of science." It starts by saying that "While large majorities of Americans respect science and scientists, they are not always willing to accept scientific findings that squarely contradict their religious beliefs." Moreover, "specific factual disagreements are 'not common today', though 40% to 50% of Americans do not accept the evolution of humans and other living things, with the 'strongest opposition' coming from evangelical Christians at 65% saying life did not evolve." It continues by saying that "in the U.S., biological evolution is the only concrete example of conflict where a significant portion of the American public denies scientific consensus for religious reasons." This *is* exemplary reporting of the propositional belief results summarized in Chapter 6, but certainly does not flag for the reader that this is a fundamentally different perspective than what has been discussed for the previous 9,500 words.

Most notably, this says nothing about moral conflict. Moral conflict is only gestured to with one sentence summarizing a study that I described in Chapter 7. The general conclusion from the Wikipedia page is that religion and science are about systemic knowledge. Elites are concerned with systemic knowledge conflict, but if you get to the last 5 percent of the entry, you will see that the public is only concerned with a few knowledge claims (propositional belief). The idea that the relationship between religion and science could be moral essentially does not exist.

IMPLICATIONS FOR THE ACADEMIC RELIGION AND SCIENCE DEBATE

In the preceding pages I have shown, using data from a wide range of sources, that despite the assumptions of academics and participants in the public sphere, the religious members of the general public are not in systemic knowledge conflict with science. I show instead that some religious groups are in propositional conflict, which means that there are some distinct religiously-based claims that some religious people believe that science says are false. However, these knowledge claims are merely propositions—they are not linked to other facts about nature— and religious people in propositional belief conflict would believe the majority of scientific claims. In this version of conflict, if a conservative Protestant thinks the earth is six thousand years old, it does not mean they will reject scientific claims about global warming.

I have also built the case that for the public the strongest and most motivating type of conflict between religion and science is moral. This of course flies in the face of scientists' image of themselves as engaged in morally neutral investigation of the world. But, existing research on the views of the public and on the nature of contemporary American religion and my own empirical examinations in Chapter 7 suggest that the most likely conflict is indeed over morality. For example, the much more likely driver of conflict for the contemporary religious public is the morality of embryonic stem cell research, not the age of the Earth.

What I have presented above suggests that for the good of a healthy debate in the public sphere, scholars should make it clear when they are talking about elites or the public—or even explicitly say that what they write may have little to do with how the contemporary public views religion and science. As I demonstrated with my case study of an internet search, an uninformed person will conclude that, for the public, religion and science are locked in a systemic knowledge relationship that sometimes results in conflict.

It will be useful for the academic fields involved with the religion and science debate to be aware of the contemporary public's views. We might think that this would be irrelevant for historians, because they only examine the past. However, history has a bias toward explaining the historical origins of what is relevant today. For example, I suspect that there would be much less historical analysis of Darwin and his interlocutors if Darwinism were no longer a live debate. If moral conflict is central today, it would be extremely interesting for historians to look more closely at the historic origins of this and other conflicts.

For sociologists, an extremely large issue, beyond the scope of this book, is to ask what the deep premises of the discipline should be if these premises are not based on systemic knowledge conflict. Closer to the ground, sociologists of religion and science should not presume that those they study are in systemic conflict, but they *should* continue to focus on instances of propositional belief conflict. That is, opposition to scientific claims about human origins remains an important sociological phenomena—it just does not stand in for a conflict over the nature of knowledge. A key question will be what predicts a person believing a religious claim about nature instead of a scientific claim, and I sketch out a number of hypotheses in the second half of Chapter 6. Moreover, as I will argue below, sociologists have a long tradition of addressing debates over morality, and these tools will be useful in examining contemporary religion and science.

Theology and philosophy are, in ideal form, not concerned with what the public thinks, because the public may just be wrong, and the point is to lead people to the correct answer. However, in general it would be useful for theologians and philosophers to be aware of the public's views before they try to change these views. At a minimum, they need to be aware of the misperceptions the public holds and how far they have to go to get to the correct answer. For example, it is useful for Catholic theologians to know that their most observant members are actually quite heterodox regarding evolution, believing in the conservative Protestant version. For theological traditions like Protestantism where the individual believer is also a source of truth, the collected views of the members of a tradition could provide theological input to the theologians. Theology and philosophy should continue to try to integrate systemic knowledge structures, because that is what their fields are about. It is important to emphasize to their readers that their systemic view of knowledge is probably not held by average religious practitioners, and to be very clear when claims are about nature and when they are about morality.

IMPLICATIONS FOR SCIENTISTS

Additional social science research on religion and science would be the most useful for scientists. Scientists are aware that society—whether the scientists like it or not—can determine what the scientists do by either creating explicit public policies or more subtly by influencing government funding. Many scientists think that there is a Republican war on science, which means that one political party and its supporters are limiting the resources that flow to science and ignoring the information it provides.[4] Science is then inevitably political, and it would be extremely useful for scientists to have accurate information about the source of opposition they actually face. For example, if scientists continue to think that the Republican war on science is driven by conservative religious people—which is possibly true—they should know that it is unlikely driven by these religious people's view of knowledge per se, but by morality. Scientists should acknowledge and deal with this moral difference to resolve this lack of support from the political system. That some Protestant fundamentalists do not believe scientists' accounts of the age of the Earth really is not the problem, but pretending that it is is comforting for science, because it keeps the debate on the scientists' turf of facts. But, this comfort comes at the price of ultimately hurting science.

What is worse for science in the U.S. is that what I am calling the systemic knowledge conflict narrative is likely hurting scientists in the eyes of the public. The public is being told that they must, in the weak systemic knowledge conflict version, believe all scientific claims, even if irrelevant to their lives. For example, to believe in science, they have to believe in an ancient Earth. In the strong version, science requires metaphysical naturalism and atheism—God cannot exist. I am certainly not the first to suggest that promoting the idea of knowledge conflict is bad for science. Typical is eminent primatologist Frans de Waal, who writes:

> Most Americans feel that the Bible is either an inspired text not intended to be taken literally or a book of legends and moral precepts. This is great to know for those trying to get an evolutionary message across. The nonliteralist majority is (or should be) their target audience, since they are more likely to listen. Except, of course, if the discussion opener is a slap in the face. Unfortunately, all this talk about how science and religion are irreconcilable is not free of consequences. It tells religious people that, however open-minded and undogmatic they may be, worthy of science they are not. They will first need to jettison all beliefs held dear. I find the neo-atheist insistence on purity curiously religious. All that is lacking is some sort of baptism ceremony at which believers publicly repent before they join the "rational elite" of nonbelievers. Ironically, the last one to qualify would have been an Augustinian friar growing peas in a monastery garden.[5]

It is also likely that some of the moral agenda of some scientists hurt science. For example, consider attempts to have science set meaning for society. In Peter Harrison's words, "In the twenty-first century, attempts to imbue science with quasi-religious significance play little role in routine scientific activities, but are common in some influential popular presentations of science, particularly among those who seek to promote the image of an essential antagonism between science and religion."[6] While more research is needed, the survey analysis in Chapter 7 suggests that religious people have a particularly strong reaction against scientists' trying to determining meaning and direction for society. I suspect that the vast majority of practicing scientists do not want this role for their profession, so why have they allowed it to be seen as a part of the scientific agenda?

The analysis in previous chapters leads me to conclude that scientists should admit their own moral stance and engage with the religious public in moral debate. Consider climate change again. Conservative Protestants, and all the other religious groups I examine, do not seem to have religious motivations to not believe scientists, but rather political motivations.

Climate scientists obviously have a moral position on climate change. Yes, it is a highly consensual moral position—that we want to limit the suffering of humans—but it is a moral position nonetheless. I would bet that most climate scientists are also concerned that the poor of the world will disproportionately suffer due to the actions of the wealthy who have created the problem in the first place. The current pope recently made a statement that accepted all of the science on global warming and then turned to morality—for example, that the people most negatively impacted by global warming will be the poorest.[7] Mainline Protestants have long had similar views, and the National Association of Evangelicals takes a very similar stand.[8] The climate science community and the largest religious traditions in the U.S. appear to be in moral agreement.

By explicitly turning to morality, scientists might be able to crack the real problem with climate change mitigation—the Republican party. Like it or not, most Americans probably view issues of intergenerational responsibility and the future of the species through a religious lens. Scientists could take components of the morality expressed by religious leaders, such as concern for the poor, and use this to facilitate the divorce of conservative Protestants from the Republican Party—at least on this issue. Groups like the Evangelical Environmental Network are working on exactly this project.[9] But scientists will not be able to help facilitate this divorce if they imply that conservative Protestant religion somehow precludes believing scientific claims about global warming, or if scientists cannot be explicit about their own moral values.

Grabbing a different moral bull by the horns would also be useful to science. I can see why scientists and others are bothered by the propositional belief conflict that does exist. My research above suggests that the concern that not believing in Darwin means that people cannot become doctors is overblown. But, it is plausible that creationist activists are limiting the education of some children in the U.S. by stopping schools from effectively teaching scientific topics.

If scientists simply acknowledged that many people have moral concerns about science, they could mitigate some conflict without having to take a moral position themselves. For example, pretending that the debate about human origins is only about knowledge claims makes that debate go on and on, because the two "sides" are talking past each other. The courts have decided that science has greater authority, but that is not going to resolve any debate.

If scientists acknowledged that people have moral concerns about Darwin, they could at least join with the religious people to counter-program against these supposed moral impacts. For example, scientists could advocate detangling facts from morals. We can imagine science teachers talking about moral concerns with Darwinism, and teach that, for example, the survival of the fittest organism is not a moral model for human society. They could note that the role of random mutations in evolution does not mean that human morality is random. The moral lessons of Darwinism that concern religious critics could be counteracted in schools without compromising the idea that Darwinism is true or violating the separation of church and state. Some scientists already do this moral deprogramming. For example, in his response to the movie advocating Intelligent Design titled *Expelled*, Richard Dawkins wrote:

> Natural selection is a good object lesson in how NOT to organize a society. As I have often said before, as a scientist I am a passionate Darwinian. But as a citizen and a human being, I want to construct a society which is about as un-Darwinian as we can make it. I approve of looking after the poor (very un-Darwinian). I approve of universal medical care (very un-Darwinian). It is one of the classic philosophical fallacies to derive an 'ought' from an 'is.'[10]

Scientists might think that such an exercise is a silly waste of time, because that is not how they view religion and science. Even if scientists think the concern that scientific research teaches morality is fanciful, it would benefit them to acknowledge that others, rightly or wrongly, have these concerns. If Richard Dawkins can take the time to give these moral qualifiers, anybody can, given that Dawkins has been called the "high priest of the religion of scientism."[11]

A FUTURE DEBATE

Religious groups and scientists are going to be in conflict with each other in the public sphere as long as some religious groups oppose the moral goals of scientists. In these debates, scientists may come to disagree with their religious opponents, and vice versa. That is fine and a part of democracy, but people should disagree with each other for the right reasons. I hope that after reading this book we can conclude that the religious opponents of the scientists are not "anti-science" but rather opposed to the moral values promoted by scientists. Our public debates would be better if the participants were clear about this fact.

The final problem is where this moral deliberation between science and society, including the religious groups in society, would occur. We might think that the field of bioethics would be such a location, but as I have argued elsewhere, beginning in the mid-1980s mainstream bioethics evolved into a field that surreptitiously promoted the morality of scientists while claiming that this morality was that of the public.[12] What is worse is that with the advent of the George W. Bush administration, the final polarization of the field occurred, as it split into liberal and conservative factions or, in the terms of one of the liberals, between those who "celebrate the transformative power of science and those who fear it."[13] Religion became associated with conservative bioethics, and mainstream science participates in liberal bioethics, which still promotes the moral values of scientists. This is unfortunately not the venue of a conversation between religion and science about morality.

We are left with the public sphere—with the internet, opinion editorials, conferences, and TV shows. Before this can effectively occur we need to better understand the structural impediments to having a debate between religion and science in the public sphere. A recent study of religion and science debates in the public sphere by sociologist Michael Evans suggests a number of problems. At least in current media debates, when representatives of "science" and "religion" appear to discuss contentious issues, they do not engage in debate but just assert or advocate. Actual dialogue is a rare commodity.

The most severe problem for an actual debate between religion and science over morality is that the public thinks that "religion" means "religious right," and the religious right is seen as violating the expectations of an appropriate debate in the public sphere. So, the liberal religious people who typically engage in debates with science are discredited along with the religious right. What is worse is that, for science, the dominant model of scientific credibility removes the credibility of science from any one scientist. Thus, science is more legitimate if it is faceless, without a representative, and the public then generally disapproves of scientists in public debates. How a debate without representatives could occur is unclear. Even worse for science is that people think that scientists are trying to cut off deliberation by deploying expert knowledge.[14] Thus, we need more social science research on the nature of debates in the public sphere before a productive debate about morality between science and religion can occur.

CALL FOR MORE RESEARCH

As I have written in previous pages, the claims in this book are somewhat tentative because most of the existing data on the relationship between religion and science was designed while assuming the systemic knowledge conflict. I have tried to repurpose these data for my analyses. My point is to show enough disparate strands of data to spur others to conduct more research in this area. For example, I proposed a number of explanations for the existence of propositional belief conflict in Chapter 6, all of which would require more social science research. Much of the existing data is about knowledge claims and can then be, to some extent, repurposed to examine propositional conflict. The most pressing need in this area is further studies of the moral relationship between religion and science for the public, in particular the area of moral conflict. Examination of the moral values taught by religion is a recognizable field in social science, so I will focus my suggestions on a more heterodox call for a similar investigation of science. I see three primary areas of inquiry.

The Moral Values of Science

Religion and science are both institutions that exist to replicate certain ideas and practices. Both have either explicit or implicit moral values that are taught to those embedded in these institutions—and these moral values may be behind more surface-level conflicts concerning beliefs about nature.

The first deeper institutional value of science that should be investigated to see if it actually exists among scientists—and if the public perceives it as well—is the aggressive attitude of science versus the more cautious approach of nonscientists. Science, at least in its cutting-edge forms, has a persistent "We know what is good for you, we know what is right, just get out of our way" attitude. As Wuthnow writes, in many people's view: "Scientists are drunk on hubris, in it for the money or their own glory, and sadly incapable of any humility." Wuthnow quotes C. P. Snow as writing that the scientific culture "is expansive, not restrictive, confident at the roots, the more confident after its bout of Oppenheimerian self-criticism, certain that history is on its side, impatient, intolerant." Concerns remain that the "can-do attitude of science presumably overwhelms questions about deeper values."[15]

This "can-do attitude"—this "impatient, intolerant" view on "progress"—is likely a major cultural and moral divide with the rest of the population, and another reason why the public thinks that scientists are promoting a morality different than the public's morality. Scientists probably think that the public is far too cautious, and that if we had listened to public concerns about safety there would be no test tube babies or organ transplants, both of which occurred with only the dimmest understanding of what would happen. The public has a more cautious view, and this may be a trigger for public groups to engage in moral conflict with science.

A second institutional value to investigate is scientism, defined as "a matter of putting too high a value on natural science in comparison with other branches of learning or culture."[16] An extreme version of this idea is that the natural sciences are the only source of real knowledge. Poetry, literature, philosophy, and obviously religion would all be, at minimum, second-class ways of thinking, even for questions that have nothing to do with the physical world, such as what our ethics should be. If scientists are explicitly or implicitly projecting this view and the public perceives it, I think this would again be another source of moral conflict with science.

A third and related potential source of moral conflict to investigate is the extent to which scientists look to science to set the goals for humanity. As noted previously, at various points in recent history prominent scientists and their allies have not wanted to be limited to investigate the world but have rather wanted to change it to be consistent with their own eschatological vision of human progress. For example, the eugenics movements of the twentieth century wanted to use science to improve the human species through selective breeding. In developing these movements, scientists often create idea systems that are structurally similar to religions. It would be good to see whether scientists approve of these attempts and if the public perceives scientists as trying to create a religion of science.

Fourth, and finally, research should try to enumerate the values forwarded by scientists on some public issue, like embryonic stem cell research, and compare these to the values forwarded by the public. For example, I think that medical research scientists explicitly learn only two values from their scientific training—the relief of suffering and the value of human understanding of the world. Individual scientists may have additional values, but they did not learn these from institutional science. Religious people share these values, but probably have a number of additional ones. If this is true, then moral conflict will occur, because religious citizens are using moral values that scientists do not recognize. More research is necessary to determine whether this is really true. In all four of these open questions, what requires examination is not only whether scientists hold these views but whether the public sees the scientists as holding these views and whether this changes their orientation toward scientists in the public sphere.

The Morally Expressive Nature of Science and Technology

A second major area that needs more social science research is in the area of the morally expressive nature of scientific discoveries. As bioethicist Erik Parens summarizes, "Technology is value-laden and it shapes us in ways that usually elude our attention." For example, no pregnant woman has to take the test for Down syndrome, but the existence of such a test has a moral message, that people may want to avoid having a baby with Down syndrome. Social pressures then emerge for its use and then, in Parens' words, "the fact that a technology exists can swiftly, if imperceptibly, turn into an ethical obligation to use it for a specific purpose."[17]

In a recent study, I examined belief in an extreme version of a biological definition of a human, where humans are biological machines defined by their DNA. I showed that among the public this view is associated with being less concerned about human rights violations such as buying organs from poor people, not stopping genocides, taking blood from prisoners against their will, and people committing suicide to save money for their families.[18] This suggests that certain biological claims are expressive of a certain moral orientation toward people.

Again, the question is whether the knowledge and technology promoted by scientists really do teach the public a certain morality, as social scientists and humanists have long claimed.[19] If so, this could be the source of a moral conflict between religion and science. Research is needed on a range of scientific claims and technologies to see whether they really do teach people a moral value, whether the public perceives this to be the case, and whether what is taught is at odds with what the public's values are.

Moral Conflict Over Specific Scientific Experiments and Technologies

The third type of moral conflict where much more research is needed is in public conflicts over specific scientific experiments and technologies, like embryonic stem cell research. It is extremely easy to show with public opinion data that the public is more opposed to embryonic research than are scientists. That is not the interesting question. The question is whether the religious public perceives "science" to be behind calls for embryonic stem cell research and whether any disagreement they have with science in this one area spills out into opposition to scientists' involvement with other issues. Moreover, how does the public perceive scientific advocates of these technologies? Are they perceived as medical researchers focused on the relief of suffering—or as one of the negative Frankenstein-type figures so popular in our culture? A similar and interesting question would be what the public hears when it hears about a new technology, such as "gene editing" of human embryos. Does it attribute the morally contentious technology to scientists? If so, what do they perceive the values of these scientists to be, and do they perceive them as being in opposition to their own?

It has long been said that religion and science are the two great ways of understanding the world, and this view has justified the enormous energy that has been spent on the relationship between these two great institutions. I would still say that religion and science are the two great ways of understanding the world, but by understanding I mean the relationships between humans in the world and the relationship between humans and nature. These relations are the stuff of morality, and we should turn our eyes to this new era of this ongoing relationship.

NOTES

ACKNOWLEDGMENTS

1. There are twenty-two paragraphs in Chapter 4 reproduced from Michael S. Evans and John H. Evans, "Arguing Against Darwinism: Religion, Science and Public Morality," in *The New Blackwell Companion to the Sociology of Religion,* ed. Bryan Turner (New York: Blackwell, 2010), 286–308. There are twenty-eight paragraphs in Chapter 7 reproduced from John H. Evans, "Future Vision in Transhumanist Writings and the Religious Public," in *Perfecting Human Futures: Transhuman Visions and Technological Imaginations,* ed. J. Benjamin Hurlbut and Hava Tirosh-Samuelson (Dordrecht, Netherlands: Springer-Verlag, 2016), 291–306.

1. INTRODUCTION

1. Alister E. McGrath, *Science and Religion: An Introduction* (Malden, MA: Blackwell Publishers, 1999).
2. Andrew Dickson White, *A History of the Warfare of Science with Theology in Christendom* (New York: Dover Publications, 1960 [1896]).
3. Accessed April 20, 2015.
4. http://www.huffingtonpost.com/2013/08/15/rush-limbaugh-climate-change_n_3762978.html
5. It has been well demonstrated that climate denial is indeed funded by "big money." Naomi Oreskes and Erik M. Conway, *Merchants of Doubt* (New York: Bloomsbury Press, 2010).
6. http://www.huffingtonpost.com/victor-stenger/the-folly-of-faith_b_863179.html

7. http://www.huffingtonpost.com/victor-stenger/global-warming-and-religi_b_864014.html

8. John H. Evans and Justin Feng, "Conservative Protestantism and Skepticism of Scientists Studying Climate Change," *Climatic Change* 121 (2013): 595–608.

9. http://www.huffingtonpost.com/rev-jim-ball/leaving-the-carnival-climate-change_b_888664.html

10. Merriam-Webster online.

11. Social scientists will recognize a belief system as one term for the idea systems that people supposedly hold. The most well-known term is "ideology," which is roughly analogous to concepts in the social sciences such as worldview, cultural system, and symbol system. These concepts are, by one social scientist's account, "vast receptacle[s] for all conscious and relatively organized ideational phenomena." All definitions of ideology include the idea that they are internally coherent sets of ideas, while the American intellectual tradition also assumes that these are, in the words of two theorists, "organized in a hierarchical fashion, in which more specific attitudes interact with attitudes toward the more general class of objects in which the specific object is seen to belong." John Gerring, "Ideology: A Definitional Analysis," *Political Research Quarterly* 50, no. 4 (1997): 969, 975.

12. Upon occasion a very high-level component of a pyramid is overthrown due to logical inconsistencies from below, in what Kuhn called a "paradigm shift" or a change in "worldview." See Thomas S. Kuhn, *The Structure of Scientific Revolutions* (Chicago, IL: University of Chicago Press, 1970). For example, in biology, a lot of the lower-level beliefs could not be made logically coherent until Darwin replaced the high-level belief in this deductive structure with something like "life forms evolve due to random mutations that are selected by their environments." In theology, the high-level concept of the Trinity resolved some logical inconsistencies between beliefs lower in the pyramid such as "God is transcendent," "Jesus was the son of God," and "Jesus was fully human." As we will see in the next chapter, the theologians in the religion and science debate are essentially engaged in trying to make belief statements from science fit logically into a theological pyramid where "God exists" is still near the top.

13. Peter Harrison, *The Territories of Science and Religion* (Chicago: University of Chicago Press, 2015).

14. Ronald L. Numbers, "Science Without God: Natural Laws and Christian Beliefs," in *When Science and Christianity Meet,* ed. David C. Lindberg and Ronald L. Numbers (Chicago: University of Chicago Press, 2003), 266.

15. Numbers, "Science Without God: Natural Laws and Christian Beliefs," 320.

16. Numbers, "Science Without God: Natural Laws and Christian Beliefs," 320.

17. Much of what has been attributed to this debate is actually mythological. What does remain clear is that there was a debate between these two figures in 1860 over the legitimacy of Darwin's way of describing the natural world. See David N. Livingstone, "That Huxley Defeated Wilberforce in Their Debate Over Evolution and Religion," in *Galileo Goes to Jail and Other Myths About Science and Religion,* ed. Ronald L. Numbers (Cambridge, MA: Harvard University Press, 2009), 152–60.

18. I mean proposition in the philosophical logic sense of a statement that affirms or denies something, so that it could be characterized as true or false. See "proposition" at www.dictionary.com.

19. Steven Hitlin and Stephen Vaisey, "Back to the Future: Reviving the Sociology of Morality," in *Handbook of the Sociology of Morality*, ed. Steven Hitlin and Stephen Vaisey (New York: Springer, 2010), 5.

20. Erik Parens, *Shaping Our Selves: On Technology, Flourishing, and a Habit of Thinking* (New York: Oxford University Press, 2015).

21. Ronald L. Numbers, *The Creationists: The Evolution of Scientific Creationism, Expanded Edition* (Cambridge, MA: Harvard University Press, 2006).

22. Ronald Numbers, "Creationism in 20th-Century America," *Science* 217 (1982): 538. See also Stephen Jay Gould, *Rocks of Ages: Science and Religion in the Fullness of Life* (New York: Ballantine, 1999), 150–70.

23. Some research has begun to emerge on American religious minorities' views of science. Brandon Vaidyanathan et al., "Rejecting the Conflict Narrative: American Jewish and Muslim Views on Science and Religion," *Social Compass* 63, no. 4 (2016): 478–96; Donald Everhart and Salman Hameed, "Muslims and Evolution: A Study of Pakistani Physicians in the United States," *Evolution: Education and Outreach* 6, no. 2 (2013): 1–8.

2. THE RELIGION AND SCIENCE ADVOCATES IN THE ACADEMIC DEBATE

1. Peter Harrison, *The Territories of Science and Religion* (Chicago: University of Chicago Press, 2015), 35, 84, 93, 92, 94.

2. Harrison, *The Territories of Science and Religion*, 106.

3. Harrison, *The Territories of Science and Religion*, 108, 114, 189.

4. John C. Besley and Matthew Nisbet, "How Scientists View the Public, the Media and the Political Process," *Public Understanding of Science* 22, no. 6 (2011): 647.

5. Besley and Nisbet, "How Scientists View the Public, the Media and the Political Process," 646, 653, 654–55.

6. Matthew C. Nisbet and Dietram A. Scheufele, "What's Next for Science Communication? Promising Directions and Lingering Distractions," *American Journal of Botany* 96, no. 10 (2009): 1767.

7. Nisbet and Scheufele, "What's Next for Science Communication? Promising Directions and Lingering Distractions," 1767. Allum and his colleagues similarly describe the phenomena as: "the deficit model sees public resistance to science and technology as underpinned by ignorance, superstition, and fear. Public skepticism about technological innovations such as nuclear energy, microwave cooking, and genetic science would be markedly reduced if citizens were better able to grasp the science upon which they are based. That is, a judgment when informed by scientific fact would tend to be more favorable and consistent with expert opinion than one expressed without recourse to such 'objective' knowledge." Their meta-analysis of 193 surveys across 40 countries concludes that there is "a small but positive relationship" between knowledge and attitudes toward science. The knowledge deficit model is summarized by the aphorism "to know science is to love it." Nick Allum et al., "Science Knowledge and Attitudes Across Cultures: A Meta-Analysis," *Public Understanding of Science* 17 (2008): 35–36, 51, 52.

8. In Christopher Frayling, *Mad, Bad and Dangerous? The Scientist and the Cinema* (London: Reaktion Books, 2005), 44.

9. Keith Thomson, "Introduction. The Religion and Science Debate: Why Does It Continue?" in *The Religion and Science Debate: Why Does It Continue?* ed. Harold W. Attridge (New Haven, CT: Yale University Press, 2009), 2.

10. Harold W. Attridge, ed., *The Religion and Science Debate: Why Does It Continue?* (New Haven, CT: Yale University Press, 2009), ix. The location of the "controversy" they had in mind is the public, not academia. For example, the back cover of the resulting published volume starts by talking about the Scopes trial, asks whether the "tensions" have "impacted the public debate about so-called 'intelligent design,'" and the manifestations of these "tensions" "within American culture," with the goal of "creating a society that reconciles scientific inquiry with the human spirit."

11. The sociologist was Robert Wuthnow, whose work will be prominent in later chapters.

12. Thomson, "Introduction. The Religion and Science Debate: Why Does It Continue?" 2, 5, 6.

13. Lawrence M. Krauss, "Religion Vs. Science?" in *The Religion and Science Debate: Why Does It Continue?* ed. Harold W. Attridge (New Haven, CT: Yale University Press, 2009), 130.

14. Kenneth R. Miller, "Darwin, God, and Dover: What the Collapse of "Intelligent Design" Means for Science and Faith in America," in *The Religion and Science Debate: Why Does It Continue?* ed. Harold W. Attridge (New Haven, CT: Yale University Press, 2009), 58.

15. Miller, "Darwin, God, and Dover: What the Collapse of "Intelligent Design" Means for Science and Faith in America," 86, 88.

16. Christopher P. Scheitle and Elaine Howard Ecklund, "The Influence of Science Popularizers on the Public's View of Religion and Science: An Experimental Assessment," *Public Understanding of Science* 26, no. 1 (2017): 31.

17. http://www.lrb.co.uk/v28/n20/terry-eagleton/lunging-flailing-mispunching

18. http://edthemanicstreetpreacher.wordpress.com/2013/12/20/against-theology/

19. Jerry A. Coyne, *Faith Versus Fact: Why Science and Religion Are Incompatible* (New York: Viking, 2015), xi-xvi.

20. Coyne, *Faith Versus Fact: Why Science and Religion Are Incompatible*, 13–14.

21. Coyne, *Faith Versus Fact: Why Science and Religion Are Incompatible*, 229.

22. Coyne, *Faith Versus Fact: Why Science and Religion Are Incompatible*, 239, 241, 243.

23. Dennett is a philosopher who makes similar claims as the scientific atheists. Scientist and theologian Alister McGrath describes the works of two prominent New Atheists—Dennett and Dawkins—as expressing "the fundamental belief that the Darwinian theory of evolution has such explanatory power that it erodes many traditional metaphysical notions—such as belief in God—through its 'universal acid.' . . . Darwinism has been transposed in recent atheist apologetics from a provisional scientific theory to an antitheistic ideology." See Alister E. McGrath, "The Ideological Uses of Evolutionary Biology in Recent Atheist Apologetics," in *Biology and Ideology: From Descartes to Dawkins*, ed. Denis R. Alexander and Ronald L. Numbers (Chicago: University of Chicago Press, 2010), 329–31.

24. Ronald L. Numbers, "Aggressors, Victims, and Peacemakers: Historical Actors in the Drama of Science and Religion," in *The Religion and Science Debate: Why Does It Continue?* ed. Harold W. Attridge (New Haven, CT: Yale University Press, 2009), 46.

25. Thomas F. Gieryn, "Boundary-Work and the Demarcation of Science from Non-Science: Strains and Interests in Professional Ideologies of Scientists," *American Sociological Review* 48 (1983): 781.

26. Gieryn, "Boundary-Work and the Demarcation of Science from Non-Science: Strains and Interests in Professional Ideologies of Scientists," 785.

27. Thomas F. Gieryn, George M. Bevins, and Stephen C. Zehr, "Professionalization of American Scientists: Public Science in the Creation/Evolution Trials," *American Sociological Review* 50 (1985): 406.

28. Harrison, *The Territories of Science and Religion*, 160, 187, 196–97. In one of the introductory chapters to the encyclopedia titled *The History of Science and Religion in the Western Tradition*, historian Colin Russell asks "given that the warfare model is so inaccurate, one may wonder why it has lasted so long." His conclusion is that "by establishing the conflict thesis," various Victorian-era figures "could perpetrate a myth as part of their strategy to enhance the public appreciation of science." Colin A. Russell, "The Conflict of Science and Religion," in *Science and Religion: A Historical Introduction*, ed. Gary B. Ferngren (Baltimore, MD: The Johns Hopkins University Press, 2002), 10.

29. Ronald Numbers, ed., *Galileo Goes to Jail: And Other Myths About Science and Religion* (Cambridge, MA: Harvard University Press, 2009).

30. Thomas M. Lessl, "The Galileo Legend as Scientific Folklore," *Quarterly Journal of Speech* 85 (1999): 163, 153.

31. Jon H. Roberts, "'The Idea That Wouldn't Die': The Warfare Between Science and Christianity," *Historically Speaking* 48 (2003): 21–24.

32. Lessl, "The Galileo Legend as Scientific Folklore," 149, 164.

33. For brevity I have not separately considered philosophers, but they make the same assumptions as scientists and theologians. Consider the short book, set up as a back and forth debate for university students, titled *Science and Religion: Are They Compatible?* by Daniel Dennett and Alvin Plantinga. See Daniel C. Dennett and Alvin Plantinga, *Science and Religion: Are They Compatible?* (New York, NY: Oxford University Press, 2011). The former is one of the most influential philosophers of biology and a noted atheist, the latter the most prominent conservative Protestant philosopher and a leader in Christian epistemology. It is not surprising that these authors only address epistemic issues—primarily whether God could have used evolution and the basic empirical question of whether God exists. What is important for my argument is that the book is not called "science and religion *knowledge claims:* are they compatible?" It does not need to say so because of the deep assumption that the religion and science debate only concerns knowledge claims about the physical world.

34. http://en.wikipedia.org/wiki/Ian_Barbour

35. Ian G. Barbour, *When Science Meets Religion* (San Francisco: Harper and Row, 2000), xi, 4. He explored "ethical issues" in a different book. The two books were from his Gifford lectures. The first book, published in 1990, summarizes knowledge conflict, and was rewritten as a different book in 2000. The second Gifford lecture book, published in 1993, is titled *Ethics in the Age of Technology*. See Ian Barbour, *Ethics in an Age of Technology* (San Francisco: Harper and Row, 1993). Google Scholar shows that the first book, along with the 2000 rewrite, has about 900 cites and the second book has 235 cites. It is notable that it was

these knowledge relationships for which he is famous, and for which he basically wrote this second book summarizing an earlier book.

36. Barbour, *When Science Meets Religion*, 11.
37. Barbour, *When Science Meets Religion*, 2.
38. Stephen Jay Gould, *Rocks of Ages: Science and Religion in the Fullness of Life* (New York: Ballantine, 1999).
39. Barbour, *When Science Meets Religion*, 17–22, 163.
40. Barbour, *When Science Meets Religion*, 3, 23.
41. Barbour, *When Science Meets Religion*, 29, 31.
42. Barbour, *When Science Meets Religion*, 2–4.
43. Alister E. McGrath, *Science and Religion: An Introduction* (Malden, MA: Blackwell Publishers, 1999).
44. Alister E. McGrath, *The Foundations of Dialogue in Science and Religion* (Malden, MA: Blackwell, 1998), 29, 81. "The present work aims to establish the foundations for dialogue in science and religion by exploring the critically important area of methodology. Much work in the field of 'science and religion' has focused on single issues, perhaps most importantly the issue of compatibility. For example, is the Christian understanding of human nature compatible with the neo-Darwinian theory of evolution? . . . Systematic engagement with the issues just noted rests upon a prior substantial engagement with question of method—including such issues as the way in which knowledge is gained and confirmed, the manner in which evidence is accumulated and assimilated, and particularly the manner in which the world is represented."
45. McGrath, *The Foundations of Dialogue in Science and Religion*, 29.
46. John Polkinghorne, "Science and Theology in the Twenty-First Century," *Zygon* 35, no. 4 (2000): 942–43.
47. Merriam-Webster online.
48. Francis S. Collins, *The Language of God: A Scientist Presents Evidence for Belief* (New York: Free Press, 2006).
49. As of this writing, the new president is Deborah Haarsma, who formerly taught astronomy at Calvin College (a center of conservative Protestant intellectual life). Jeff Schloss, an evolutionary biologist at the evangelical Westmount College, is Senior Scholar. The board of directors and advisory council is a veritable who's who of people engaged in the evangelical religion and science dialogue. Accessed April 2017.
50. Jocelyn Kaiser, "White House taps former genome chief Francis Collins as NIH director," *Science* 17 July, 2009, 250–55; Sam Harris, "Science Is in the Details," *New York Times*, July 26, 2009, A21.
51. Collins' 2006 book was a *New York Times* bestseller, extensively reviewed, and comes complete with a discussion group guide. The core of the book is only about conflict between religion and science over knowledge claims—primarily evolution. There is a section titled "The Moral Practice of Science and Medicine: Bioethics." Tellingly, in terms of what is portrayed as important, it is an appendix to the book. Moreover, it does not really consider religion and science to be in ethical conflict, as the ethical principles advanced in bioethics are portrayed as universally held by all. Religious positions on embryos are gestured at. In contrast to the knowledge part of the book, where religion is considered to be true

and has a legitimate voice, in the last three paragraphs of the ethics section he implicitly acknowledges conflict over embryos and the like, but argues against the legitimacy of religious involvement in ethical debates. He writes "Does a person's grounding in one of the great world faiths assist his or her ability to resolve these moral and ethical dilemmas? Professional bioethicists would generally say no, since as we have already noted, the principles of ethics, such as autonomy, beneficence, nonmaleficence, and justice are held true by believers and nonbelievers alike. On the other hand, given the uncertain ethical grounding of the postmodernist era, which discounts the existence of absolute truth, ethics grounded on specific principles of faith can provide a certain foundational strength that may otherwise be lacking. I hesitate, however, to advocate very strongly for faith-based bioethics. The obvious danger is the historical record that believers can and will sometimes utilize their faith in a way never intended by God, and to move from loving concern to self-righteousness, demagoguery, and extremism." Collins, *The Language of God: A Scientist Presents Evidence for Belief*, 271.

52. The final two "core commitments are: "We strive for *humility and gracious dialogue* with those who hold other views" and "We aim for *excellence* in all areas, from science to education to business practices."

53. http://biologos.org/about

54. http://biologos.org/questions

55. To make the claims below I examined all of the web pages of DoSER, the texts linked to those web pages, and the materials distributed at their 2015 "Perceptions" conference. Web pages accessed April, 2015.

56. 2013 Annual Report, p. 2. http://www.aaas.org/sites/default/files/AAAS_2013-Annual-Report.pdf

57. http://www.aaas.org/page/doser-overview

58. There are actually six goals, but only two are relevant to my analysis. The second goal is to simply encourage scholarship on the first: "Promote and facilitate scholarship on the ethical, religious, and theological implications of contemporary scientific discoveries and technological innovations." The other three are organizational: "Increase the engagement of scientific communities in the dialogue on science, ethics, and religion;" "Facilitate collaboration among scientists, ethicists, and religion scholars and leaders to address critical multidisciplinary issues related to science, ethics, and religion;" and "Further public understanding of the dialogue on science, ethics, and religion." http://www.aaas.org/page/doser-overview

59. http://www.aaas.org/page/physics-cosmos

60. http://www.aaas.org/page/neuroscience-brain-mind

61. https://www.aaas.org/page/neuroscience-brain-mind

62. In the spirit of full disclosure, I was on the advisory board to this project, and went to three meetings. My primary purpose was to offer advice on the nationally representative public opinion survey that was conducted for this project, carried out by Elaine Howard Ecklund of Rice University.

63. http://perceptionsproject.org/wp-content/uploads/2014/10/AAAS-Choicework.pdf

64. http://perceptionsproject.org/wp-content/uploads/2014/10/AAAS-Choicework.pdf

65. http://perceptionsproject.org/2014/08/26/environmental-science-front-and-center-in-denver/

66. http://perceptionsproject.org/2014/11/13/can-scientists-and-evangelical-leaders-work-together/

67. National Association of Evangelicals, *When God and Science Meet: Surprising Discoveries of Agreement* (Washington, DC: National Association of Evangelicals, 2015), 7–8.

68. National Association of Evangelicals, *When God and Science Meet: Surprising Discoveries of Agreement*, 44, 63, 44.

69. Robert L. Herrmann, *Sir John Templeton: Supporting Scientific Research for Spiritual Discoveries* (Radnor, PA: Templeton Foundation Press, 2004), 32.

70. Terry Barnes, "Unity (Unity School of Christianity)," in *The Popular Encyclopedia of Church History*, ed. Ed Hindson and Dan Mitchell (Eugene, OR: Harvest House Publishers, 2013), 330–31.

71. Sir John Templeton, *Possibilities of Over One Hundredfold More Spiritual Information: The Humble Approach in Theology and Science* (Radnor, PA: Templeton Foundation Press, 2000), 3.

72. Templeton, *Possibilities of Over One Hundredfold More Spiritual Information: The Humble Approach in Theology and Science*, 5–6.

73. Herrmann, *Sir John Templeton: Supporting Scientific Research for Spiritual Discoveries*, 183, 189, 191.

3. THE ACADEMIC ANALYSTS OF THE RELATIONSHIP BETWEEN RELIGION AND SCIENCE

1. John Hedley Brooke, *Science and Religion: Some Historical Perspectives* (New York: Cambridge University Press, 1991).

2. Brooke, *Science and Religion: Some Historical Perspectives*, 144.

3. Brooke, *Science and Religion: Some Historical Perspectives*, 336ff.

4. Peter J. Bowler, *Reconciling Science and Religion: The Debate in Early-Twentieth-Century Britain* (Chicago, IL: University of Chicago Press, 2001), 87, 90–91.

5. Gary B. Ferngren, ed., *The History of Science and Religion in the Western Tradition: An Encylopedia* (New York: Garland Publishing, 2000).

6. The first three are overviews—"The Historiography of Science and Religion," "The Conflict of Science and Religion," and "the Demarcation of Science and Religion." Then there are chapters on "Epistemology," "Causation," "Views of Nature," "God, Nature and Science," "Varieties of Providentialism," "Natural Theology," The Design Argument," "Miracles," "Theodicy," "Genesis and Science,"and "Nineteenth-Century Biblical Criticism." All of these are about nature, and how you make claims about nature.

7. Chapters are: "Plato and Platonism," "Aristotle and Aristotelianism," "Atomism," "Epicureanism," "Stoicism," "Augustine of Hippo," "Thomas Aquinas and Thomism," "Skepticism," "Cartesianism," "Mechanical Philosophy," "The Cambridge Platonists," "Deism," "Enlightenment," "Baconianism," "German Nature Philosophy," "Materialism," "Atheism," "Positivism," "Pragmatism," "Evolutionary Ethics," "Scientific Naturalism," "Secular Humanism," Process Philosophy and Theology," "The Social Construction of Science," "Gender" and "Postmodernism."

8. "Judaism to 1700," "Early Christian Attitudes Toward Nature," "Islam," "Medieval Science and Religion," "Orthodoxy," "Roman Catholicism Since Trent," "Early-Modern Protestantism," "Judaism Since 1700," "Modern American Mainline Protestantism," "Evangelicalism and Fundamentalism," "America's Innovative Nineteenth-Century Religions," and "Creationism Since 1859."

9. David B. Wilson, "The Historiography of Science and Religion," in *The History of Science and Religion in the Western Tradition*, ed. Gary B. Ferngren (New York: Garland Publishing, 2000), 3–11.

10. Collin A. Russell, "The Conflict of Science and Religion," in *The History of Science and Religion in the Western Tradition*, ed. Gary B. Ferngren (New York: Garland Publishing, 2000), 12–13.

11. Russell, "The Conflict of Science and Religion," 13–14.

12. Russell, "The Conflict of Science and Religion," 13.

13. Ronald L. Numbers, *Science and Christianity in Pulpit and Pew* (New York: Oxford University Press, 2007), 142.

14. Numbers, *Science and Christianity in Pulpit and Pew*, 18.

15. Numbers, *Science and Christianity in Pulpit and Pew*, 12. Numbers speculates that to the extent ordinary people paid attention at all, they focused on their immediate needs, which is consistent with the contemporary era: "A focus on Copernicus, Galileo, Newton, and Darwin barely touches the issues troubling the greatest number of believers, most of whom remained oblivious to the alleged theological implications of elite science.... While intellectuals wrestled with the theological ramifications of heliocentrism and the mechanical philosophy, the nature of force and matter, the manifestations of vitalism, the meaning of thermodynamics, relativity theory, and quantum physics, and the implications of positivism and scientific naturalism, the common people, to the extent that they paid any attention to science at all, concerned themselves largely with developments that impinged on their daily lives and self-understanding: diseases, disasters, and descent from apes." See Numbers, *Science and Christianity in Pulpit and Pew*, 36–37.

16. Bowler, *Reconciling Science and Religion: The Debate in Early-Twentieth-Century Britain*.

17. Bernard Lightman, *Victorian Popularizers of Science: Designing Nature for New Audiences* (Chicago: University of Chicago Press, 2007).

18. James A. Secord, *Victorian Sensation: The Extraordinary Publication, Reception, and Secret Authorship of Vestiges of the Natural History of Creation* (Chicago: University of Chicago Press, 2000).

19. Thomas Aechtner, "Galileo Still Goes to Jail: Conflict Model Persistence Within Introductory Anthropology Materials," *Zygon* 50, no. 1 (2015): 211, 216–17, 220.

20. Thomas Aechtner, "Social Scientists," in *'The Idea That Wouldn't Die;' The Warfare Between Science and Religion*, ed. Jeff Hardin and Ronald L. Numbers (forthcoming).

21. Peter L. Berger, *The Sacred Canopy: Elements of a Sociological Theory of Religion* (New York: Doubleday, 1967), 112–13.

22. James Leuba, *The Belief in God and Immortality, a Psychological, Anthropological and Statistical Study* (Boston: Sherman, French and Company, 1916); James Leuba, "Religious Beliefs of American Scientists," *Harper's Magazine* 169 (1934): 291–300.

23. Rodney Stark, "On the Incompatibility of Religion and Science: A Survey of American Graduate Students," *Journal for the Scientific Study of Religion* 3 (1963): 3–20.

24. Edward C. Lehman Jr. and Donald W. Shriver Jr., "Academic Discipline as Predictive of Faculty Religiosity," *Social Forces* 47 (1968): 171–82; Fred Thalheimer, "Religiosity and Secularization in the Academic Professions," *Sociology of Education* 46 (1973): 183–202.

25. Lehman and Shriver, "Academic Discipline as Predictive of Faculty Religiosity."; Robert Wuthnow, *The Struggle for America's Soul: Evangelicals, Liberals and Secularism* (Grand Rapids, MI: William B. Eerdmans Publishing Co., 1989), 142–57.

26. Edward J. Larson and Larry Witham, "Scientists Are Still Keeping the Faith," *Nature* 386 (1997): 435–36.

27. Elaine Howard Ecklund, *Science Vs. Religion: What Scientists Really Think* (New York: Oxford University Press, 2010), 15.

28. Edward J. Larson and Larry Witham, "Leading Scientists Still Reject God," *Nature* 394 (1998): 313.

29. Elaine Howard Ecklund and Christopher P. Scheitle, "Religion Among Academic Scientists: Distinctions, Disciplines, and Demographics," *Social Problems* 54, no. 2 (2007): 289–307.

30. Ecklund and Scheitle, "Religion Among Academic Scientists: Distinctions, Disciplines, and Demographics," 291.

31. Ecklund and Scheitle, "Religion Among Academic Scientists: Distinctions, Disciplines, and Demographics," 294.

32. In order, these three claims are made in Ecklund and Scheitle, "Religion Among Academic Scientists: Distinctions, Disciplines, and Demographics."; Elaine Howard Ecklund, Jerry Z. Park, and Phil Todd Veliz, "Secularization and Religious Change Among Elite Scientists," *Social Forces* 86, no. 4 (2008): 1805–39; and Elaine Howard Ecklund, Jerry Z. Park, and Katherine L. Sorrell, "Scientists Negotiate Boundaries Between Religion and Science," *Journal for the Scientific Study of Religion* 50, no. 3 (2011): 552–69.

33. Christopher G. Ellison and Marc A. Musick, "Conservative Protestantism and Public Opinion Toward Science," *Review of Religious Research* 36, no. 3 (1995): 246–47.

34. Darren E. Sherkat, "Religion and Verbal Ability," *Social Science Research* 39 (2010): 3.

35. Maury D. Granger and Gregory N. Price, "The Tree of Science and Original Sin: Do Christian Religious Beliefs Constrain the Supply of Scientists?" *Journal of Socio-Economics* 36 (2007): 145.

36. "Genesis, the first book, is perhaps the most explicit in identifying the costs of obtaining knowledge that could either invoke the wrath of God and/or are associated with harsh judgement in some post-temporal realm . . . The costs of man's acquisition of knowledge emerge most clearly from the accounts of man's exit from the Garden of Eden, and the Tower of Babel episode . . . Thus, in the Christian account of creation, man pays a high cost for acquiring knowledge. . . . Thus, an alternative description and definition of the forbidden tree is that it is the "tree of science." This is instructive for a particular, and compelling interpretation of the type of knowledge prohibited by God, and the consequences for having acquired it. . . . the first book of the Bible, from its inception, opposes the intention and

possibility of the objects of human knowledge." Granger and Price, "The Tree of Science and Original Sin: Do Christian Religious Beliefs Constrain the Supply of Scientists?" 146–47.

37. Sherkat, "Religion and Verbal Ability," 3.

38. Others make a similar but more narrow claim that religions that are theologically oriented away from the present world will be in conflict with science. Kosmin and his colleagues suggest that "the other-worldly outlook of Pentecostals and other ecstatic denominations, as well as to millennial or revolutionist sects such as Jehovah's Witnesses . . . focus attention away from this world or predict the world's imminent demise. Such an outlook appears to make their followers hostile to scientific rationalism and therefore disinterested in secular studies, particularly college education." Barry A. Kosmin, Ariela Keysar, and Nava Lerer, "Secular Education and the Religious Profile of Contemporary Black and White Americans," *Journal for the Scientific Study of Religion* 31, no. 4 (1992): 531.

39. Andrew Greeley and Michael Hout, *The Truth About Conservative Christians: What They Think and What They Believe* (Chicago: University of Chicago Press, 2006), 34–35.

40. Darren E. Sherkat, "Religion and Scientific Literacy in the United States," *Social Science Quarterly* 92, no. 5 (2011): 1137–38. In an earlier paper Sherkat (with Darnell) also combines explanations for conservative Protestants having less educational attainment. One reason is opposition to the humanism of public education, and the teaching of "secular humanist values." They quote Beverley LaHaye, who wrote that "one of the dangers of secular college education today is that the whole educational system has been taken over by an atheistic, humanist philosophy that is largely anti-God, anti-moral, and anti-American. . . . We have seen scores of fine Christian young people go down the drain or lose interest in spiritual things while attending such [secular] colleges." In this mechanism, the problem is conflict with the history department, not the biology department. The other reason for not attending college is opposition to science writ large, because "fundamentalists also find fault with the scientific method—an approach to learning that seeks to discover truths rather than claiming to know 'The Truth.' Scientific discoveries are seen as promoting alternatives to divine truths already specified in scripture—a course of inquiry considered inappropriate by many fundamentalists." Alfred Darnell and Darren E. Sherkat, "The Impact of Protestant Fundamentalism on Education," *American Sociological Review* 62, no. 2 (1997): 308. For the same argument, also see Darren E. Sherkat and Alfred Darnell, "The Effect of Parents' Fundamentalism on Children's Educational Attainment: Examining Differences by Gender and Children's Fundamentalism," *Journal for the Scientific Study of Religion* 38, no. 1 (1999): 23–35.

41. Lisa A. Keister, "Conservative Protestants and Wealth: How Religion Perpetuates Asset Poverty," *American Journal of Sociology* 113, no. 5 (2008): 1240.

42. Kraig Beyerlein, "Specifying the Impact of Conservative Protestantism on Educational Attainment," *Journal for the Scientific Study of Religion* 43, no. 4 (2004): 506–07.

43. Beyerlein, "Specifying the Impact of Conservative Protestantism on Educational Attainment," 506.

44. Ronald L. Numbers, "Science Without God: Natural Laws and Christian Beliefs," in *When Science and Christianity Meet*, ed. David C. Lindberg and Ronald L. Numbers (Chicago: University of Chicago Press, 2003), 320.

45. Dorothy Ross, *The Origins of American Social Science* (New York: Cambridge University Press, 1991), 4.

46. Andrew Wernick, "Comte, Auguste," in *Encyclopedia of Social Theory*, ed. George Ritzer (Thousand Oaks, CA: Sage Publications, 2005), 128, 130.

47. Glenn A. Goodwin and Joseph A. Scimecca, *Classical Sociological Theory* (Belmont, CA: Wadsworth, 2006), 2, 4.

48. Malcolm Williams, *Science and Social Science: An Introduction* (New York: Routledge, 2000), 18.

49. Timothy Larsen, "Anthropology," in *Science and Religion: A Historical Introduction, Second Edition*, ed. Gary B. Ferngren (Baltimore: Johns Hopkins University Press, 2017), 410, 414.

50. Larsen, "Anthropology," 410, 414.

51. Robert Wuthnow, *Meaning and Moral Order* (Berkeley, CA: University of California Press, 1987), 31. These two paragraphs rely upon pages 23–33.

52. Jon H. Roberts and James Turner, *The Sacred and the Secular University* (Princeton, NJ: Princeton University Press, 2000), 23. Ross describes the era similarly: "The gentry intellectuals who attacked religious control did not want to destroy the harmony between religion and science but to recast it. Positivist science was to set the terms of the agreement rather than orthodox religion. Few of them actually became agnostics; most adjusted the basis of their Christian faith to avoid cognitive conflict with natural science. For all of them, however, the influence of positivism forced for the first time in America a divorce between natural knowledge and revealed Christianity and a determination to develop natural knowledge on its own terms" Ross, *The Origins of American Social Science*, 57.

53. Roberts and Turner, *The Sacred and the Secular University*, 29.

54. Roberts and Turner, *The Sacred and the Secular University*, 43.

55. Roberts and Turner, *The Sacred and the Secular University*, 47, 53. On the "scientific" orientation of the first sociologists in America, see also Stephen Turner and Jonathan Turner, *The Impossible Science: An Institutional Analysis of American Sociology* (Newbury Park, CA: Sage Publications, 1990), 7, 17.

56. Michael S. Evans, "Defining the Public, Defining Sociology: Hybrid Science-Public Relations and Boundary-Work in Early American Sociology," *Public Understanding of Science* 185, no. 14 (2009): 7.

57. In Christian Smith, "Secularizing American Higher Education: The Case of Early American Sociology," in *The Secular Revolution: Power, Interests, and Conflict in the Secularization of American Public Life*, ed. Christian Smith (Berkeley, CA: University of California Press, 2003), 110.

58. Evans, "Defining the Public, Defining Sociology: Hybrid Science-Public Relations and Boundary-Work in Early American Sociology," 9.

59. Evans, "Defining the Public, Defining Sociology: Hybrid Science-Public Relations and Boundary-Work in Early American Sociology."; Smith, "Secularizing American Higher Education: The Case of Early American Sociology."

60. Smith, "Secularizing American Higher Education: The Case of Early American Sociology," 111.

61. In Smith, "Secularizing American Higher Education: The Case of Early American Sociology," 117, 119, 127, 126.

4. EXISTING RESEARCH ON THE PUBLIC

1. Peter L. Berger, *The Sacred Canopy: Elements of a Sociological Theory of Religion* (New York: Doubleday, 1967), 175–77.
2. Peter L. Berger, "Some Second Thoughts on Substantive Versus Functional Definitions of Religion," *Journal for the Scientific Study of Religion* 13, no. 2 (1974): 127–28; Roger O'Toole, *Religion: Classic Sociological Approaches* (New York: McGraw-Hill, 1984), 142.
3. Clifford Geertz, *Interpretation of Cultures* (New York: Basic Books, 1973), 90.
4. Geertz, *Interpretation of Cultures*, 92, 95.
5. Berger, *The Sacred Canopy: Elements of a Sociological Theory of Religion*.
6. Andrew Buckser, "Religion, Science, and Secularization Theory on a Danish Island," *Journal for the Scientific Study of Religion* 35, no. 4 (1996): 439.
7. Pierre Bourdieu, "The Specificity of the Scientific Field and the Conditions for the Progress of Reason," *Social Science Information* 14 (1975): 19–47; Bruno Latour and Steve Woolgar, *Laboratory Life: The Construction of Scientific Facts* (Princeton, NJ: Princeton University Press, [1979] 1986); Karin D. Knorr-Cetina, *The Manufacture of Knowledge: An Essay on the Constructivist and Contextual Nature of Science* (New York: Pergamon Press, 1981).
8. Thomas F. Gieryn, "Boundary-Work and the Demarcation of Science from Non-Science: Strains and Interests in Professional Ideologies of Scientists," *American Sociological Review* 48 (1983): 781–95; Thomas F. Gieryn, George M. Bevins, and Stephen C. Zehr, "Professionalization of American Scientists: Public Science in the Creation/Evolution Trials," *American Sociological Review* 50 (1985): 392–409.
9. Pippa Norris and Ronald Inglehart, *Sacred and Secular: Religion and Politics Worldwide* (New York: Cambridge University Press, 2004), 7.
10. Anthony Wallace, *Religion: An Anthropological View* (New York: Random House, 1966), 265.
11. Christian Smith, ed., *The Secular Revolution* (Berkeley, CA: University of California Press, 2003).
12. Richard W. Flory, "Promoting a Secular Standard: Secularization and Modern Journalism," in *The Secular Revolution: Power, Interests, and Conflict in the Secularization of American Public Life*, ed. Christian Smith (Berkeley, CA: University of California Press, 2003), 395–433.
13. Roger Finke and Rodney Stark, *The Churching of America, 1776–1990: Winners and Losers in Our Religious Economy* (New Brunswick, NJ: Rutgers University Press, 1992); R. Stephen Warner, "Work in Progress Toward a New Paradigm for the Sociological Study of Religion in the United States," *American Journal of Sociology* 98 (1993): 1044–93; Rodney Stark and William S. Bainbridge, *The Future of Religion* (Berkeley: University of California Press, 1985).
14. Finke and Stark, *The Churching of America, 1776–1990: Winners and Losers in Our Religious Economy*, 19.
15. Norris and Inglehart, *Sacred and Secular: Religion and Politics Worldwide*.
16. David A. Hollinger, *After Cloven Tongues of Fire: Protestant Liberalism in Modern American History* (Princeton, NJ: Princeton University Press, 2013), Chapter 4.

17. Robert K. Merton, *The Sociology of Science* (Chicago: University of Chicago Press, 1973).

18. Late nineteenth-century advocates included T. H. Huxley, Herbert Spencer, John Tyndall. Twentieth century-advocates included John Dewey and Walter Lippmann.

19. Hollinger, *After Cloven Tongues of Fire: Protestant Liberalism in Modern American History*, 93, 94.

20. Andrew Jewett, *Science, Democracy, and the American University: From the Civil War to the Cold War* (New York: Cambridge University Press, 2012), 22.

21. Hollinger, *After Cloven Tongues of Fire: Protestant Liberalism in Modern American History*, 99.

22. John H. Evans, *Playing God? Human Genetic Engineering and the Rationalization of Public Bioethical Debate* (Chicago: University of Chicago Press, 2002); John H. Evans, *The History and Future of Bioethics: A Sociological View* (New York: Oxford University Press, 2012). The account of Hurlbut, which covers the same time period but focusing on debates about human embryos, reaches the same conclusion. See J. Benjamin Hurlbut, *Experiments in Democracy: Human Embryo Research and the Politics of Bioethics* (New York: Columbia University Press, 2017).

23. Robert Edwards, *Life Before Birth: Reflections on the Embryo Debate* (New York: Basic Books, 1989), 165.

24. Gordon Wolstenholme, *Man and His Future*, ed. Gordon Wolstenholme (London: J. & A. Churchill Ltd., 1963), 372.

25. Paul Ramsey, *Fabricated Man: The Ethics of Genetic Control* (New Haven, CT: Yale University Press, 1970), 143–44.

26. Bernard Davis, "Novel Pressures on the Advance of Science," *Annals of the New York Academy of Sciences* 265 (1976): 198.

27. Bernard D. Davis, "Prospects for Genetic Intervention in Man," *Science* 170 (1970): 1279.

28. Davis, "Novel Pressures on the Advance of Science," 195.

29. The previous eight paragraphs are a summary of my argument in Evans, *The History and Future of Bioethics: A Sociological View.*

30. Peter Harrison, *The Territories of Science and Religion* (Chicago: University of Chicago Press, 2015), 179.

31. Harrison, *The Territories of Science and Religion*, 178–79.

32. John H. Evans and Cynthia E. Schairer, "Bioethics and Human Genetic Engineering," in *Handbook of Genetics and Society: Mapping the New Genomic Era*, ed. Paul Atkinson, Peter Glasner, and Margaret Lock (London: Routledge, 2009), 349–66.

33. J. Benjamin Hurlbut and Hava Tirosh-Samuelson, *Perfecting Human Futures: Transhuman Visions and Technological Imaginations* (Wiesbaden, Germany: Springer-Verlag, 2016).

34. Michael Hauskeller, "Reinventing Cockaigne: Utopian Themes in Transhumanist Thought," *The Hastings Center Report* 42, no. 2 (2012): 39.

35. In Hauskeller, "Reinventing Cockaigne: Utopian Themes in Transhumanist Thought," 40.

36. Andrew Pollack. "A genetic entrepreneur sets his sights on aging and death," *New York Times*, March 5, 2014, B1.

37. Margarita Boenig-Lipstin and J. Benjamin Hurlbut, "Technologies of Transcendence at Singularity University," in *Perfecting Human Futures: Transhuman Visions and Technological Imaginations,* ed. J. Benjamin Hurlbut and Hava Tirosh-Samuelson (Wiesbaden, Germany: Springer-Verlag, 2016), 239.

38. Linell E. Cady, "Religion and the Technowonderland of Transhumanism," in *Building Better Humans? Refocusing the Debate on Transhumanism,* ed. Hava Tirosh-Samuelson and Kenneth L. Mossman (Frankfurt am Main: Peter Lang, 2012), 83.

39. William Sims Bainbridge, "The Transhuman Heresy," *Journal of Evolution and Technology* 14, no. 2 (2005): 91.

40. Brent Waters, "Whose Salvation? Which Eschatology? Transhumanism and Christianity as Contending Salvific Religions," in *Transhumanism and Transcendence,* ed. Ronald Cole-Turner (Washington, DC: Georgetown University Press, 2011), 164.

41. Michael Mulkay, *The Embryo Research Debate* (Cambridge, UK: Cambridge University Press, 1997), 97, 114.

42. Hurlbut, *Experiments in Democracy: Human Embryo Research and the Politics of Bioethics.*

43. Hurlbut, *Experiments in Democracy: Human Embryo Research and the Politics of Bioethics,* Chapter 6. For more on Proposition 71 that is generally consistent with Hurlbut's view, see Ruha Benjamin, *People's Science: Bodies and Rights on the Stem Cell Frontier* (Stanford, CA: Stanford University Press, 2013); Charis Thompson, *Good Science: The Ethical Choreography of Stem Cell Research* (Cambridge, MA: MIT Press, 2013), 85–112.

44. Hurlbut, *Experiments in Democracy: Human Embryo Research and the Politics of Bioethics,* 212, 252.

45. Hurlbut, *Experiments in Democracy: Human Embryo Research and the Politics of Bioethics,* 252, 254.

46. Hurlbut, *Experiments in Democracy: Human Embryo Research and the Politics of Bioethics,* 241.

47. Hurlbut, *Experiments in Democracy: Human Embryo Research and the Politics of Bioethics,* 245.

48. Hurlbut, *Experiments in Democracy: Human Embryo Research and the Politics of Bioethics,* 246, 335.

49. While this book is largely focused on the U.S. and on Christianity, it is worth noting that this account of religious reactions to Darwin is consistent with the reaction by Muslims in Europe. Salman Hameed concludes that rejection of evolution "may not be a matter of epistemological clash, but rather on being a Muslim in a secular, non-Muslim society." This rejection "may be becoming another contested [identity] marker for Muslim minorities in schools." Anti-evolutionism is not about knowledge per se, but a way of saying we Muslims are different from you secular Europeans. In particular, the most common version of Muslim creationism in Europe "frames the rejection of evolution in moral terms along with the rhetoric against racism and terrorism." Salman Hameed, "Making Sense of Islamic Creationism in Europe," *Public Understanding of Science* 24, no. 4 (2015): 393.

50. Harrison, *The Territories of Science and Religion,* 197.

51. Gowan Dawson, *Darwin, Literature and Victorian Respectability* (Cambridge, UK: Cambridge University Press, 2007), 5, 32, 33.

52. Dorothy Nelkin, *The Creation Controversy: Science or Scripture in the Schools* (New York: W.W. Norton, 1982); Edward J. Larson, *Summer of the Gods: The Scopes Trial and America's Continuing Debate Over Science and Religion* (New York: Basic Books, 1997).

53. George William Hunter, *A Civic Biology: Presented in Problems* (New York: American Book Company, 1914), 261.

54. For extended analysis of this book, see Adam R. Shapiro, *Trying Biology: The Scopes Trial, Textbooks, and the Antievolution Movement in American Schools* (Chicago: University of Chicago Press, 2013).

55. Larson, *Summer of the Gods: The Scopes Trial and America's Continuing Debate Over Science and Religion*.

56. Ronald Numbers, "Creationism in 20th-Century America," *Science* 217 (1982): 538. See also Stephen Jay Gould, *Rocks of Ages: Science and Religion in the Fullness of Life* (New York: Ballantine, 1999), 150–70.

57. Mark A. Noll, *The Scandal of the Evangelical Mind* (Grand Rapids, MI: Eerdmans, 1994), 153, 189.

58. Gould, *Rocks of Ages: Science and Religion in the Fullness of Life*, 163.

59. Larson, *Summer of the Gods: The Scopes Trial and America's Continuing Debate Over Science and Religion*, 27–28.

60. Shapiro, *Trying Biology: The Scopes Trial, Textbooks, and the Antievolution Movement in American Schools*, 75, 83.

61. Nelkin, *The Creation Controversy: Science or Scripture in the Schools*, 31.

62. Ronald L. Numbers, *Darwinism Comes to America* (Cambridge, MA: Harvard University Press, 1998), 85.

63. Judith V. Grabiner and Peter D. Miller, "Effects of the Scopes Trial," *Science* 185 (1974): 835; Numbers, *Darwinism Comes to America*, 91; Shapiro, *Trying Biology: The Scopes Trial, Textbooks, and the Antievolution Movement in American Schools*, Chapters 7 and 8.

64. Nelkin, *The Creation Controversy: Science or Scripture in the Schools*; Ronald L. Numbers, *The Creationists: The Evolution of Scientific Creationism, Expanded Edition* (Cambridge, MA: Harvard University Press, 2006); Michael Lienesch, *In the Beginning: Fundamentalism, the Scopes Trial, and the Making of the Antievolution Movement* (Chapel Hill, NC: University of North Carolina Press, 2007).

65. Francis Galton, *Inquiries Into Human Faculty and Its Development* (London: Macmillan, 1883).

66. John Berry Haycraft, *Darwinism and Race Progress* (New York: Charles Scribner, 1895), 155.

67. This source is found in the Eugenics Archive, an image archive of the American eugenics movement.

68. Frederick W. Brown, "Eugenic Sterilization in the United States: Its Present Status," *Annals of the American Academy of Political and Social Science* 149 (1930): 23, 25.

69. Eugenics Archive.

70. Diane B. Paul, *Controlling Human Heredity: 1865 to the Present* (Amherst, NY: Humanity Books, 1995), 86.

71. Daniel Kevles, *In the Name of Eugenics: Genetics and the Uses of Human Heredity* (Berkeley: University of California Press, 1985), 118.

72. Lienesch, *In the Beginning: Fundamentalism, the Scopes Trial, and the Making of the Antievolution Movement*.

73. Nelkin, *The Creation Controversy: Science or Scripture in the Schools*.

74. John C. Whitcomb Jr. and Henry M. Morris, *The Genesis Flood: The Biblical Record and Its Scientific Implications* (Phillipsburg: Presbyterian and Reformed Publishing Company, 1961), 447.

75. Reproduced in Christopher P. Toumey, *God's Own Scientists: Creationists in a Secular World* (New Brunswick, NJ: Rutgers University Press, 1994), 96.

76. Henry M. Morris, *Scientific Creationism* (San Diego, CA: Creation-Life Publishers, 1974).

77. Gilkey, *Creationism on Trial: Evolution and God at Little Rock* (Minneapolis, MN: Winston Press, 1985); Numbers, *The Creationists: The Evolution of Scientific Creationism, Expanded Edition*, 272.

78. Morris and Clark, cited in McLean v. Arkansas.

79. Toumey, *God's Own Scientists: Creationists in a Secular World*, 52, 98–99.

80. Percival Davis and Dean H. Kenyon, *Of Pandas and People: The Central Question of Biological Origins* (Dallas, TX: Haughton Publishing, 1989).

81. Steve Fuller, *Science Vs. Religion? Intelligent Design and the Problem of Evolution* (New York: Polity, 2007).

82. Discovery Institute, "The Wedge," n.d., http://www.antievolution.org/features/wedge.pdf

83. Motive Entertainment, *Expelled Leader's Guide* (Westlake Village, CA: Motive Entertainment, 2008), 14.

84. Robert T. Pennock, ed., *Intelligent Design Creationism and Its Critics* (Cambridge, MA: MIT Press, 2001); Barbara Forrest and Paul R. Gross, *Creationism's Trojan Horse: The Wedge of Intelligent Design* (Oxford: Oxford University Press, 2004).

5. EXISTING RESEARCH ON THE PUBLIC

1. Noah Efron, "Judaism," in *'The Idea That Wouldn't Die;' The Warfare Between Science and Religion*, ed. Jeff Hardin, Ronald L. Numbers, and Ronald A. Binzley (Baltimore: Johns Hopkins University Press, forthcoming).

2. Efron, "Judaism."

3. Ira M. Sheskin and Harriet Hartman, "Denominational Variations Across American Jewish Communities," *Journal for the Scientific Study of Religion* 54, no. 2 (2015): 210.

4. In reflection of what went wrong with the Galileo affair, Pope John Paul II said that: "The error of the theologians of the time . . . was to think that our understanding of the physical world's structure was in some way imposed by the literal sense of Sacred Scripture . . . In fact the Bible does not concern itself with the details of the physical world. . . . There exist two realms of knowledge, one that has its source in revelation and one that reason can discover by its own power . . . The methodologies proper to each make it possible to bring out different aspects of reality."

Steven J. Harris, "Roman Catholicism Since Trent," in *Science and Religion: A Historical Introduction,* ed. Gary B. Ferngren (Baltimore, MD: The Johns Hopkins University Press,

2002), 256–57. This is consistent with the Augustinian view that scripture should not be read as a guide to nature but as a guidebook to salvation.

5. David Mislin, "Catholicism," in *'The Idea That Wouldn't Die;' The Warfare Between Science and Religion,* ed. Jeff Hardin, Ronald L. Numbers, and Ronald A. Binzley (Baltimore: Johns Hopkins University Press, Forthcoming), 2.

6. Cited in John A. Heitmann, "Doing 'True Science': The Early History of the Institutum Divi Thomae, 1935–1951," *Catholic Historical Review* 88, no. 4 (2002): 702.

7. In James L. Heft, "Catholicism and Science: Renewing the Conversation," *Journal of Ecumenical Studies* 39, no. 3–4 (2002): 377.

8. Mislin, "Catholicism."

9. Mislin, "Catholicism."

10. John Hooper, "Pope Prepares to Embrace Theory of Intelligent Design," *The Guardian* (London), August 28, 2006.

11. Richard Owen, "Vatican Buries the Hatchet with Charles Darwin," *The Times* (London), February 11, 2009, online.

12. Heft, "Catholicism and Science: Renewing the Conversation," 377.

13. Eva Marie Garroutte, "The Positivist Attack on Baconian Science and Religious Knowledge in the 1870s," in *The Secular Revolution,* ed. Christian Smith (Berkeley, CA: University of California Press, 2003), 197–98; George M. Marsden, "Everyone One's Own Interpreter? The Bible, Science, and Authority in Mid-Nineteenth-Century America," in *The Bible in America: Essays in Cultural History,* ed. Nathan O. Hatch and Mark A. Noll (New York: Oxford University Press, 1982), 82; Peter Harrison, *The Territories of Science and Religion* (Chicago: University of Chicago Press, 2015), Chapter 6.

14. Garroutte, "The Positivist Attack on Baconian Science and Religious Knowledge in the 1870s," 198.

15. Marsden, "Everyone One's Own Interpreter? The Bible, Science, and Authority in Mid-Nineteenth-Century America," 82–83.

16. Mark A. Noll, *The Scandal of the Evangelical Mind* (Grand Rapids, MI: Eerdmans, 1994), 68.

17. Garroutte, "The Positivist Attack on Baconian Science and Religious Knowledge in the 1870s," 199.

18. Harrison, *The Territories of Science and Religion,* 154.

19. Ronald L. Numbers, *The Creationists: The Evolution of Scientific Creationism, Expanded Edition* (Cambridge, MA: Harvard University Press, 2006), 369.

20. George M. Marsden, "Evangelicals and the Scientific Culture: An Overview," in *Religion and Twentieth-Century American Intellectual Life,* ed. Michael J. Lacey (New York: Cambridge University Press, 1989), 28–29.

21. Herbert Hovenkamp, *Science and Religion in America 1800–1860* (Philadelphia: University of Pennsylvania Press, 1978), ix.

22. Christopher P. Toumey, *God's Own Scientists: Creationists in a Secular World* (New Brunswick, NJ: Rutgers University Press, 1994), 16.

23. Marsden, "Everyone One's Own Interpreter? The Bible, Science, and Authority in Mid-Nineteenth-Century America," 90–91, 83.

24. Noll, *The Scandal of the Evangelical Mind,* 98.

25. Marsden, "Everyone One's Own Interpreter? The Bible, Science, and Authority in Mid-Nineteenth-Century America," 90–91.
26. Noll, *The Scandal of the Evangelical Mind*, 98. See also Harrison, *The Territories of Science and Religion*, 154.
27. Noll, *The Scandal of the Evangelical Mind*, 110ff; Marsden, "Evangelicals and the Scientific Culture: An Overview," 41.
28. Noll, *The Scandal of the Evangelical Mind*, 113.
29. Noll, *The Scandal of the Evangelical Mind*, 180.
30. Marsden, "Everyone One's Own Interpreter? The Bible, Science, and Authority in Mid-Nineteenth-Century America," 93–94.
31. Noll, *The Scandal of the Evangelical Mind*, 185, 186.
32. Marsden, "Everyone One's Own Interpreter? The Bible, Science, and Authority in Mid-Nineteenth-Century America," 95.
33. Marsden, "Everyone One's Own Interpreter? The Bible, Science, and Authority in Mid-Nineteenth-Century America," 95.
34. Sydney Ahlstrom, *A Religious History of the American People* (New Haven, CT: Yale University Press, 1972), Chapter 53.
35. Jon H. Roberts, "Mainline Protestantism," in *'The Idea That Wouldn't Die;' The Warfare Between Science and Religion*, ed. Jeff Hardin, Ronald L. Numbers, and Ronald A. Binzley (Baltimore: Johns Hopkins University Press, forthcoming), 12.
36. "Liberal Protestants were convinced that in order to preserve the credibility of the Christian world view, it would be necessary to come to grips with important changes that had taken place in scientific thought during the course of the nineteenth century." Periodic fundamental reconstructions of Christian theology were necessary to make it fit with contemporary science because "the essential truths of Christian theology were characteristically expressed in idioms and categories drawn from the cultural conceptions that happened to prevail at any given time." Roberts, "Mainline Protestantism," 3–5.
37. Christian Smith, *American Evangelicalism: Embattled and Thriving* (Chicago: University of Chicago Press, 1998).
38. Smith, *American Evangelicalism: Embattled and Thriving*.
39. To take the obvious example, when white conservative Protestants were creating the Creation Research Society in 1963, African American Protestants would have been more concerned with the civil rights movement. Historian Jeffrey Moran shows that at the time of Scopes in the 1920s, African American Protestant clergy endorsed the anti-evolution position because they saw it is an important defense of the Bible. Yet, the anti-evolution cause never became a central focus of these leaders for a number of related reasons. First, African American clergy were not exposed to modernist theology because they by and large did not have theological training. Darwin was thus not a threat to the religion. Second, the clergy did not want to be painted as outsiders like the fundamentalists at the Scopes trial had been, given that they were striving for national respectability. Third, reaction against Darwinism came from its teaching in high schools, yet in this era, very few African Americans made it to the grades in high school where they would encounter biology, and even then, African American schools tended to only teach vocational subjects. Finally, and obviously, the white people who exclusively controlled public policy in this era would not have

been very concerned with what African Americans thought. In opposition to the African American religious position on evolution, secular elites in the community were supportive of evolution, seeing scientific truths as leading to their liberation from racism. These secular elites thought, for example, that Darwin showed that the distinction between races was an arbitrary social construct. See Jeffrey P. Moran, *American Genesis: The Antievolution Controversies from Scopes to Creation Science* (New York: Oxford University Press, 2012), Chapter 3.

40. Stephen Kalberg, "Max Weber's Types of Rationality: Cornerstones for the Analysis of Rationalization Processes in History," *American Journal of Sociology* 85, no. 5 (1980): 1153.

41. John Gerring, "Ideology: A Definitional Analysis," *Political Research Quarterly* 50, no. 4 (1997): 969, 975.

42. Mark A. Peffley and Jon Hurwitz, "A Hierarchical Model of Attitude Constraint," *American Journal of Political Science* 29 (1985): 876–77.

43. Peter L. Berger, *The Sacred Canopy: Elements of a Sociological Theory of Religion* (New York: Doubleday, 1967).

44. Philip E. Converse, "The Nature of Belief Systems in Mass Publics," in *Ideology and Discontent*, ed. David E. Apter (New York: Free Press, 1964), 206–61.

45. Paul DiMaggio, "Culture and Cognition," *Annual Review of Sociology* 23 (1997): 267.

46. Mark Chaves, "Rain Dances in the Dry Season: Overcoming the Religious Congruency Fallacy," *Journal for the Scientific Study of Religion* 49 (2010): 1–14.

47. John H. Evans, "Worldviews or Social Groups as the Source of Moral Value Attitudes: Implications for the Culture Wars Thesis," *Sociological Forum* 12, no. 3 (1997): 371–404.

48. Smith, *American Evangelicalism: Embattled and Thriving*, 104–07.

49. William H. Sewell Jr., "The Concept(s) of Culture," in *Beyond the Cultural Turn: New Directions in the Study of Society and Culture*, ed. Victoria E. Bonnell and Lynn Hunt (Berkeley, CA: University of California Press, 1999), 58.

50. Ann Swidler, *Talk of Love: How Culture Matters* (Chicago: University of Chicago Press, 2001), 182.

51. Robert Wuthnow, *Christianity in the Twenty-First Century* (New York: Oxford University Press, 1993), 100–01.

52. Wuthnow, *Christianity in the Twenty-First Century*, 100–01.

53. Jeremy E. Uecker, Mark D. Regnerus, and Margaret L. Vaaler, "Losing My Religion: The Social Sources of Religious Decline in Early Adulthood," *Social Forces* 85, no. 4 (2007): 1667–92.

54. Christopher P. Scheitle, "U.S. College Students' Perception of Religion and Science: Conflict, Collaboration, or Independence? A Research Note," *Journal for the Scientific Study of Religion* 50, no. 1 (2011): 175–86.

55. Joseph O. Baker, "Acceptance of Evolution and Support for Teaching Creationism in Public Schools: The Conditional Impact of Educational Attainment," *Journal for the Scientific Study of Religion* 52, no. 1 (2013): 216–28.

56. Cristine H. Legare and Aku Visala, "Between Religion and Science: Integrating Psychological and Philosophical Accounts of Explanatory Coexistence," *Human Development* 54 (2011): 169.

57. Cristine H. Legare et al., "The Coexistence of Natural and Supernatural Explanations Across Cultures and Development," *Child Development* 83, no. 3 (2012): 781, 789.

58. Legare et al., "The Coexistence of Natural and Supernatural Explanations Across Cultures and Development," 779.

59. Robert Wuthnow, *The God Problem: Expressing Faith and Being Reasonable* (Berkeley: University of California Press, 2012), 17, 34, 296.

60. Wuthnow, *The God Problem: Expressing Faith and Being Reasonable*, 40, 58–60.

61. Wuthnow, *The God Problem: Expressing Faith and Being Reasonable*, 96, 124.

62. Joseph O. Baker, "Public Perceptions of Incompatibility Between 'Science and Religion,'" *Public Understanding of Science* 21 (2012): 334.

63. Elaine Howard Ecklund and Christopher P. Scheitle, *Religion Vs. Science: What Religious People Really Think* (New York: Oxford University Press, 2018), 16.

64. Ecklund and Scheitle, *Religion Vs. Science: What Religious People Really Think*, 17.

65. Berger, *The Sacred Canopy: Elements of a Sociological Theory of Religion*.

66. Smith, *American Evangelicalism: Embattled and Thriving*.

67. Robert Wuthnow, "No Contradictions Here: Science, Religion and the Culture of All Reasonable Possibilities," in *The Religion and Science Debate: Why Does It Continue?* ed. Harold W. Attridge (New Haven, CT: Yale University Press, 2009), 173.

68. Merriam-Webster online.

69. "The Fall" is a term in Christianity to represent when Adam and Eve went from a state of obedience to God in the Garden of Eden to a state of disobedience. This brought sin into the world, and thus the need for humans to atone for that sin.

70. Peter J. Bowler, *Reconciling Science and Religion: The Debate in Early-Twentieth-Century Britain* (Chicago: University of Chicago Press, 2001), 211.

71. Alan Wolfe, *The Transformation of American Religion* (New York: Free Press, 2003), 72.

72. Donald E. Miller, *Reinventing American Protestantism: Christianity in the New Millennium* (Berkeley, CA: University of California Press, 1997), 127–29.

73. Robert Wuthnow, *After the Baby Boomers: How Twenty- and Thirty-Somethings Are Shaping the Future of American Religion* (Princeton, NJ: Princeton University Press, 2007), 133.

74. Robert Wuthnow, *After Heaven: Spirituality in America Since the 1950s* (Berkeley: University of California Press, 1998), 3.

75. Wuthnow, "No Contradictions Here: Science, Religion and the Culture of All Reasonable Possibilities," 175.

76. Wuthnow, *After Heaven: Spirituality in America Since the 1950s*, 115, 133.

77. Wuthnow, *After Heaven: Spirituality in America Since the 1950s*, 133–34.

78. Robert N. Bellah et al., *Habits of the Heart: Individualism and Commitment in American Life* (New York: Harper and Row, 1985).

79. As sociologist Richard Madsen summarizes, the "dominant form" of American religion is individualism. See Madsen 2009: 1265.

80. Wuthnow, *After the Baby Boomers: How Twenty- and Thirty-Somethings Are Shaping the Future of American Religion*, 14–15.

81. Wuthnow, *After the Baby Boomers: How Twenty- and Thirty-Somethings Are Shaping the Future of American Religion*, 113–14.

82. Wolfe, *The Transformation of American Religion*, 23–24, 74.

83. Stephen Ellingson, "The Rise of the Megachurches and Changes in Religious Culture: Review Article," *Sociology Compass* 3, no. 1 (2009): 18, 20–21, 22.

84. Christian Smith, *Soul Searching: The Religious and Spiritual Lives of American Teenagers* (New York: Oxford University Press, 2005), 162–63.

85. Smith, *Soul Searching: The Religious and Spiritual Lives of American Teenagers*, 165.

86. Kate Bowler, *Blessed: A History of the American Prosperity Gospel* (New York: Oxford University Press, 2013), 3, 7.

87. Kate Bowler, "The Prosperity Gospel's Transformation of the Popular Religious Imagination," *CCDA Theological Journal* (2014): 22.

88. Bowler, "The Prosperity Gospel's Transformation of the Popular Religious Imagination," 19.

89. Bowler, "The Prosperity Gospel's Transformation of the Popular Religious Imagination," 22.

90. Bowler, *Blessed: A History of the American Prosperity Gospel*, 6.

91. Bowler, *Blessed: A History of the American Prosperity Gospel*, 6.

92. Gary Dorrien, *Social Ethics in the Making: Interpreting an American Tradition* (New York: Wiley-Blackwell, 2010), Chapter 2.

93. Matthew Nisbet et al., "Knowledge, Reservations, or Promise? A Media Effects Model for Public Perceptions of Science and Technology," *Communication Research* 29, no. 5 (2002): 592.

94. They also used two additional categories that are not substantive but more procedural: "Middle way/alternative path" and "Conflict/strategy." See Matthew C. Nisbet and Dietram A. Scheufele, "What's Next for Science Communication? Promising Directions and Lingering Distractions," *American Journal of Botany* 96, no. 10 (2009): 1772.

95. http://www.redherry.com/2013/08/parallel-collision-orphan-black-and_3518.html

96. John H. Evans, *The History and Future of Bioethics: A Sociological View* (New York: Oxford University Press, 2012).

97. Susan E. Lederer, *Frankenstein: Penetrating the Secrets of Nature* (New Brunswick, NJ: Rutgers University Press, 2002), 1.

98. David A. Kirby, "Science and Technology in Film: Themes and Representations," in *Routledge Handbook of Public Communication of Science and Technology, 2nd Ed.*, ed. Massimiano Bucchi and Brian Trench (New York: Routledge, 2014), 100.

99. Peter Weingart, "Of Power Maniacs and Unethical Geniuses: Science and Scientists in Fiction Film," *Public Understanding of Science* 12 (2003): 279.

100. Lederer, *Frankenstein: Penetrating the Secrets of Nature*, 1.

101. Weingart, "Of Power Maniacs and Unethical Geniuses: Science and Scientists in Fiction Film," 283.

102. Christopher Frayling, *Mad, Bad and Dangerous? The Scientist and the Cinema* (London: Reaktion Books, 2005), 40.

103. Kirby, "Science and Technology in Film: Themes and Representations," 100.

104. Frayling, *Mad, Bad and Dangerous? The Scientist and the Cinema*, 43.

105. Her depiction of the archetypes is worth quoting at length: (1) "the alchemist, who reappears at critical times as the obsessed or maniacal scientist. Driven to pursue an arcane intellectual goal that carries suggestions of ideological evil, this figure has been reincarnated

recently as the sinister biologist producing new (and hence allegedly unlawful) species through the quasi-magical processes of genetic engineering." (2) "the stupid virtuoso, out of touch with the real world of social intercourse.... Preoccupied with the trivialities of his private world of science, he ignores his social responsibilities." (3) "the Romantic depiction of the unfeeling scientist who has reneged on human relationships and suppressed all human affections in the cause of science. This has been the most enduring stereotype of all and still provides the most common image of the scientist in popular thinking ... In portrayals of the 1950s there is an additional ambivalence about this figure: his emotional deficiency is condemned as inhuman, even sinister, but in a less extreme form it is also condoned, even admired, as the inevitable price scientists must pay to achieve their disinterestedness." (4) "the heroic adventurer in the physical or the intellectual world. Towering like a superman over his contemporaries, exploring new territories, or engaging with new concepts, this character emerges at periods of scientific optimism.... More subtle analyses of such heroes, however, suggest the danger of their charismatic power as, in the guise of neo-imperialist space travelers, they impose their particular brand of colonization on the universe." (5) "the helpless scientist. This character has lost control either over his discovery (which, monsterlike, has grown beyond his expectations) or, as frequently happens in wartime, over the direction of its implementation." (6) "the scientist as idealist. This figure represents the one unambiguously acceptable scientist, sometimes holding out the possibility of a scientifically sustained utopia with plenty and fulfillment for all but more frequently engaged in conflict with a technology-based system that fails to provide for individual human values." See Roslynn D. Haynes, *From Faust to Strangelove: Representations of the Scientist in Western Literature* (Baltimore: Johns Hopkins University Press, 1994), 3–4.

106. Casey H. Rawson and Megan Astolfi McCool, "Just Like All the Other Humans? Analyzing Images of Scientists in Children's Trade Books," *School Science and Mathematics* 114 (2014): 11.

107. Jonathan Knight, "Hollywood or Bust," *Nature* 430, no. 12, August (2004): 721.

108. Bastiaan T. Rutjens and Steven J. Heine, "The Immoral Landscape? Scientists Are Associated with Violations of Morality," *PLOS One* 11, no. 4 (2016).

109. http://en.wikipedia.org/wiki/The_Big_Bang_Theory

110. Margaret A. Weitekamp, "'We're Physicists': Gender, Genre and the Image of Scientists in The Big Bang Theory," *Journal of Popular Television* 3, no. 1 (2015): 75–92.

111. Rutjens and Heine, "The Immoral Landscape? Scientists Are Associated with Violations of Morality," 7.

112. Susan Carol Losh, "Stereotypes About Scientists Over Time Among US Adults: 1983 and 2001," *Public Understanding of Science* 19, no. 3 (2010): 375.

6. EMPIRICAL TESTS OF KNOWLEDGE AND BELIEF CONFLICT FOR THE RELIGIOUS PUBLIC

1. For details of coding and the precise results of this analysis, see John H. Evans, "Epistemological and Moral Conflict Between Religion and Science," *Journal for the Scientific Study of Religion* 50, no. 4 (2011): 707–27.

2. Although the phrase "millions of years" in the "moving continents" question would be contradicted by young-earth creationism, when this question is added to the two questions

in the "contested facts" index, the coherence of that index decreases. This suggests either how rare it is for a member of the population to believe in a young earth or to know how young is young. In Jonathan Hill's close analysis of survey questions on creationism, he finds that if you define creationism as denying human evolution and affirming that God created humans, 37% of the public is a creationist. This percent drops down to 25% if you include questions about believing in Adam and Eve. Hill concludes that this group has little certainty about the time frame for creation, writing that "many creationists are simply unsure whether the days of creation were literal, and they are especially unsure about when humans first came into existence." See Jonathan P. Hill, "National Study of Religion and Human Origins," Biologos Foundation (2014), 9.

3. The final question was contingent upon the previous question, so they were combined into one variable. A correct answer was given a 2 for each variable, and incorrect, refused and "don't know" responses a 1, on the premise that those who would otherwise provide an incorrect answer will refuse to answer (Chronbach alpha = .674).

4. This coding is premised on the fact that engineering involves a great degree of science. The majors coded as natural science or engineering were: biology, chemistry, computer science, engineering, geology, mathematics, medicine, pharmacy, physics, veterinary medicine, general sciences, and health. Of the people who had obtained a BA or BS degree, 22% were coded as having had a natural science or engineering major. Removing the more applied fields of engineering, computer science, and health results in 9% coded as natural science, and has no substantive effect on the results reported below. It also could be argued that the conservative Protestants were educated at conservative Protestant colleges that teach a different version of science, but I argue elsewhere that this effect is insignificant. See Evans, "Epistemological and Moral Conflict Between Religion and Science," Appendix C.

5. Occupations included all engineers; statisticians; mathematicians; physicians; clinical laboratory, biology, and chemical technicians; science, math, and engineering teachers; physics, chemical, atmospheric, space, geological, physical, agricultural, biological, life, food, forestry, conservation, and medical scientists.

6. J. Scott Long and Jeremy Freese, *Regression Models for Categorical and Limited Dependent Variables Using Stata* (College Station, TX: Stata Press, 2014), Chapter 4.

7. The available "fact-claim" data is limited in that it is hard to know whether a respondent gets one of these questions "wrong" because they disagree with it, or they actually do not know what scientists have concluded about human origins. The best approach is to try to control for scientific knowledge under the assumption that a respondent who knows what scientists say about electrons will know what they say about evolution, so getting the evolution question "wrong" means they disagree with it. I can then see if belief in the conservative Protestant contested facts predicts having less exposure to science, such as taking fewer science courses, not having a scientific occupation, and not being a science major in college. I conducted three separate regression analyses that predict the number of science courses taken, whether the respondent has a scientific occupation, and whether they were a science major if they went to college. I predicted these outcomes with a measure of a lack of knowledge of the religiously contested facts, but controlling for the three knowledge indices described above. While in these models the knowledge indices unsurprisingly often predict exposure to science education or having a scientific occupation, not "knowing" the

religiously contested facts does not add any predictive capacity. This is further evidence that belief in the religiously contested facts does not lead to lack of belief in science writ large. For these technical results, see Tables A.1, A.2, and A.3 in the online appendix (pages.ucsd.edu/~jhevans/). It could be argued that since these models control for participating in a religious tradition, and the distinction between the two types of conservative Protestants is based on biblical literalism, I am over-controlling these models. I therefore ran this and all of the subsequent models in this chapter that use the contested facts measure without the denominational controls. The results were in each case the same.

Similar analysis by J. Micah Roos reaches a different conclusion than I do. Using GSS data he finds that those who believe in contested knowledge (such as human origins) know less uncontested knowledge. What he calls "spillover" I would call evidence that propositional knowledge conflict leads to systemic knowledge conflict. There are a large number of differences between our analyses, most notably that I use regression and he is using structural equation modeling. I suspect that our findings are different due to what he says is a possibility, which is that he cannot determine whether the respondent's lack of knowledge about contested facts is due to religious belief or simply ignorance of what scientists say. He tries to account for this by controlling for the number of science classes and education, but I suspect that these specific knowledge questions—that I control for but he cannot due to his design—are a different way of measuring knowledge that must be accounted for. See J. Micah Roos, "Contested Knowledge and Spillover," *Social Currents* 4, no. 2 (2016): 360–379.

8. Peter Jacques, Riley Dunlap, and Mark Freeman, "The Organisation of Denial: Conservative Think Tanks and Environmental Scepticism," *Environmental Politics* 173, no. 3 (2008): 349–85; Aaron McCright and Riley Dunlap, "Challenging Global Warming as a Social Problem: An Analysis of the Conservative Movement's Counter Claims," *Social Problems* 47, no. 4 (2000): 499–522; Aaron McCright and Riley Dunlap, "Anti-Reflexivity: The American Conservative Movement's Success in Undermining Climate Science and Policy," *Theory, Culture and Society* 27 (2010): 100–33.

9. Gordon Gauchat, "Politicization of Science in the Public Sphere: A Study of Public Trust in the United States, 1974 to 2010," *American Sociological Review* 77, no. 2 (2012): 167–87; Aaron McCright and Riley Dunlap, "The Politicization of Climate Change and Polarization in the American Public's Views of Global Warming, 2001–2010," *The Sociological Quarterly* 52 (2011): 155–94.

10. For the technical details and full results for this analysis, see John H. Evans and Justin Feng, "Conservative Protestantism and Skepticism of Scientists Studying Climate Change," *Climatic Change* 121 (2013): 595–608.

11. In addition to the set of characteristics used in previous calculations of predicted probabilities, in these models the hypothetical respondent is also a political independent, ideological moderate who responded to the survey in 2010.

12. As before, I add the variable indicating how many of the religious fact claims the respondent knows, while controlling for basic scientific knowledge via a measure of knowing noncontested fact claims, scientific methods, and claiming to understand science. Unfortunately, two of the control variables were not asked in the 2010 GSS, so this additional analysis is limited to 2006. This drops the number of cases from 1250 to 829, which still provides a fair amount of power. For technical results, see Table A.4 in the online appendix.

13. Survey analysis by Smith and Leiserowitz extensively examines evangelical public opinion and global warming. See N. Smith and A. Leiserowitz, "American Evangelicals and Global Warming," *Global Environmental Change* 23 (2013): 1009–17. Unfortunately, the design of their analysis makes it non-comparable to mine. They do show that 61 percent of evangelicals and 78 percent of nonevangelicals think global warming is happening, as well as related measures, but they do not control for the critical variables, which include political ideology and party identification. Their other models only analyze evangelicals without comparing them to others, and focus on the influence of various psychological constructs on views of global warming, such as whether evangelicals with egalitarian vs. individualistic worldviews would be more supportive of policy to mitigate climate change. Ultimately their paper is asking a separate set of questions than I do here.

14. Penny Edgell, Joseph Gerteis, and Douglas Hartmann, "Atheists as 'Other': Moral Boundaries and Cultural Membership in American Society," *American Sociological Review* 71 (2006): 211–34.

15. All but six respondents gave the same response for both daughter and son, so the results are essentially identical. The "not care" group included the handful who said "unhappy." Statistical problems emerge because every one of the African American Protestant church attenders in the survey selected that they would be "happy" for their daughter to be a scientist, resulting in no variance to predict. Therefore, to create a statistically valid analysis, I combined the black Protestants with the nonliteralist conservative Protestant category.

16. For the technical model, see Table A.5 in the online appendix.

17. For a systematic study of what respondents actually mean in their responses to these basic survey questions, see Hill, "National Study of Religion and Human Origins."

18. Edward B. Davis and Elizabeth Chmielewski, "Galileo and the Garden of Eden: Historical Reflections on Creationist Hermeneutics," in *Nature and Scripture in the Abrahamic Religions: 1700 – Present, Volume 2*, ed. Jitse M. van der Meer and Scott Mandelbrote (Leiden: Brill, 2008), 457, 459.

19. Percival Davis and Dean H. Kenyon, *Of Pandas and People: The Central Question of Biological Origins* (Dallas, TX: Haughton Publishing, 1989).

20. Google dictionary.

21. Davis and Kenyon, *Of Pandas and People: The Central Question of Biological Origins*, 158–60.

22. Davis and Kenyon, *Of Pandas and People: The Central Question of Biological Origins*, 158–60.

23. Jeffrey Guhin, "Why Worry About Evolution? Boundaries, Practices, and Moral Salience in Sunni and Evangelical High Schools," *Sociological Theory* 34, no. 2 (2016): 151–74.

24. Joseph Gusfield, *Symbolic Crusade: Status Politics and the American Temperance Movement* (Urbana, IL: University of Illinois Press, 1963); Michael Lienesch, "Right-Wing Religion: Christian Conservatism as a Political Movement," *Political Science Quarterly* 97, no. 3 (1992): 410.

25. Lienesch, "Right-Wing Religion: Christian Conservatism as a Political Movement," 411.

26. Christian Smith, *American Evangelicalism: Embattled and Thriving* (Chicago: University of Chicago Press, 1998).

27. This is a common explanation of creationist beliefs among European Muslims, where evolution "stands for the moral degradation that allegedly comes with Western secularism." Stefaan Blancke et al., "Creationism in Europe: Facts, Gaps, and Prospects," *Journal of the American Academy of Religion* 81, no. 4 (2013): 1014.

28. Guhin, "Why Worry About Evolution? Boundaries, Practices, and Moral Salience in Sunni and Evangelical High Schools."

7. EMPIRICAL TESTS OF MORAL CONFLICT FOR THE RELIGIOUS PUBLIC

1. Merriam-Webster online.

2. John H. Evans, *The History and Future of Bioethics: A Sociological View* (New York: Oxford University Press, 2012), 5.

3. Paul Ramsey, *Fabricated Man: The Ethics of Genetic Control* (New Haven, CT: Yale University Press, 1970), 144.

4. The surveys were the 1993, 2000, and 2010 GSS.

5. Other studies have used these or similar questions to measure "general attitudes toward science." See Martin Bauer, John Durant, and Geoffrey Evans, "European Public Perceptions of Science," *International Journal of Public Opinion Research* 6, no. 2 (1994): 174; Bernadette C. Hayes and Vicki N. Tariq, "Gender Differences in Scientific Knowledge and Attitudes Toward Science: A Comparative Study of Four Anglo-American Nations," *Public Understanding of Science* 9 (2000): 433–47. I parse the meaning of each of these questions more closely than do these other studies. Preliminary analysis reveals that the three questions cannot be merged into an index because the responses are largely uncorrelated, confirming that they represent different aspects of faith in science.

6. My interpretation of this question is bolstered by the wording comparing "science" to "faith," by which I think people understand the latter to mean "religion." The respondent is being asked the extent to which they agree that "science" fulfills the role of religion, further suggesting the "meaning" interpretation. My interpretation is also supported by the "believe in" wording. To "believe in" something indicates faith, as something we count on in our society to give us direction. We do not "believe in" scientific facts, but "believe" them. We "believe in" an institution like religion or science.

7. For analytic details see John H. Evans, "Faith in Science in Global Perspective: Implications for Transhumanism," *Public Understanding of Science* 23, no. 7 (2014): 814–32.

8. John H. Evans, *What is a Human? What the Answers Mean for Human Rights* (New York: Oxford University Press, 2016).

9. The three questions are: "The next few items concern some public issues. The first issue is global warming. Global warming means a trend toward warmer temperatures throughout the world, with more extreme weather in many places and changes in food production that could affect our way of life. Some people believe that the burning of gasoline and other fossil fuels causes global warming. Others say that global warming has purely natural causes." "Here is another public issue: research that uses human embryonic stem cells. These are cells from human embryos that can develop into many different types of tissue. Some say that cells taken from human embryos are uniquely valuable in medi-

cal research. Others say that the same discoveries can be made without destroying living embryos." "Here is another public issue: Genetically modified foods. Genetically modified foods come from plants or animals whose characteristics have been changed by the alteration, addition, or deletion of DNA in their genetic material using advanced laboratory techniques. Some say that genetically modified foods are unsafe and pose risks for human health. Others say that they are safe and necessary to reduce world hunger."

10. Anthony Leiserowitz et al., "Climategate, Public Opinion, and the Loss of Trust," *American Behavioral Scientist* 57, no. 6 (2012): 818–37.

11. These groups are politicians and business people for global warming, religious leaders and politicians for stem cells. In the predicted probabilities shown in Table 3, these additional variables are set at their means.

12. For formal results, see John H. Evans, "Epistemological and Moral Conflict Between Religion and Science," *Journal for the Scientific Study of Religion* 50, no. 4 (2011): 722.

13. I included data from not only 2006 but also 2010.

14. For formal results, see John H. Evans and Justin Feng, "Conservative Protestantism and Skepticism of Scientists Studying Climate Change," *Climatic Change* 121 (2013): 595–608.

15. Robert K. Merton, *The Sociology of Science* (Chicago: University of Chicago Press, 1973).

16. Michael Mulkay, "Norms and Ideology in Science," *Social Science Information* 15 (1976): 638.

17. Michael Mulkay, "Some Aspects of Cultural Growth in the Natural Sciences," *Social Research* 36 (1969): 654.

18. For global warming the groups asked about were environmental scientists, elected officials and business leaders. For embryonic stem cell research it was medical researchers, religious leaders, and elected officials. For genetically modified food it was medical researchers, elected officials, and business leaders.

19. More technically it is an additive index with an alpha of .643. The index had values from 1 to 9, and I used OLS regression for these models.

20. The genetically modified food questions were on a separate ballot from the other two in 2006. This question was not asked at all in 2010, while the other two were. For the question concerning bias of scientists for genetically modified food, only 6 percent of the respondents selected the endpoint in the five point scale labeled "follows own narrow interests." Therefore, to avoid estimation problems, I combined this category with the next one, resulting in a four-point scale. I used OLS so that the interpretation of both "self-interestedness" analyses would use expected values. An ordered logistic regression model produced the same substantive result.

21. For the combined global warming and stem cell analysis, the respondent evaluations of the self-interestedness of two other groups of professionals per issue were combined into an index with an alpha of .740. The two other groups asked about for genetically modified foods were combined into an index with an alpha of .627. These alphas mean that respondents who think one group is self-interested tend to think that all groups are self-interested.

22. Predicted values set the trust in other groups measure at its mean. The formal model is found in Table A.6 of the online appendix.

23. Since only .6 of 1 percent selected "strongly disagree" I collapsed this response into the "disagree" category. See Table A8 in the online appendix.

24. Google dictionary.

25. Bryan S. Turner, "The Body in Western Society: Social Theory and Its Perspectives," in *Religion and the Body*, ed. Sarah Coakley (New York: Cambridge University Press, 1997), 15–41; Andrew Louth, "The Body in Western Catholic Christianity," in *Religion and the Body*, ed. Sarah Coakley (New York: Cambridge University Press, 1997), 111–30; Giuseppe Giordan, "The Body Between Religion and Spirituality," *Social Compass* 56, no. 2 (2009): 226–36.

26. Allen Verhey, "'Playing God' and Invoking a Perspective," *Journal of Medicine and Philosophy* 20 (1995): 347–64.

27. John Paul II, *Evangelium Vitae* (Vatican City, 1995).

28. Thomas Banchoff, *Embryo Politics: Ethics and Policy in Atlantic Democracies* (Ithaca, NY: Cornell University Press, 2011), 58.

29. John H. Evans, *Contested Reproduction: Genetic Technologies, Religion, and Public Debate* (Chicago: University of Chicago Press, 2010).

30. I start in 1984 and not earlier because before the 1984 GSS Protestants cannot be effectively divided between conservative and mainline because the necessary questions were not asked.

31. Robert Horwitz, *America's Right: Anti-Establishment Conservatism from Goldwater to the Tea Party* (New York: Polity Press, 2013); Robert Wuthnow, *The Restructuring of American Religion* (Princeton, NJ: Princeton University Press, 1988).

32. Turner, "The Body in Western Society: Social Theory and Its Perspectives"; Louth, "The Body in Western Catholic Christianity"; Giordan, "The Body Between Religion and Spirituality."

33. Evans, *The History and Future of Bioethics: A Sociological View*, Chapter 1.

34. I would expect to find the same effects for conservative Catholics, who were also a part of the religious right and also opposed to the positions scientists would have been associated with regarding embryos, euthanasia, and so on. However, I will not discuss Catholics further in this particular analysis because data does not allow me to distinguish traditionalist and nontraditionalist Catholics. It would only be the traditionalist Catholics who would have this growing conflict.

35. This priming first occurs as the question is framed as being about "the people running these institutions," which suggests an evaluation of their character, abilities and/or goals, not the ability of science to produce knowledge. The priming also occurs as the specific question about science is preceded with questions about the respondent's confidence in banks and financial institutions, major companies, organized religion, education, the executive branch of the federal government, organized labor, the press, medicine, TV, and the U.S. Supreme Court. It is followed by questions about confidence in the Congress and the military. Therefore, while not specifically a question about moral influence, the question is evaluating the respondent's view of the social influence of elite scientists.

36. For technical details and formal results for these analyses, see John H. Evans, "The Growing Social and Moral Conflict Between Conservative Protestantism and Science," *Journal for the Scientific Study of Religion* 52, no. 2 (2013): 368–85.

37. The respondent could pick from four categories that ranged from "a great deal" to "none at all." Since only 3.5 percent of respondents selected "none at all," this category was collapsed into the next, resulting in a three category variable ranging from "a great deal" to "a little/none at all."

38. Not shown. See Evans, "The Growing Social and Moral Conflict Between Conservative Protestantism and Science," 378–79. Subsequent analyses by other scholars concur with this finding. Making different comparisons, Johnson and his co-authors found that those who thought of themselves as more religious and attended services more often had the least confidence in scientists. See David R. Johnson, Christopher P. Scheitle, and Elaine Howard Ecklund, "Individual Religiosity and Orientation Towards Science: Reformulating Relationships," *Sociological Science* 2, no. 106–124 (2015).

39. Evans, "The Growing Social and Moral Conflict Between Conservative Protestantism and Science," 381–82.

40. Evans, *Contested Reproduction: Genetic Technologies, Religion, and Public Debate*.. In 2003 and 2004 my research team and I interviewed 145 members of religious congregations in the U.S. and 35 nonreligious people. The number of religious respondents from each of the large religious traditions in the U.S. was set to match the percentage of congregational members from each of those groups in the general population. The groups were Catholics, evangelicals, and mainline Protestants, with an over sample of Jews. The analysis presented here is not in *Contested Reproduction*.

41. Pre-implantation genetic diagnosis is a technology where perhaps six embryos are created in a petri dish by combining the egg and sperm of a couple. The embryos are allowed to grow until they reach the 8-cell stage. One cell is then removed from each and the genetics tested. Embryos that have undesirable genetic qualities, typically diseases, are discarded. Embryos with desirable qualities are implanted in the woman to ideally start a pregnancy.

42. For a copy of the interview guide, see Appendix B in Evans, *Contested Reproduction: Genetic Technologies, Religion, and Public Debate*.

43. Ronald Cole-Turner, *The New Genesis: Theology and the Genetic Revolution* (Louisville, KY: Westminster/John Knox Press, 1993).

8. CONCLUSION

1. David C. Lindberg and Ronald L. Numbers, eds., *When Science and Christianity Meet* (Chicago: University of Chicago Press, 2003).

2. Conducted April, 2015. When using the internet as data we must be clear on what this is representing. Obviously the content of the internet does not represent "American culture" or "the information available." Rather, by looking at a Google search we simply see the information that would be shown to a person who did the same search. Given that this is how I believe the general public finds academic information, this Google search will show the information that will dominate in shaping views of the public.

3. http://www.nas.edu/evolution/Compatibility.html

4. Chris Mooney, *The Republican War on Science* (New York: Basic Books, 2005).

5. Frans de Waal, *The Bonobo and the Atheist: In Search of Humanism Among the Primates* (New York: W.W. Norton, 2013), 102. That friar referred to in the last sentence is Gregor Mendel, whose experiments in the mid-nineteenth century are credited as the first scientific experiments in modern genetics.

6. Peter Harrison, *The Territories of Science and Religion* (Chicago: University of Chicago Press, 2015), 178–81.

7. "Laudato Si." http://w2.vatican.va/content/francesco/en/encyclicals/documents/papa-francesco_20150524_enciclica-laudato-si.html

8. https://www.nae.net/caring-for-gods-creation/

9. http://creationcare.org/

10. Richard Dawkins, "Lying for Jesus," Retrieved 11 September 2008 from http://richarddawkins.net/article,2394,Lying-for-Jesus,Richard-Dawkins.

11. For this particular example of this typical comment about Dawkins, see Larry S. Chapp, *The God of Covenant and Creation: Scientific Naturalism and Its Challenge to the Christian Faith* (London: T&T Clark International, 2011), 27.

12. John H. Evans, *The History and Future of Bioethics: A Sociological View* (New York: Oxford University Press, 2012).

13. Evans, *The History and Future of Bioethics: A Sociological View*, xxxv.

14. Michael S. Evans, *Seeking Good Debate: Religion, Science, and Conflict in American Public Life* (Berkeley: University of California Press, 2016).

15. Robert Wuthnow, "No Contradictions Here: Science, Religion and the Culture of All Reasonable Possibilities," in *The Religion and Science Debate: Why Does It Continue?* ed. Harold W. Attridge (New Haven, CT: Yale University Press, 2009), 167, 168.

16. http://www.aaas.org/page/what-scientism

17. Erik Parens, *Shaping Our Selves: On Technology, Flourishing, and a Habit of Thinking* (New York: Oxford University Press, 2015), 72, 87.

18. John H. Evans, *What is a Human? What the Answers Mean for Human Rights* (New York: Oxford University Press, 2016), 63.

19. Evans, *What is a Human? What the Answers Mean for Human Rights*, Chapter 2. Critics "worry that our technological way of being in the world will turn us into objects in a different sense: the more our technologies proliferate, the more we will be tempted to treat each other as if we were 'mere objects,' not human. They worry that, if we don't check our technological imperative, we will become dehumanized." See Parens, *Shaping Our Selves: On Technology, Flourishing, and a Habit of Thinking*, 87.

WORKS CITED

Aechtner, Thomas. 2015. Galileo Still Goes to Jail: Conflict Model Persistence Within Introductory Anthropology Materials. *Zygon* 50(1): 209-26.
———. Forthcoming. Social Scientists. In *"The Idea That Wouldn't Die": The Warfare Between Science and Religion*, ed. J. Hardin and R. L. Numbers.
Ahlstrom, Sydney. 1972. *A Religious History of the American People*. New Haven, CT: Yale University Press.
Allum, Nick, Patrick Sturgis, Dimitra Tabourazi, and Ian Brunton-Smith. 2008. Science Knowledge and Attitudes Across Cultures: A Meta-Analysis. *Public Understanding of Science* 17: 35-54.
Attridge, Harold W., ed. 2009. *The Religion and Science Debate: Why Does It Continue?* New Haven, CT: Yale University Press.
Bainbridge, William Sims. 2005. The Transhuman Heresy. *Journal of Evolution and Technology* 14(2): 91-100.
Baker, Joseph O. 2012. Public Perceptions of Incompatibility Between "Science and Religion." *Public Understanding of Science* 21: 340-53.
———. 2013. Acceptance of Evolution and Support for Teaching Creationism in Public Schools: The Conditional Impact of Educational Attainment. *Journal for the Scientific Study of Religion* 52(1): 216-28.
Banchoff, Thomas. 2011. *Embryo Politics: Ethics and Policy in Atlantic Democracies*. Ithaca, NY: Cornell University Press.
Barbour, Ian G. 2000. *When Science Meets Religion*. San Francisco: Harper and Row.
Barbour, Ian. 1993. *Ethics in an Age of Technology*. San Francisco: Harper and Row.
Barnes, Terry. 2013. Unity (Unity School of Christianity). In *The Popular Encyclopedia of Church History*, ed. E. Hindson and D. Mitchell, 330-31. Eugene, OR: Harvest House Publishers.

Bauer, Martin, John Durant, and Geoffrey Evans. 1994. European Public Perceptions of Science. *International Journal of Public Opinion Research* 6(2): 163–86.

Bellah, Robert N., Richard Madsen, William M. Sullivan, Ann Swidler, and Steven M. Tipton. 1985. *Habits of the Heart: Individualism and Commitment in American Life*. New York: Harper and Row.

Benjamin, Ruha. 2013. *People's Science: Bodies and Rights on the Stem Cell Frontier*. Stanford, CA: Stanford University Press.

Berger, Peter L. 1967. *The Sacred Canopy: Elements of a Sociological Theory of Religion*. New York: Doubleday.

———. 1974. Some Second Thoughts on Substantive Versus Functional Definitions of Religion. *Journal for the Scientific Study of Religion* 13(2): 125–33.

Besley, John C. and Matthew Nisbet. 2011. How Scientists View the Public, the Media and the Political Process. *Public Understanding of Science* 22(6): 644–59.

Beyerlein, Kraig. 2004. Specifying the Impact of Conservative Protestantism on Educational Attainment. *Journal for the Scientific Study of Religion* 43(4): 505–18.

Blancke, Stefaan, Hans Henrik Hjermitslev, Johan Braeckman, and Peter C. Kjaergaard. 2013. Creationism in Europe: Facts, Gaps, and Prospects. *Journal of the American Academy of Religion* 81(4): 996–1028.

Boenig-Lipstin, Margarita and J. Benjamin Hurlbut. 2016. Technologies of Transcendence at Singularity University. In *Perfecting Human Futures: Transhuman Visions and Technological Imaginations*, ed. J. B. Hurlbut and H. Tirosh-Samuelson, 239–67. Wiesbaden, Germany: Springer-Verlag.

Bourdieu, Pierre. 1975. The Specificity of the Scientific Field and the Conditions for the Progress of Reason. *Social Science Information* 14: 19–47.

Bowler, Kate. 2013. *Blessed: A History of the American Prosperity Gospel*. New York: Oxford University Press.

———. 2014. The Prosperity Gospel's Transformation of the Popular Religious Imagination. *CCDA Theological Journal*, 19–23.

Bowler, Peter J. 2001. *Reconciling Science and Religion: The Debate in Early-Twentieth-Century Britain*. Chicago: University of Chicago Press.

Brooke, John Hedley. 1991. *Science and Religion: Some Historical Perspectives*. New York: Cambridge University Press.

Brown, Frederick W. 1930. Eugenic Sterilization in the United States: Its Present Status. *Annals of the American Academy of Political and Social Science* 149: 22–35.

Buckser, Andrew. 1996. Religion, Science, and Secularization Theory on a Danish Island. *Journal for the Scientific Study of Religion* 35(4): 432–41.

Cady, Linell E. 2012. Religion and the Technowonderland of Transhumanism. In *Building Better Humans? Refocusing the Debate on Transhumanism*, ed. H. Tirosh-Samuelson and K. L. Mossman, 83–104. Frankfurt am Main: Peter Lang.

Chapp, Larry S. 2011. *The God of Covenant and Creation: Scientific Naturalism and Its Challenge to the Christian Faith*. London: T&T Clark International.

Chaves, Mark. 2010. Rain Dances in the Dry Season: Overcoming the Religious Congruency Fallacy. *Journal for the Scientific Study of Religion* 49: 1–14.

Cole-Turner, Ronald. 1993. *The New Genesis: Theology and the Genetic Revolution.* Louisville, KY: Westminster/John Knox Press.
Collins, Francis S. 2006. *The Language of God: A Scientist Presents Evidence for Belief.* New York: Free Press.
Converse, Philip E. 1964. The Nature of Belief Systems in Mass Publics. In *Ideology and Discontent,* ed. D. E. Apter, 206–61. New York: Free Press.
Coyne, Jerry A. 2015. *Faith Versus Fact: Why Science and Religion Are Incompatible.* New York: Viking.
Darnell, Alfred, and Darren E. Sherkat. 1997. The Impact of Protestant Fundamentalism on Education. *American Sociological Review* 62(2): 306–15.
Davis, Bernard D. 1970. Prospects for Genetic Intervention in Man. *Science* 170: 1279–83.
Davis, Bernard. 1976. Novel Pressures on the Advance of Science. *Annals of the New York Academy of Sciences* 265: 193–202.
Davis, Edward B., and Elizabeth Chmielewski. 2008. Galileo and the Garden of Eden: Historical Reflections on Creationist Hermeneutics. In *Nature and Scripture in the Abrahamic Religions: 1700—Present, Volume 2,* ed. J. M. van der Meer and S. Mandelbrote, 437–64. Leiden: Brill.
Davis, Percival, and Dean H. Kenyon. 1989. *Of Pandas and People: The Central Question of Biological Origins.* Dallas, TX: Haughton Publishing.
Dawson, Gowan. 2007. *Darwin, Literature and Victorian Respectability.* Cambridge, UK: Cambridge University Press.
de Waal, Frans. 2013. *The Bonobo and the Atheist: In Search of Humanism Among the Primates.* New York: W.W. Norton.
Dennett, Daniel C., and Alvin Plantinga. 2011. *Science and Religion: Are They Compatible?* New York: Oxford University Press.
DiMaggio, Paul. 1997. Culture and Cognition. *Annual Review of Sociology* 23: 263–87.
Discovery Institute. N.d. The Wedge. http://www.antievolution.org/features/wedge.pdf.
Dorrien, Gary. 2010. *Social Ethics in the Making: Interpreting an American Tradition.* New York: Wiley-Blackwell.
Ecklund, Elaine Howard. 2010. *Science Vs. Religion: What Scientists Really Think.* New York: Oxford University Press.
Ecklund, Elaine Howard, Jerry Z. Park, and Katherine L. Sorrell. 2011. Scientists Negotiate Boundaries Between Religion and Science. *Journal for the Scientific Study of Religion* 50(3): 552–69.
Ecklund, Elaine Howard, Jerry Z. Park, and Phil Todd Veliz. 2008. Secularization and Religious Change Among Elite Scientists. *Social Forces* 86(4): 1805–39.
Ecklund, Elaine Howard, and Christopher P. Scheitle. 2007. "Religion Among Academic Scientists: Distinctions, Disciplines, and Demographics." *Social Problems* 54(2): 289–307.
———. 2018. *Religion Vs. Science: What Religious People Really Think.* New York: Oxford University Press.
Edgell, Penny, Joseph Gerteis, and Douglas Hartmann. 2006. Atheists as "Other": Moral Boundaries and Cultural Membership in American Society. *American Sociological Review* 71: 211–34.

Edwards, Robert. 1989. *Life Before Birth: Reflections on the Embryo Debate.* New York: Basic Books.
Efron, Noah. Forthcoming. Judaism. In *"The Idea That Wouldn't Die:" The Warfare Between Science and Religion,* ed. J. Hardin, R. L. Numbers, and R. A. Binzley. Baltimore: Johns Hopkins University Press.
Ellingson, Stephen. 2009. The Rise of the Megachurches and Changes in Religious Culture: Review Article. *Sociology Compass* 3(1): 16–30.
Ellison, Christopher G., and Marc A. Musick. 1995. Conservative Protestantism and Public Opinion Toward Science. *Review of Religious Research* 36(3): 245–62.
Evans, John H. 1997. Worldviews or Social Groups as the Source of Moral Value Attitudes: Implications for the Culture Wars Thesis. *Sociological Forum* 12(3): 371–404.
———. 2002. *Playing God? Human Genetic Engineering and the Rationalization of Public Bioethical Debate.* Chicago: University of Chicago Press.
———. 2010. *Contested Reproduction: Genetic Technologies, Religion, and Public Debate.* Chicago: University of Chicago Press.
———. 2011. Epistemological and Moral Conflict Between Religion and Science. *Journal for the Scientific Study of Religion* 50(4): 707–27.
———. 2012. *The History and Future of Bioethics: A Sociological View.* New York: Oxford University Press.
———. 2013. The Growing Social and Moral Conflict Between Conservative Protestantism and Science. *Journal for the Scientific Study of Religion* 52(2): 368–85.
———. 2014. Faith in Science in Global Perspective: Implications for Transhumanism. *Public Understanding of Science* 23(7): 814–32.
———. 2016. Future Vision in Transhumanist Writings and the Religious Public. In *Perfecting Human Futures: Transhuman Visions and Technological Imaginations,* ed. J. B. Hurlbut and H. Tirosh-Samuelson, 291–306. Dordrecht, Netherlands: Springer-Verlag.
———. 2016. *What is a Human? What the Answers Mean for Human Rights.* New York: Oxford University Press.
Evans, John H., and Justin Feng. 2013. Conservative Protestantism and Skepticism of Scientists Studying Climate Change. *Climatic Change* 121: 595–608.
Evans, John H., and Cynthia E. Schairer. 2009. Bioethics and Human Genetic Engineering. In *Handbook of Genetics and Society: Mapping the New Genomic Era,* ed. P. Atkinson, P. Glasner, and M. Lock, 349–66. London: Routledge.
Evans, Michael S. 2009. Defining the Public, Defining Sociology: Hybrid Science-Public Relations and Boundary-Work in Early American Sociology. *Public Understanding of Science* 185(14): 5–22.
———. 2016. *Seeking Good Debate: Religion, Science, and Conflict in American Public Life.* Berkeley, CA: University of California Press.
Evans, Michael S., and John H. Evans. 2010. Arguing Against Darwinism: Religion, Science and Public Morality. In *The New Blackwell Companion to the Sociology of Religion,* ed. B. Turner, 286–308. New York: Blackwell.
Everhart, Donald, and Salman Hameed. 2013. Muslims and Evolution: A Study of Pakistani Physicians in the United States. *Evolution: Education and Outreach* 6(2): 1–8.

Ferngren, Gary B., ed. 2000. *The History of Science and Religion in the Western Tradition: An Encylopedia.* New York: Garland Publishing.

Finke, Roger, and Rodney Stark. 1992. *The Churching of America, 1776–1990: Winners and Losers in Our Religious Economy.* New Brunswick, NJ: Rutgers University Press.

Flory, Richard W. 2003. Promoting a Secular Standard: Secularization and Modern Journalism. In *The Secular Revolution: Power, Interests, and Conflict in the Secularization of American Public Life*, ed. C. Smith, 395–433. Berkeley, CA: University of California Press.

Forrest, Barbara, and Paul R. Gross. 2004. *Creationism's Trojan Horse: The Wedge of Intelligent Design.* Creationism's Trojan Horse: The Wedge of Intelligent Design. Oxford: Oxford University Press.

Frayling, Christopher. 2005. *Mad, Bad and Dangerous? The Scientist and the Cinema.* London: Reaktion Books.

Fuller, Steve. 2007. *Science Vs. Religion? Intelligent Design and the Problem of Evolution.* New York: Polity.

Galton, Francis. 1883. *Inquiries Into Human Faculty and Its Development.* London: Macmillan.

Garroutte, Eva Marie. 2003. The Positivist Attack on Baconian Science and Religious Knowledge in the 1870s. In *The Secular Revolution*, ed. Christian Smith. Berkeley, CA: University of California Press.

Gauchat, Gordon. 2012. Politicization of Science in the Public Sphere: A Study of Public Trust in the United States, 1974 to 2010. *American Sociological Review* 77(2): 167–87.

Geertz, Clifford. 1973. *Interpretation of Cultures.* New York: Basic Books.

Gerring, John. 1997. Ideology: A Definitional Analysis. *Political Research Quarterly* 50(4): 957–94.

Gieryn, Thomas F. 1983. Boundary-Work and the Demarcation of Science from Non-Science: Strains and Interests in Professional Ideologies of Scientists. *American Sociological Review* 48: 781–95.

Gieryn, Thomas F., George M. Bevins, and Stephen C. Zehr. 1985. Professionalization of American Scientists: Public Science in the Creation/Evolution Trials. *American Sociological Review* 50: 392–409.

Gilkey, Langdon. 1985. *Creationism on Trial: Evolution and God at Little Rock.* Minneapolis, MN: Winston Press.

Giordan, Giuseppe. 2009. The Body Between Religion and Spirituality. *Social Compass* 56(2): 226–36.

Goodwin, Glenn A., and Joseph A. Scimecca. 2006. *Classical Sociological Theory.* Belmont, CA: Wadsworth.

Gould, Stephen Jay. 1999. *Rocks of Ages: Science and Religion in the Fullness of Life.* New York: Ballantine.

Grabiner, Judith V., and Peter D. Miller. 1974. Effects of the Scopes Trial. *Science* 185:832–37.

Granger, Maury D., and Gregory N. Price. 2007. The Tree of Science and Original Sin: Do Christian Religious Beliefs Constrain the Supply of Scientists? *Journal of Socio-Economics* 36: 144–60.

Greeley, Andrew, and Michael Hout. 2006. *The Truth About Conservative Christians: What They Think and What They Believe.* Chicago: University of Chicago Press.

Guhin, Jeffrey. 2016. Why Worry About Evolution? Boundaries, Practices, and Moral Salience in Sunni and Evangelical High Schools. *Sociological Theory* 34(2): 151–74.

Gusfield, Joseph. 1963. *Symbolic Crusade: Status Politics and the American Temperance Movement.* Urbana, IL: University of Illinois Press.

Hameed, Salman. 2015. Making Sense of Islamic Creationism in Europe. *Public Understanding of Science* 24(4): 388–99.

Harris, Steven J. 2002. Roman Catholicism Since Trent. In *Science and Religion: A Historical Introduction,* ed. G. B. Ferngren, 247–60. Baltimore, MD: The Johns Hopkins University Press.

Harrison, Peter. 2015. *The Territories of Science and Religion.* Chicago: University of Chicago Press.

Hauskeller, Michael. 2012. Reinventing Cockaigne: Utopian Themes in Transhumanist Thought. *The Hastings Center Report* 42(2): 39–47.

Haycraft, John Berry. 1895. *Darwinism and Race Progress.* New York: Charles Scribner.

Hayes, Bernadette C., and Vicki N. Tariq. 2000. Gender Differences in Scientific Knowledge and Attitudes Toward Science: A Comparative Study of Four Anglo-American Nations. *Public Understanding of Science* 9: 433–47.

Haynes, Roslynn D. 1994. *From Faust to Strangelove: Representations of the Scientist in Western Literature.* Baltimore: Johns Hopkins University Press.

Heft, James L. 2002. Catholicism and Science: Renewing the Conversation. *Journal of Ecumenical Studies* 39(3–4): 376–80.

Heitmann, John A. 2002. Doing "True Science": The Early History of the Institutum Divi Thomae, 1935–1951. *Catholic Historical Review* 88(4): 702–22.

Herrmann, Robert L. 2004. *Sir John Templeton: Supporting Scientific Research for Spiritual Discoveries.* Radnor, PA: Templeton Foundation Press.

Hill, Jonathan P. 2014. National Study of Religion and Human Origins. Biologos Foundation. https://www.dropbox.com/s/k8pm1s48uaqvvm3/NSRHO%20Report.pdf?dl = 0

Hitlin, Steven, and Stephen Vaisey. 2010. Back to the Future: Reviving the Sociology of Morality. In *Handbook of the Sociology of Morality,* ed. S. Hitlin and S. Vaisey, 3–14. New York: Springer.

Hollinger, David A. 2013. *After Cloven Tongues of Fire: Protestant Liberalism in Modern American History.* Princeton, NJ: Princeton University Press.

Hooper, John. 2006. Pope Prepares to Embrace Theory of Intelligent Design. *The Guardian* (London), August 28.

Horwitz, Robert. 2013. *America's Right: Anti-Establishment Conservatism from Goldwater to the Tea Party.* New York: Polity Press.

Hovenkamp, Herbert. 1978. *Science and Religion in America 1800–1860.* Philadelphia, PA: University of Pennsylvania Press.

Hunter, George William. 1914. *A Civic Biology: Presented in Problems.* New York: American Book Company.

Hurlbut, J. Benjamin. 2017. *Experiments in Democracy: Human Embryo Research and the Politics of Bioethics.* New York: Columbia University Press.

Hurlbut, J. Benjamin, and Hava Tirosh-Samuelson. 2016. *Perfecting Human Futures: Transhuman Visions and Technological Imaginations.* Wiesbaden, Germany: Springer-Verlag.

Jacques, Peter, Riley Dunlap, and Mark Freeman. 2008. The Organisation of Denial: Conservative Think Tanks and Environmental Scepticism. *Environmental Politics* 173(3): 349–85.

Jewett, Andrew. 2012. *Science, Democracy, and the American University: From the Civil War to the Cold War.* New York: Cambridge University Press.

John Paul II. 1995. *Evangelium Vitae.* Vatican City.

Johnson, David R., Christopher P. Scheitle, and Elaine Howard Ecklund. 2015. Individual Religiosity and Orientation Towards Science: Reformulating Relationships. *Sociological Science* 2(106–124).

Kalberg, Stephen. 1980. Max Weber's Types of Rationality: Cornerstones for the Analysis of Rationalization Processes in History. *American Journal of Sociology* 85(5): 1145–79.

Keister, Lisa A. 2008. Conservative Protestants and Wealth: How Religion Perpetuates Asset Poverty. *American Journal of Sociology* 113(5): 1237–71.

Kevles, Daniel. 1985. *In the Name of Eugenics: Genetics and the Uses of Human Heredity.* Berkeley, CA: University of California Press.

Kirby, David A. 2014. Science and Technology in Film: Themes and Representations. In *Routledge Handbook of Public Communication of Science and Technology, 2nd ed.,* ed. M. Bucchi and B. Trench, 97–112. New York: Routledge.

Knight, Jonathan. 2004. Hollywood or Bust. *Nature* 430(12, August): 720–22.

Knorr-Cetina, Karin D. 1981. *The Manufacture of Knowledge: An Essay on the Constructivist and Contextual Nature of Science.* New York: Pergamon Press.

Kosmin, Barry A., Ariela Keysar, and Nava Lerer. 1992. Secular Education and the Religious Profile of Contemporary Black and White Americans. *Journal for the Scientific Study of Religion* 31(4): 523–32.

Krauss, Lawrence M. 2009. Religion Vs. Science? In *The Religion and Science Debate: Why Does It Continue?* ed. by H. W. Attridge, 125–53. New Haven, CT: Yale University Press.

Kuhn, Thomas S. 1970. *The Structure of Scientific Revolutions.* Chicago: University of Chicago Press.

Larsen, Timothy. 2017. Anthropology. In *Science and Religion: A Historical Introduction, Second Edition,* ed. G. B. Ferngren, 409–22. Baltimore: Johns Hopkins University Press.

Larson, Edward J. 1997. *Summer of the Gods: The Scopes Trial and America's Continuing Debate Over Science and Religion.* New York: Basic Books.

Larson, Edward J., and Larry Witham. 1997. Scientists Are Still Keeping the Faith. *Nature* 386: 435–36.

———. 1998. Leading Scientists Still Reject God. *Nature* 394: 313.

Latour, Bruno, and Steve Woolgar. [1979] 1986. *Laboratory Life: The Construction of Scientific Facts.* Princeton, NJ: Princeton University Press.

Lederer, Susan E. 2002. *Frankenstein: Penetrating the Secrets of Nature.* New Brunswick, NJ: Rutgers University Press.

Legare, Cristine H., E. Margaret Evans, Karl S. Rosengren, and Paul L. Harris. 2012. The Coexistence of Natural and Supernatural Explanations Across Cultures and Development. *Child Development* 83(3): 779–893.

Legare, Cristine H., and Aku Visala. 2011. Between Religion and Science: Integrating Psychological and Philosophical Accounts of Explanatory Coexistence. *Human Development* 54: 169–84.

Lehman, Edward C. Jr., and Donald W. Jr Shriver. 1968. Academic Discipline as Predictive of Faculty Religiosity. *Social Forces* 47: 171–82.

Leiserowitz, Anthony, Edward W. Maibach, Connie Roser-Renouf, Nicholas Smith, and Erica Dawson. 2012. Climategate, Public Opinion, and the Loss of Trust. *American Behavioral Scientist* 57(6): 818–37.

Lessl, Thomas M. 1999. The Galileo Legend as Scientific Folklore. *Quarterly Journal of Speech* 85: 146–68.

Leuba, James. 1916. *The Belief in God and Immortality, a Psychological, Anthropological and Statistical Study.* Boston, MA: Sherman, French, and Company.

———. 1934. Religious Beliefs of American Scientists. *Harper's Magazine* 169: 291–300.

Lienesch, Michael. 1992. Right-Wing Religion: Christian Conservatism as a Political Movement. *Political Science Quarterly* 97(3): 403–25.

———. 2007. *In the Beginning: Fundamentalism, the Scopes Trial, and the Making of the Antievolution Movement.* Chapel Hill, NC: University of North Carolina Press.

Lightman, Bernard. 2007. *Victorian Popularizers of Science: Designing Nature for New Audiences.* Chicago: University of Chicago Press.

Lindberg, David C., and Ronald L. Numbers, Editors. 2003. *When Science and Christianity Meet.* Chicago: University of Chicago Press.

Livingstone, David N. 2009. That Huxley Defeated Wilberforce in Their Debate Over Evolution and Religion. In *Galileo Goes to Jail and Other Myths About Science and Religion*, ed. R. L. Numbers, 152–60. Cambridge, MA: Harvard University Press.

Long, J. Scott, and Jeremy Freese. 2014. *Regression Models for Categorical and Limited Dependent Variables Using Stata.* College Station, TX: Stata Press.

Losh, Susan Carol. 2010. Stereotypes About Scientists Over Time Among US Adults: 1983 and 2001. *Public Understanding of Science* 19(3): 372–82.

Louth, Andrew. 1997. The Body in Western Catholic Christianity. In *Religion and the Body*, ed. S. Coakley, 111–30. New York: Cambridge University Press.

Madsen, Richard. 2009. The Archipelago of Faith: Religious Individualism and Faith Community in America Today. *American Journal of Sociology* 114(5): 1263–301.

Marsden, George M. 1982. Everyone One's Own Interpreter? The Bible, Science, and Authority in Mid-Nineteenth-Century America. In *The Bible in America: Essays in Cultural History*, ed. N. O. Hatch and M. A. Noll, 79–100. New York: Oxford University Press.

———. 1989. Evangelicals and the Scientific Culture: An Overview. In *Religion and Twentieth-Century American Intellectual Life*, ed. M. J. Lacey, 23–48. New York: Cambridge University Press.

McCright, Aaron, and Riley Dunlap. 2000. Challenging Global Warming as a Social Problem: An Analysis of the Conservative Movement's Counter Claims. *Social Problems* 47(4): 499–522.

———. 2010. Anti-Reflexivity: The American Conservative Movement's Success in Undermining Climate Science and Policy. *Theory, Culture and Society* 27: 100–33.

———. 2011. The Politicization of Climate Change and Polarization in the American Public's Views of Global Warming, 2001–2010. *The Sociological Quarterly* 52: 155–94.

McGrath, Alister E. 1998. *The Foundations of Dialogue in Science and Religion*. Malden, MA: Blackwell.

———. 1999. *Science and Religion: An Introduction*. Malden, MA: Blackwell Publishers.

———. 2010. The Ideological Uses of Evolutionary Biology in Recent Atheist Apologetics. In *Biology and Ideology: From Descartes to Dawkins*, ed. D. R. Alexander and R. L. Numbers, 329–51. Chicago: University of Chicago Press.

Merton, Robert K. 1973. *The Sociology of Science*. Chicago: University of Chicago Press.

Miller, Donald E. 1997. *Reinventing American Protestantism: Christianity in the New Millennium*. Berkeley, CA: University of California Press.

Miller, Kenneth R. 2009. Darwin, God, and Dover: What the Collapse of "Intelligent Design" Means for Science and Faith in America. In *The Religion and Science Debate: Why Does It Continue?* ed. H. W. Attridge, 55–92. New Haven, CT: Yale University Press.

Mislin, David. Forthcoming. Catholicism. In *"The Idea That Wouldn't Die;" The Warfare Between Science and Religion*, ed. J. Hardin, R. L. Numbers, and R. A. Binzley. Baltimore, MD: Johns Hopkins University Press.

Mooney, Chris. 2005. *The Republican War on Science*. New York: Basic Books.

Moran, Jeffrey P. 2012. *American Genesis: The Antievolution Controversies from Scopes to Creation Science*. New York: Oxford University Press.

Morris, Henry M. 1974. *Scientific Creationism*. San Diego, CA: Creation-Life Publishers.

Motive Entertainment. 2008. *Expelled Leader's Guide*. Westlake Village, CA: Motive Entertainment.

Mulkay, Michael. 1969. Some Aspects of Cultural Growth in the Natural Sciences. *Social Research* 36: 22–52.

———. 1976. Norms and Ideology in Science. *Social Science Information* 15: 637–56.

———. 1997. *The Embryo Research Debate*. Cambridge, UK: Cambridge University Press.

National Association of Evangelicals. 2015. *When God and Science Meet: Surprising Discoveries of Agreement*. Washington, DC: National Association of Evangelicals.

Nelkin, Dorothy. 1982. *The Creation Controversy: Science or Scripture in the Schools*. New York: W.W. Norton.

Nisbet, Matthew C., and Dietram A. Scheufele. 2009. What's Next for Science Communication? Promising Directions and Lingering Distractions. *American Journal of Botany* 96(10): 1767–78.

Nisbet, Matthew, Dietram A. Scheufele, James Shanahan, Patricia Moy, Dominique Brossard, and Bruce Lewenstein. 2002. Knowledge, Reservations, or Promise? A Media Effects Model for Public Perceptions of Science and Technology. *Communication Research* 29(5): 584–608.

Noll, Mark A. 1994. *The Scandal of the Evangelical Mind*. Grand Rapids, MI: Eerdmans.

Norris, Pippa, and Ronald Inglehart. 2004. *Sacred and Secular: Religion and Politics Worldwide*. New York: Cambridge University Press.

Numbers, Ronald L. 1982. Creationism in 20th-Century America. *Science* 217: 538–54.

———. 1998. *Darwinism Comes to America*. Cambridge, MA: Harvard University Press.

———. 2003. Science Without God: Natural Laws and Christian Beliefs. In *When Science and Christianity Meet*, ed. D. C. Lindberg and R. L. Numbers, 265–85. Chicago: University of Chicago Press.

———. 2006. *The Creationists: The Evolution of Scientific Creationism, Expanded Edition*. Cambridge, MA: Harvard University Press.

———. 2007. *Science and Christianity in Pulpit and Pew*. New York: Oxford University Press.

———. 2009. Aggressors, Victims, and Peacemakers: Historical Actors in the Drama of Science and Religion. In *The Religion and Science Debate: Why Does It Continue?* Ed. H. W. Attridge, 15–53. New Haven, CT: Yale University Press.

———, ed. 2009. *Galileo Goes to Jail: And Other Myths About Science and Religion*. Cambridge, MA: Harvard University Press.

O'Toole, Roger. 1984. *Religion: Classic Sociological Approaches*. New York: McGraw-Hill.

Oreskes, Naomi, and Erik M. Conway. 2010. *Merchants of Doubt*. New York: Bloomsbury Press.

Owen, Richard. 2009. Vatican Buries the Hatchet with Charles Darwin. *The Times* (London), February 11, online edition.

Parens, Erik. 2015. *Shaping Our Selves: On Technology, Flourishing, and a Habit of Thinking*. New York: Oxford University Press.

Paul, Diane B. 1995. *Controlling Human Heredity: 1865 to the Present*. Amherst, NY: Humanity Books.

Peffley, Mark A., and Jon Hurwitz. 1985. A Hierarchical Model of Attitude Constraint. *American Journal of Political Science* 29(4): 871–90.

Pennock, Robert T., ed. 2001. *Intelligent Design Creationism and Its Critics*. Cambridge, MA: MIT Press.

Polkinghorne, John. 2000. Science and Theology in the Twenty-First Century. *Zygon* 35(4): 941–53.

Ramsey, Paul. 1970. *Fabricated Man: The Ethics of Genetic Control*. New Haven, CT: Yale University Press.

Rawson, Casey H., and Megan Astolfi McCool. 2014. Just Like All the Other Humans? Analyzing Images of Scientists in Children's Trade Books. *School Science and Mathematics* 114: 10–18.

Roberts, Jon H. 2003. "The Idea That Wouldn't Die": The Warfare Between Science and Christianity. *Historically Speaking* 48: 21–24.

———. Forthcoming. Mainline Protestantism. In *"The Idea That Wouldn't Die" The Warfare Between Science and Religion*, ed. J. Hardin, R. L. Numbers, and R. A. Binzley. Baltimore, MD: Johns Hopkins University Press.

Roberts, Jon H., and James Turner. 2000. *The Sacred and the Secular University*. Princeton, NJ: Princeton University Press.

Roos, J. Micah. 2016. Contested Knowledge and Spillover. *Social Currents* 4(4): 360–79.

Ross, Dorothy. 1991. *The Origins of American Social Science*. New York: Cambridge University Press.

Russell, Colin A. 2002. The Conflict of Science and Religion. In *Science and Religion: A Historical Introduction*, ed. G. B. Ferngren, 3–12. Baltimore, MD: The Johns Hopkins University Press.

Russell, Collin A. 2000. The Conflict of Science and Religion. In *The History of Science and Religion in the Western Tradition*, ed. G. B. Ferngren, 12–16. New York: Garland Publishing.

Rutjens, Bastiaan T., and Steven J. Heine. 2016. The Immoral Landscape? Scientists Are Associated with Violations of Morality. *PLOS One* 11(4).

Scheitle, Christopher P. 2011. U.S. College Students' Perception of Religion and Science: Conflict, Collaboration, or Independence? A Research Note. *Journal for the Scientific Study of Religion* 50(1): 175–86.

Scheitle, Christopher P., and Elaine Howarrd Ecklund. 2017. The Influence of Science Popularizers on the Public's View of Religion and Science: An Experimental Assessment. *Public Understanding of Science* 26(1): 25–39.

Secord, James A. 2000. *Victorian Sensation: The Extraordinary Publication, Reception, and Secret Authorship of Vestiges of the Natural History of Creation*. Chicago: University of Chicago Press.

Sewell, William H Jr. 1999. The Concept(s) of Culture. In *Beyond the Cultural Turn: New Directions in the Study of Society and Culture*, ed. V. E. Bonnell and L. Hunt, 35–61. Berkeley, CA: University of California Press.

Shapiro, Adam R. 2013. *Trying Biology: The Scopes Trial, Textbooks, and the Antievolution Movement in American Schools*. Chicago: University of Chicago Press.

Sherkat, Darren E. 2010. Religion and Verbal Ability. *Social Science Research* 39: 2–13.

———. 2011. Religion and Scientific Literacy in the United States. *Social Science Quarterly* 92(5): 1134–50.

Sherkat, Darren E., and Alfred Darnell. 1999. The Effect of Parents' Fundamentalism on Children's Educational Attainment: Examining Differences by Gender and Children's Fundamentalism. *Journal for the Scientific Study of Religion* 38(1): 23–35.

Sheskin, Ira M., and Harriet Hartman. 2015. Denominational Variations Across American Jewish Communities. *Journal for the Scientific Study of Religion* 54(2): 205–21.

Smith, Christian. 1998. *American Evangelicalism: Embattled and Thriving*. Chicago: University of Chicago Press.

———, ed. 2003. *The Secular Revolution*. Berkeley, CA: University of California Press.

———. 2003. Secularizing American Higher Education: The Case of Early American Sociology. In *The Secular Revolution: Power, Interests, and Conflict in the Secularization of American Public Life*, ed. C. Smith, 97–159. Berkeley, CA: University of California Press.

———. 2005. *Soul Searching: The Religious and Spiritual Lives of American Teenagers*. New York: Oxford University Press.

Smith, N., and A. Leiserowitz. 2013. American Evangelicals and Global Warming. *Global Environmental Change* 23: 1009–17.

Stark, Rodney. 1963. On the Incompatibility of Religion and Science: A Survey of American Graduate Students. *Journal for the Scientific Study of Religion* 3: 3–20.

Stark, Rodney, and William S. Bainbridge. 1985. *The Future of Religion*. Berkeley, CA: University of California Press.

Swidler, Ann. 2001. *Talk of Love: How Culture Matters*. Chicago: University of Chicago Press.

Templeton, Sir John. 2000. *Possibilities of Over One Hundredfold More Spiritual Information: The Humble Approach in Theology and Science*. Radnor, PA: Templeton Foundation Press.

Thalheimer, Fred. 1973. Religiosity and Secularization in the Academic Professions. *Sociology of Education* 46: 183–202.

Thompson, Charis. 2013. *Good Science: The Ethical Choreography of Stem Cell Research*. Cambridge, MA: MIT Press.

Thomson, Keith. 2009. Introduction. The Religion and Science Debate: Why Does It Continue? In *The Religion and Science Debate: Why Does It Continue?* ed. H. W. Attridge, 1–14. New Haven, CT: Yale University Press.

Toumey, Christopher P. 1994. *God's Own Scientists: Creationists in a Secular World*. New Brunswick, NJ: Rutgers University Press.

Turner, Bryan S. 1997. The Body in Western Society: Social Theory and Its Perspectives. In *Religion and the Body*, ed. S. Coakley, 15–41. New York: Cambridge University Press.

Turner, Stephen, and Jonathan Turner. 1990. *The Impossible Science: An Institutional Analysis of American Sociology*. Newbury Park, CA: Sage Publications.

Uecker, Jeremy E., Mark D. Regnerus, and Margaret L. Vaaler. 2007. Losing My Religion: The Social Sources of Religious Decline in Early Adulthood. *Social Forces* 85(4):1667–92.

Vaidyanathan, Brandon, David R. Johnson, Pamela J. Prickett, and Elaine Howard Ecklund. 2016. Rejecting the Conflict Narrative: American Jewish and Muslim Views on Science and Religion. *Social Compass* 63(4): 478–96.

Verhey, Allen. 1995. "Playing God" and Invoking a Perspective. *Journal of Medicine and Philosophy* 20: 347–64.

Wallace, Anthony. 1966. *Religion: An Anthropological View*. New York: Random House.

Warner, R. Stephen. 1993. Work in Progress Toward a New Paradigm for the Sociological Study of Religion in the United States. *American Journal of Sociology* 98: 1044–93.

Waters, Brent. 2011. Whose Salvation? Which Eschatology? Transhumanism and Christianity as Contending Salvific Religions. In *Transhumanism and Transcendence*, ed. R. Cole-Turner, 163–75. Washington, DC: Georgetown University Press.

Weingart, Peter. 2003. Of Power Maniacs and Unethical Geniuses: Science and Scientists in Fiction Film. *Public Understanding of Science* 12: 279–87.

Weitekamp, Margaret A. 2015. "We're Physicists": Gender, Genre and the Image of Scientists in The Big Bang Theory. *Journal of Popular Television* 3(1): 75–92.

Wernick, Andrew. 2005. Comte, Auguste. In *Encyclopedia of Social Theory*, ed. G. Ritzer, 128–34. Thousand Oaks, CA: Sage Publications.

Whitcomb, John C. Jr., and Henry M. Morris. 1961. *The Genesis Flood: The Biblical Record and Its Scientific Implications*. Phillipsburg, NJ: Presbyterian and Reformed Publishing Company.

White, Andrew Dickson. 1960 [1896]. *A History of the Warfare of Science with Theology in Christendom*. New York: Dover Publications.

Williams, Malcolm. 2000. *Science and Social Science: An Introduction*. New York: Routledge.

Wilson, David B. 2000. The Historiography of Science and Religion. In *The History of Science and Religion in the Western Tradition*, ed. G. B. Ferngren, 3–11. New York: Garland Publishing.

Wolfe, Alan. 2003. *The Transformation of American Religion*. New York: Free Press.
Wolstenholme, Gordon. 1963. *Man and His Future*, ed. G. Wolstenholme. London: J. & A. Churchill Ltd.
Wuthnow, Robert. 1987. *Meaning and Moral Order*. Berkeley, CA: University of California Press.
———. 1988. *The Restructuring of American Religion*. Princeton, NJ: Princeton University Press.
———. 1989. *The Struggle for America's Soul: Evangelicals, Liberals and Secularism*. Grand Rapids, MI: William B. Eerdmans Publishing Co.
———. 1993. *Christianity in the Twenty-First Century*. New York: Oxford University Press.
———. 1998. *After Heaven: Spirituality in America Since the 1950s*. Berkeley, CA: University of California Press.
———. 2007. *After the Baby Boomers: How Twenty-and Thirty-Somethings Are Shaping the Future of American Religion*. Princeton, NJ: Princeton University Press.
———. 2009. No Contradictions Here: Science, Religion and the Culture of All Reasonable Possibilities. In *The Religion and Science Debate: Why Does It Continue?* ed. H. W. Attridge, 155–77. New Haven, CT: Yale University Press.
———. 2012. *The God Problem: Expressing Faith and Being Reasonable*. Berkeley, CA: University of California Press.

INDEX

abortion, 135, 141, 151
academia: specialization within, 60. *See also* schools
academic debate, 8, 17; implications for, 163–64. *See also* advocates; analysts
advocates, 13, 16–43, 61–62. *See also* scientists; theologians
African Americans: civil rights movement, 95, 191n39; Protestants, 95, 123, 139, 191–92n39, 198n15; Tuskegee syphilis study, 113
age of the Earth, 5; belief and knowledge about, 7, 9; Catholics and, 89; conservative Protestants and, 92–96, 160, 163; fundamentalist Protestants and, 6, 23, 64–65, 92–96; lack of coherence in beliefs about, 98–99; theological synthesizers and, 28
Allum, Nick, 175n7
American Academy for the Advancement of Science (AAAS), 19, 36–40
American Civil Liberties Union, 78
American Scientific Affiliation, 38, 40
analysts: academic, 13–14, 44–62. *See also* historians; sociologists
angels, belief in, 106–7
Anglicans, 45, 47, 104–5
anthropology, 58
Are Science & Religion at War?, 161
Arizona, sterilization laws, 80
Armageddon, 4
assisted dying, 24

atheists, 121, 161; new, 64–65, 72, 176n23; scientist, 10, 13, 21–25, 39–40, 43, 57
Atkins, Peter, 25
Augustine, St., 21, 40, 89, 190n4
avoidance: of appearance of knowledge conflict, 100–101; of science, 52, 121–22, 136, 147

Baconian science, 90–93, 131–34, 136
Ball, Jim, 4–5
Barbour, Ian, 28–31, 36, 94, 162, 177–78n35
BBC, *Orphan Black*, 112–14
belief, 7, 108; in angels, 106–7. *See also* faith/confidence
belief systems, 7–9, 108, 174n11; conservative Protestants' educational attainment and, 54; logical consistency, 96–97, 118, 174n12; religions as, 17, 111. *See also* propositional belief conflict
Benedict XVI, Pope, 89
Berg, Paul, 76
Berger, Peter, 50, 65, 103–4
Beyerlein, Kraig, 55
Bible, 21, 32, 33, 109; and age of the Earth, 9, 95; BioLogos and, 34, 35; Catholic authority and, 88–89; common sense philosophy and, 91–93; conservative Protestants' educational attainment and, 54–55; creation science based on, 81; evangelicals and, 40, 65, 94–95, 136; evolution vs., 92–93, 134; fundamentalist Protestants and, 43, 64–65, 92–96, 105;

Genesis, 28, 40, 65, 94, 132, 134, 182–83n36; hermeneutics, 91, 95, 133–34; inerrancy of, 43, 54, 91, 93, 162; John Paul II on, 189–90n4; liberal Christians and, 60, 136; one of two books of God, 35, 40, 91–93. *See also* literalists, biblical
Big Bang, 28, 29, 31, 131–32, 133
The Big Bang Theory, 116–17
bioethics, 70, 72–76, 113, 168, 170, 178–79n51; faith-based, 179n51; theologians, 138, 147
Biological Sciences Curriculum Study program, 81, 82
BioLogos, 34–36
biology: biomedical technologies, 76, 141; conservative Protestants avoiding, 52; materialist view, 83; and meaning of life, 71–72; school curriculum, 78–82. *See also* bioethics; Darwinism
Bluestone, Jeff, 76
body. *See* human body
Bowler, Kate, 110, 111
Bowler, Peter, 46, 48
Brave New World (Huxley), 112
bricolage, 107–8
A Brief History of Time (Hawking), 27
Britain, 13, 46, 74, 104, 112–13
Bronowski, Jacob, 70, 71
Brooke, John Hedley, 45–46, 47, 159
Bryan, William Jennings, 11, 13, 78–80, 84
Buckser, Andrew, 66
Bush, George W., 76, 168

California: biomedical industry, 76; Institute of Technology, 116–17; Proposition 71, 75–76; Silicon Valley, 73
catechisms, 17
Catholics, 87–89, 95, 103; and children becoming scientists, 130; conservative, 130–31, 146, 201n34; embryology, 145; Galileo and, 16, 27, 64, 76, 189–90n4; Inquisition, 76; moral theologians, 33; proper practice, 18; propositional belief conflict, 130–31, 136; rationalism and, 67; scientists, 21, 51; sociologists and, 50; systemic knowledge conflict, 89, 123, 125; theological synthesizers, 28, 89. *See also* Popes
cervical cancer, vaccination against, 24
Christians, 13, 15; Anglicans, 45, 47, 104–5; anthropology and, 58; catechisms, 17; early, 17; essential tenets, 93–94; founders of the scientific revolution, 29; and Judaism, 87,

88; vs. morality of evolution, 82; scientists and, 21, 22, 27, 34–36, 38, 51; and sexual activity, 24; transhumanism and, 73–74. *See also* Bible; Catholics; liberal Christians; Protestants; theologians
Christian Science, 24
Christian Social Ethicists, 33
citizens. *See* public
A Civic Biology (Hunter), 78, 79
civil rights, 95, 191n39
climate change, 2–4, 24, 126–29, 141, 173n5. *See also* global warming
Climategate, 141
cloning, 75, 112–13, 151–52
Closer to Truth?, 161
Cobb, John B., 28
cognitive psychology, 97
Cold Spring Harbor Laboratory, 80
Collins, Francis, 21, 34, 98, 161, 178–79n51
common sense philosophy, 90–93, 101, 132–33
communism, 143
Comte, Auguste, 57–58, 60, 61
conflict, 5–13, 30, 31, 177n28. *See also* moral conflict; propositional belief conflict; systemic knowledge conflict
conservative Catholics, 130–31, 146, 201n34
conservative politics, 96, 97, 126–29, 142
conservative Protestants, 14, 168; and age of the Earth, 92–96, 160, 163; Baconian science, 92–93, 131–34, 136; biology avoided by, 52; and climate change/global warming, 2–5, 126–29, 128 *table*, 132, 141–43, 160, 163; common sense and observation, 91–93, 132–33; and Darwinism/evolution/ human origins, 45, 55, 77, 92–93, 131–36, 139–41, 147–48, 162; and doctrine, 105–6; educational attainment, 53–55, 125–26, 183n40; faith/confidence in science, 139, 147–50; human reproductive technologies, 135, 151–59; identity formation, 134–35, 136; megachurches, 105–6, 109, 110–11; moral conflict, 14–15, 135–59; narcissism, 109–10; "new paradigm" or "seeker," 105, 106–9; Proposition 71 and, 76; propositional belief conflict, 93, 106, 108, 121, 122, 126, 130–36; Prosperity Gospel, 110–11; religion about social relationships, 102, 108–11; sociological surveys of, 53–55, 106; systemic knowledge conflict, 14, 35, 86–96, 102, 108–9, 119–36, 147–48; therapeutic individualism, 108–11, 118. *See also* literalists, biblical

INDEX 221

Constitution, First Amendment Establishment Clause, 82–83
Copernicus, N., 1, 47
Cornwall Alliance, 4
Coyne, Jerry A., 23–25
creationism, 3, 12–13, 55, 77, 78–84, 162; creation science, 81–83, 162; dictionary, 91; evolutionary, 34–35; geocentrists and, 132; intelligent design (ID), 20–21, 25, 77, 83–84, 89, 132–33, 136; Muslims and, 187n49, 199n27; status politics and, 135; Young Earth Creationism, 77, 78–83, 94, 120, 196–97n2
Crick, Francis, 25
Cumberland Presbyterian Church, 41

Darnell, Alfred, 183n40
Darrow, Clarence, 11
Darwin, Charles, 78–81, 174n12; *Descent of Man*, 78; *The Origin of Species*, 78
Darwinism, 1, 11–14, 29, 63–64, 77–84; African Americans and, 191–92n39; Anglicans and, 45, 104–5; atheists and, 25, 176n23; Baconian science and, 133; Catholics and, 89; Collins and, 21, 98; "evil fruits," 82; historians and, 46, 47; Huxley vs. Wilberforce, 11, 174n18; materialist, 30, 83; moral conflict, 12–14, 77–85, 136; neo-Darwinism, 89; Protestants and, 3, 45, 55, 77, 92–93, 131–36, 139–41, 147–48, 162; Scopes trial, 11, 13, 78–83, 176n10, 191n39; social, 79; sociologists and, 49–50. *See also* evolution
Davis, Bernard, 71
Dawkins, Richard, 21–23, 51, 72, 162, 176n23
Dawson, Gowan, 78
Dennett, Daniel, 25, 161, 176n23
Descartes, R., 45, 48, 107
Descent of Man (Darwin), 78
diabetes, 75–76
dialogue: associations, 33–40, 42, 162; theological synthesizers and, 30, 31, 33, 36–37, 42, 162
Dialogue on Science, Ethics, and Religion (DoSER), 36–40
Diamandis, Peter, 73
DiMaggio, Paul, 97
Discovery Institute, 83
disinterestedness, of scientists, 143, 144
doctrine: collapse of, 104–6; Fall, 104–5, 193n69
Dollar, Creflo, 110
Do Science & Religion Conflict?, 161
DoSER (Dialogue on Science, Ethics, and Religion (DoSER)), 36–40

Down syndrome, 12
Durkheim, Emile, 58–59, 61
"dwelling religion," 106, 107

Eagleton, Terry, 22
Ecklund, Elaine Howard, 52, 101–2
Edinburgh School, 66–67
education: conservative Protestants' attainment, 53–55, 125–26, 183n40; in science, 99, 112; survey measure, 122, 125. *See also* schools
Edwards, Jonathan, 109
Edwards, Robert, 70, 71, 138
Edwards v. Aguillard, 83
Efron, Noah, 88
elites, 6–9, 16. *See also* scientists; theologians
Ellison, Christopher G., 52–53
embryology, 145
embryonic stem cell research, 12, 15, 24, 74–76, 141–46, 148, 163, 178–79n51
Enlightenment, 56–60, 67, 93, 94, 160; Scottish, 92
environmental problems, 139
Epperson v. Arkansas, 82
"ether theory," 46
eugenics, 73, 78–81, 112–13, 150, 155, 170
Eugenics Record Office, 80, 112–13
Europe: Muslims, 187n49, 199n27; secularization theory, 67, 68; sociology, 58–59, 61. *See also* Britain; Germany
euthanasia, 24
evangelicals, 90–96; and Bible, 40, 65, 94–95, 136; BioLogos and, 36; and doctrine, 105; DoSER and, 38–40; educational attainment, 55; Evangelical Environmental Network, 4–5; and evolution, 134, 135; and global warming, 126–27; National Association of Evangelicals, 38, 40; propositional belief conflict, 131; vs. Prosperity Gospel, 110–11; scientists, 21, 34–36, 38, 51; "symbolic boundary" with the secular United States, 135; Templeton, 41
Evans, Michael, 60, 168
evolution: African Americans and, 191–92n39; Bible vs., 92–93, 134; Catholics and, 89; cloning and, 112; collapse of doctrine and, 104–5; educational attainment and, 99; "evil fruits," 82; evolutionary creationism, 34–35; Huxley vs. Wilberforce, 11, 174n18; logical coherence about, 99; moral conflict, 12–14, 77–85, 136; Muslims and, 187n49, 199n27; Protestants and, 3, 45, 55, 77, 92–93, 131–36, 139–41, 147–48, 162;

in schools, 6, 78, 80, 81, 141; scientific atheists and, 25, 176n23; "scientific evidence," 30; Scopes trial, 11, 13, 78–83, 176n10, 191n39; social, 89; sociologists and, 49–50; systemic knowledge conflict, 77–84, 178n51; theistic, 34–35; theological development on, 29. *See also* Darwinism

Expelled: No Intelligence Allowed, 84

faith/confidence, 199n6; in institutions, 15, 137, 147–50; in religion, 138–39; in science, 138–39, 147–50, 202n38. *See also* belief

faith healing, 24

Faith versus Fact (Coyne), 23–25

Fall, doctrine of, 104–5, 193n69

Fillmore, Charles and Myrtle, 41

"The Folly of Faith" (Stenger), 3–4

The Foundations of Dialogue in Science and Religion (McGrath), 32

Fox News, 4, 129

Frankenstein monster, 114

Franklin, Benjamin, 109

Frayling, Christopher, 115

Frazer, James, 58

Freudian psychology, 107

fundamentalism, 23. *See also* fundamentalist Protestants

fundamentalist Protestants, 90, 92–96; and age of the Earth, 6, 23, 64–65, 92–96; Baconian science, 92–93, 132–33; and Bible, 43, 64–65, 92–96, 105; BioLogos and, 35–36; creation science, 162; and doctrine, 105; educational attainment, 55; and evolution, 3; vs. liberal Protestants, 90, 94, 134; propositional belief conflict, 95, 134; scientific atheists and, 23, 43; truth, 53

Galileo Galilei, 1, 162; Catholic Church and, 16, 27, 64, 76, 189–90n4

Galton, Francis, 80

Garroutte, Eva, 90

Geertz, Clifford, 65, 66

gender, and religiosity, 123

General Social Survey (GSS), 120, 124 *table*, 128 *table*, 138, 140 *table*, 141–44, 149 *table*, 197n7

Genesis, 28, 40, 65, 94, 132, 134, 182–83n36

The Genesis Flood (Whitcomb and Morris), 81–82

genetic modification: cloning, 75, 112–13, 151–52; of food, 141–42, 144; of humans, 15, 73, 114–15, 145, 150–58; pre-implantation genetic diagnosis, 146, 151, 202n41; reproductive technologies, 15, 46, 75, 135, 145–46, 151–59, 202n41

geocentrists, 132

Germany, World War I, 13, 81

Gieryn, Thomas, 26

global warming, conservative Protestants and, 2–5, 126–29, 128 *table*, 132, 141–43, 160, 163

"Global Warming and Religion" (Stenger), 4

God: climate controlled by, 2–3; Enlightenment and, 57; existence of, 10, 22–23, 28, 57, 94; "The God Problem," 100–101; human genetic role, 155–58; humans made in image of, 94, 141; nonreligious belief in, 121; playing, 71, 145, 156; sociologists and, 57, 60; Templeton and, 41, 42; two books of, 35, 40, 91–92

The God Delusion (Dawkins), 22

Google searches, 161, 202n2

Gould, Steven J., 30, 36, 79, 94

Greeley, Andrew, 54

Guhin, Jeffrey, 135

Gusfield, Joseph, 135

"Habits of the Heart," 107

Hameed, Salman, 187n49

Harris, John, 73

Harrison, Peter: on new atheists, 72; on religion, 9, 17, 18; on religion and science, 9, 26, 49, 77

Hawking, Stephen, 27, 31

Haycraft, John, 80

Haynes, Roslynn, 115, 194–95n105

Hebrew Union College, 88

Hegel, G. W. F., 66

hermeneutics, biblical, 91, 95, 133–34

Hill, Jonathan, 196n2

historians, 13–14, 44–49, 62, 164; recent, 63, 69–86.

historical science, 132–33

history: natural, 17; recent, 63, 69–86; stages of, 58. *See also* historians

History of Science and Religion in the Western Tradition encyclopedia, 46–47, 177n28

A History of the Warfare of Science with Theology in Christendom (White), 1

Hitler, A., 84

Hollinger, David, 69–70

Holocaust, 81

horror movies, about scientists, 114

Hout, Michael, 54

Huffington Post: and climate change, 2, 24; on science vs. religion, 3, 4–5, 8, 8 *fig*, 161

human body, 146–47, 170–71; biomedical technologies, 76, 141; embryonic stem cell research, 12, 15, 24, 74–76, 141–46, 148, 163, 178–79n51; eugenics, 73, 78–81, 112–13, 150, 155, 170; human genome mapping, 34, 73; moral concerns with, 145–59; sexuality, 24, 78, 145, 146. *See also* genetic modification; reproduction
humanism, of public education, 183n40
Human Longevity, 73
human origins, 29, 95, 104–5, 127–36, 147–48; intelligent design (ID), 20–21, 25, 77, 83–84, 89, 132–33, 136. *See also* creationism; evolution
Hurlbut, J. Benjamin, 74–75, 76
Huxley, Aldous, 112
Huxley, Thomas Henry, 11, 47, 174n17

identity formation, conservative Protestants, 134–35, 136
ideology, 174n11; political conservatives, 96, 97, 126–29, 142. *See also* belief systems
Immigration Reform Act, U.S., 81
independence relationship, 30, 36, 94
individualism: of American culture, 94, 193n79; religious, 107–8; therapeutic, 108–11, 118
inductive science, 132–33
Inglehart, Ronald, 68
Inherit the Wind, 80
Inquisition, 76
institutions: AAAS, 36; faith/confidence in, 15, 137, 147–50. *See also* religion; science
integration, of scientific and religious knowledge and values, 28–31
intellectual gospel, 69–70
intelligent design (ID), 20–21, 25, 77, 83–84, 89, 132–33, 136

Jakes, T. D., 110
Jehovah's Witnesses, 24
Jewett, Andrew, 69
Job, social and moral message about suffering, 65–66
John Paul II, Pope, 88, 89, 189–90n4
Johnson, David R., 202n38
Judaism, 13, 87, 88, 95
Jurassic Park, 114

Kansas, sterilization laws, 80–81
Kantianism, 113
Kevles, Daniel, 81

Kitzmiller v. Dover, 84
knowledge: defined, 7; existence of God claim, 22–23; Genesis and, 182–83n36; neutral, 66–67, 163; science as only real, 169–70. *See also* knowledge systems
knowledge deficit model, 19, 36, 175n7
knowledge systems: doctrine, 106; low coherence in, 96–102, 111; studies of religion and science as, 98–100. *See also* pyramid, knowledge; systemic knowledge conflict
Kosmin, Barry A., 183n38
Krauss, Lawrence, 20–21
Kuhn, Thomas S., 174n12

LaHaye, Beverley, 183n40
Larson, Edward, 79
Legare, Cristine, 99
Leiserowitz, A., 198n13
Lessl, Thomas, 27
liberal Christians, 59–60, 90, 93–95, 168, 191n36; and Bible, 60, 136; propositional belief conflict, 130–31, 134–35, 136; Social Gospel movement, 111; systemic knowledge conflict, 123, 125. *See also* synthesizers, theological
liberal politics, 2–4
Lightman, Bernard, 48
Limbaugh, Rush, 2–3, 7
literalists, biblical, 120–21, 123, 125, 134; Baconian science, 132; and children becoming scientists, 130; and Darwinism/evolution, 30, 99, 135; educational attainment, 55, 99; faith in scientists, 139, 148–50; and global warming, 127, 142–43; in knowledge pyramid, 7; liberal Christians and, 60, 95, 134; self-interestedness of scientists, 144–45
Louisiana, Creationism Act, 83
Luther, Martin, 71, 73–74

Madsen, Richard, 193n79
mainline Christians. *See* liberal Christians
Marsden, George, 90–93
Marx, Karl, 58–59, 61
materialism, 46; Darwinian, 30, 83; positivist, 90; scientific, 52–53, 54, 72
McGrath, Alister, 31–32, 176n23, 178n44
McLean v. Arkansas, 82–83
Medawar, Sir Peter, 19
media: science education from, 112. *See also* movies; television; *individual periodicals and books*
"medieval synthesis," 1

megachurches, 105–6, 109, 110–11
Mendel, Gregor (Augustinian friar), 165, 203n5
Merton, Robert, 69, 143
metaphysical naturalism, 10, 51; atheist scientists and, 21–22, 39–40, 43, 57; BioLogos and, 35; and Darwinism, 79; defining religion, 64; DoSER and, 36; sociologists and, 56–61; Templeton and, 41; theological synthesizers and, 28
methodological naturalism, 10, 32, 57, 162; atheist scientists and, 43; BioLogos and, 35; conservative Protestants and, 94; DoSER and, 36; intelligent design and, 21; natural sciences and, 57–61; religious belief system and, 87; sociologists and, 56–61; theological synthesizers and, 28
Middle Ages, 45
Miller, Kenneth R., 21
modernists. *See* liberal Christians
modernity, Berger on, 103
moral conflict, 2, 6, 9, 12–16, 102, 111, 137–59, 163, 167–71; conservative Protestants, 14–15, 135–59; Darwinism/evolution, 12–14, 77–85, 136; empirical tests, 15, 137–59; historians and, 45, 46, 47, 63, 69–85; public and, 5, 85, 86, 111–17, 129–30, 137–59, 169–70; scientists and, 18–26, 29–40, 63–64, 69–85, 87, 138–59, 169–70; sociologists and, 54–57, 63, 164; synthesizers and, 27–33, 36–37, 41–42; and technology, 15, 138, 139, 141–59, 203n19; theologians and, 29–30, 32, 33, 63–64, 69–85, 138, 147, 164. *See also* bioethics
morality: defined, 12; neutral, 163; religion about, 65, 102; science concerned about, 111–12; of scientists, 74–76, 113–17, 118, 137, 143–44, 168; transhumanism and, 73–74. *See also* moral conflict; moral values
moral philosophy, 60
moral theologians, 33
moral values, 33; Coyne and, 23; religion, 2, 12, 66, 111, 169; science, 2, 12–13, 40, 71, 111, 166–71. *See also* moral conflict; morality
Moran, Jeffrey, 191n39
Morris, Henry M., 81–82
movies, morality of scientists, 114, 115
Mulkay, Michael, 143
Musick, Marc A., 52–53
Muslims, Europe, 187n49, 199n27
myths: foundational conflict between religion and science, 1, 3, 26–27, 177n28; knowledge deficit model, 19

narcissism, 109–10
National Academy of Sciences, 51, 161–62
National Association of Evangelicals, 38, 40
National Institutes of Health (NIH), 34
National Science Foundation, 117, 120
natural history, 17
naturalism, 25, 59, 100. *See also* metaphysical naturalism; methodological naturalism
natural philosophy, 17
natural sciences, 57–61
nature, one of two books of God, 35, 40, 91–93
Nazis, 81, 84
neuroscience, 37
Newton, Isaac, 1, 45, 48, 83, 89
New York Times, 34
Nielsen Media, 110
Noll, Mark, 79, 92–93
nomological science, 132
non-overlapping magisteria, 30, 36, 94, 162
Norris, Pippa, 68
Numbers, Ronald, 12–13, 25, 48, 78–79, 91, 181n15

observers. *See* analysts
Of Pandas and People: The Central Question of Biological Origins, 83, 132, 133
"Of Power Maniacs and Unethical Geniuses," 114
operation science, 132
original sin, 31, 105, 193n69
The Origin of Species (Darwin), 78
origins science, 132
Orphan Black, BBC, 112–14
Orthodox Jews, 88
Osteen, Joel, 110

Paley, William, 83
pantheism, 41
"paradigm shift," 174n12
Parens, Erik, 12, 170
Parsons, Keith, 3
Paul, Diane, 81
Paul the Fifth, Pope, 76
PBS, 161
Pentecostals, 55, 183n38
philosophy, 164, 177n33; Cartesian, 45, 48, 107; common sense, 90–93, 101, 132–33; logically consistent beliefs, 96, 98; moral, 60; natural, 17; and public, 164
Pius XI, Pope, 88

politics: Bryan, 78–79; civil rights movement, 95, 191n39; conservative, 96, 97, 126–29, 142; liberal, 2–4; logical consistency, 96–97; religious right, 146, 168, 201n34; Republican party, 4, 76, 126–27, 142; scientists' moral projects, 74–76; status, 134–35
Polkinghorne, John, 32–33, 162
pollution, 139
Popes: Benedict XVI, 89; John Paul II, 88, 89, 189–90n4; Paul the Fifth, 76; Pius XI, 88
positivism, 57–58, 92, 184n52; materialist, 90; messianic, 71
prayer: power of, 101; therapeutic, 109
pre-implantation genetic diagnosis, 146, 151, 202n41
Principia Mathematica (Newton), 89
printing press, 17
progress, 58, 150
proposition, 11–12, 174n18
Proposition 71, California, 75–76
propositional belief conflict, 9, 11–12, 15–17, 31, 33, 53, 118–19, 136–37, 163–64, 169; Catholics, 130–31, 136; conservative Protestants, 93, 106, 108, 121, 122, 126, 130–36; empirical tests, 15, 119–36; fundamentalist Protestants, 95, 134; and global warming, 126–28, 132; liberal Christians, 130–31, 134–35, 136; not perceived as systemic knowledge conflict, 100; public, 11–12, 86–88, 119, 163
Prosperity Gospel, 110–11
Protestants, 87, 90–96; African American, 95, 123, 139, 191–92n39, 198n15; Christian Social Ethicists, 33; proper belief, 18; Reformation, 9, 17, 50; sociologists and, 50; theological synthesizers, 28. *See also* conservative Protestants; evangelicals; fundamentalist Protestants; liberal Christians
Provine, William, 25
psychology: cognitive, 97; Freudian, 107; and perceptions of scientists, 116, 117; systemic knowledge conflict model, 99
public, 6–9, 63–136, 168; empirical tests, 15, 119–59; historians and, 44–49, 62; lacking systemic knowledge structures, 96–102, 161–63; moral conflict, 5, 85, 86, 111–17, 129–30, 137–59, 169–70; and morality of scientists, 116; propositional belief conflict, 11–12, 86, 119, 163; Protestants dominating, 18, 91; scientists and, 18–40, 87, 111–17, 169–70; sociologists and, 44–62, 66, 164; synthesizers and, 27–33, 36–37, 41–42; and systemic knowledge, 14, 18–21, 44–62, 85–87, 96–136, 161–64; theologians and, 29, 31–32, 33, 164
pyramid, knowledge, 7–11, 8 *fig*, 162, 174n12; dialogue associations and, 34–35, 37; historians and, 45, 47; intelligent design and, 21; perfect religion and, 17; Protestantism and, 90, 95, 126, 131; public and, 96–106; scientific atheists and, 22–25; sociological researchers and, 52, 56; Templeton foundations and, 42; theological synthesizers and, 28–31

quantum physics, 29, 31–33, 37, 42

racial hygiene, 80, 81. *See also* eugenics
radiometric dating, 7, 9
Ramsey, Paul, 70–71, 73, 138, 145
rationalism, 67–68. *See also* Enlightenment
Rauschenbusch, Walter, 60
Reformation, 16th Century, 9, 17, 50
Reform Jews, 88
regression analysis, 122–23, 144, 147, 196–97n7, 200nn19,20
religion: anthropology and, 58; changes in, 63–85, 102–18; collapse of doctrine, 104–6; defined, 17, 23–24, 26, 64–68; "dwelling," 106, 107; faith in, 138–39; First Amendment Establishment Clause, 82–83, 84; functional definitions, 64, 65; Marx and, 59; metaphysical naturalism and, 57–58; moral values, 2, 12, 66, 111, 169; non-participation in, 121; of science, 170; "seeking," 105, 106–9; sociology of, 33, 50–53, 98–118; substantive definitions, 64; therapeutic, 108–11, 118; transhumanism and, 73–74. *See also* Christians; conflict; Judaism; Muslims
religiosity: decline in, 99; and gender, 123; of scientists, 51–52, 162–63
religious minorities, 13, 87, 121, 175n23
religious right, 146, 168, 201n34
reproduction, 146; abortion, 135, 141, 151; technologies, 15, 46, 75, 135, 145–46, 151–59, 202n41
Republican party, 4, 76, 126–27, 142
research: embryonic stem cell, 12, 15, 24, 74–76, 141–46, 148, 163, 178–79n51; ethics, 113–14; on public, 85–136; social science, 9, 14, 49, 52–55, 86–87, 96–159, 168–71. *See also* survey research
Resurrection, 87

rewards, for academics and other elites, 9, 11, 17, 96, 160
right, religious, 146, 168, 201n34
Roberts, Jon H., 27, 59, 60, 94
Robertson, Pat, 55, 101
Roos, J. Micah, 197n7
Ross, Dorothy, 184n52
Rousseau, Jean-Jacques, 58
Royal College of Physicians, 80
Royal Society, 48
"Rush Limbaugh: 'If You Believe In God . . . You Cannot Believe In Man-Made Global Warming,'" 2–3
Russell, Colin, 47, 177n28

Scheitle, Christopher, 52, 101–2
"schema alignment," 101
schools: African American, 191n39; biology curriculum, 78–82; creationism, 81–82, 135; evolution, 6, 78, 80, 81, 141; intelligent design (ID), 83–84; religious right and, 146; Tennessee, 79. *See also* education
science: aggressive, 169; avoidance of, 52, 121–22, 136, 147; Baconian, 90–93, 131–34, 136; "can-do attitude," 169; creation science, 81–83, 162; in dialogue associations, 33–40; education in, 99, 112; established scientific facts, 122; ethics of, 69, 70; faith/confidence in, 138–39, 147–50, 202n38; historical, 132–33; inductive, 132–33; mid-eighteenth-century American, 45; morally expressive nature, 170–71; moral values, 2, 12–13, 40, 71, 111, 166–71; natural, 57–61; neutral, 66–67, 163; nomological, 132; norms of, 143; operation; 132; origins, 132; public's view of, 111–12; religion of, 170; scientific method, 122, 125, 132; theological synthesizers, 13, 27–33, 36–37, 41–42, 43, 87, 89; "tree of," 182n36; as worldview, 103. *See also* conflict; knowledge; scientists; social science
Science and Religion: An Introduction (McGrath), 31–32
Science and Religion: Some Historical Perspectives (Brooke), 45–46, 47
science communication, 18–19
Science magazine, 34, 36
Scientific Creationism (Morris), 82
scientific materialism, 52–53, 54, 72
scientific revolution, 29, 57
scientific sociologists, 60
scientism, 169–70
scientists, 16–27, 57–59; AAAS, 19, 36–40; atheist, 10, 13, 21–25, 39–40, 43, 57; boundary drawing, 26; disinterestedness of, 143, 144; evangelical, 21, 34–36, 38, 51; and global warming, 127–29, 128 *table*, 141, 160; implications for, 165–67; influence in public debates, 141–44, 147–48, 159, 201n35; and meaning of life, 71–72; and moral conflict, 18–26, 29–40, 63–64, 69–85, 87, 138–59, 169–70; morality of, 74–76, 113–17, 118, 137, 143–44, 168; myths of religion-science conflict, 26–27; not like "ordinary" people, 116–18; in popular culture, 112–17, 118, 194–95n105; and public, 18–40, 87, 111–17, 169–70; recent, 63, 69–86; religiosity of, 51–52, 162–63; self-interested, 143–45; systemic knowledge conflict and, 16–40, 43, 69–85, 104–6, 147; Victorian era, 44; wanting children to be, 129–30, 137, 198n15. *See also* science
Scopes, John, 78, 79
Scopes trial, 11, 13, 78–83, 176n10, 191n39
Scottish Common Sense Realism, 90–93, 132–33
Secord, James, 48
secularization, 52, 60, 66–68, 103, 134
"seeking" religion, 105, 106–9
Sewell, William Jr., 97
sexuality, 24, 78, 145, 146
Shapiro, Adam, 79
Sheilaism, 107
Sherkat, Darren, 53–55, 183n40
Silicon Valley, 73
Singularity University, 73
skepticism, organized, 143
Smith, Christian, 60, 61, 103, 109–10
Smith, N., 198n13
Snow, C. P., 169
social Darwinism, 79
Social Gospel movement, 60–61, 111
"social power," 47
social relationships: religion about, 65–67, 102, 108–11; science about, 112; of scientists, 117
social science: origins of, 56–60; recent, 64–68; research, 9, 14, 49, 52–55, 86–87, 96–159, 168–71; scientists, 51, 56; specialization within, 60
sociologists, 13–14, 26, 44–62, 98–118; cultural analysis, 97; and moral conflict, 54–57, 63, 164; and public, 44–62, 66, 164; recent, 63–85; scientific, 60; Social Gospel, 60–61
sociology, 44, 49–62; America, 59–85; bias toward seeing knowledge conflict, 56–61; birth of, 56, 57; classical, 58–59, 61; Europe, 58–59, 61; of religion, 33, 50–53, 98–118;

research, 52–55, 96–159; of science, 66–67; of scientific knowledge, 67; surveys, 52–55, 96–159, 195–200
specialization, within academia, 60
Spencer, Herbert, 60, 80, 89
Stanford Medical Magazine, 76
Stanford Medical School, Dean, 76
Star Trek, 113–14
statistical significance, 123
status politics, 134–35
Stenger, Victor, 3–4, 162
sterilization, forced, 80–81
supernatural, 64, 87, 100, 106–7, 160. *See also* God
Supreme Court, U.S., 83
survey research: General Social Survey (GSS), 120, 124 *table*, 128 *table*, 138, 140 *table*, 141–44, 149 *table*, 197n7; knowledge conflict, 120–26; moral conflict, 137, 141–59; National Science Foundation, 117; sociological, 52–55, 96–159, 195–200
Swidler, Ann, 97
symbols: identity, 135, 136; religious, 65, 105
synthesizers, theological, 13, 27–33, 43, 87, 161, 162; Catholics, 28, 89; DoSER and, 36–37; evangelicals, 94–95; sociologists and, 59; Templeton and, 41–42, 43
systemic knowledge conflict, 2–5, 7–12, 15, 16–43, 86, 102, 119–36, 159–63, 168–69; avoidance of appearance of, 100–101; Barbour and, 28–31, 36, 94, 162, 177–78n35; Catholics, 89, 123, 125; and climate change/global warming, 2–5, 24, 126–29, 132, 141–43, 160, 163; Darwinism/evolution, 77–84, 178n51; empirical tests, 15, 119–36; historians and, 44–49, 62, 69–85; hypothetical, 8 *fig*; knowledge deficit model, 19, 36, 175n7; logical coherence and, 11, 22, 31, 96–102, 111; Protestants, 14, 35, 86–136, 147–48; public and, 14, 18–21, 44–62, 85–87, 96–136, 161–64; scientists and, 16–40, 43, 69–85, 104–6, 147; secularization theory and, 67–68; sociologists and, 49–62, 66, 164; strong version, 21, 35, 52, 56; synthesizers and, 13, 28–33, 36–37, 41–42, 43, 87, 89, 94–95; theologians and, 16–18, 27–33, 69–85, 104–6, 164; weak version, 21, 28, 35, 42, 56

technology: biomedical, 76, 141; evangelicals and, 94; moral conflict over, 15, 138, 139, 141–59, 203n19; morally expressive nature, 170–71; and transhumanism, 73

television: *The Big Bang Theory*, 116–17; documentaries on religion and science, 161; Fox News, 4, 129; *Orphan Black*, 112–14; Osteen, 110; scientist portrayals, 112–15; *Star Trek*, 113–14
temperance movements, 135
Templeton, Sir John M., 41–42
Templeton foundations, 41–42, 43
Templeton Prize, 28, 32
Templeton Religion Trust, 41
Templeton World Charity Foundation, 41
Tennessee, public education, 79
Terry Lectures (2005), Yale, 20, 25
theistic evolution, 34–35
theologians, 16–18, 189n4; bioethics, 138, 147; dichotomy between God and humans in creation, 155–56; logical consistency, 96, 174n12; moral, 33; and moral conflict, 29–30, 32, 33, 63–64, 69–85, 138, 147, 164; and public, 29, 31–32, 33, 164; recent, 69–85; systemic knowledge conflict, 16–18, 27–33, 69–85, 104–6, 164; theoretical rationality, 96. *See also* synthesizers, theological
theology, defined, 33
"theology of nature" tradition, 31
therapeutic individualism, 108–11, 118
Thomas Aquinas, 89
Thomson, Keith, 20
Time magazine, 110
transhumanism, 73–74
truth: fundamentalist Protestants and, 53; "two truths," 88; uncertainty about, 103–4
Turner, James, 59, 60
Tuskegee syphilis study, 113
two books of God, 35, 40, 91–93
"two truths," 88
Tylor, Edward, 58
Tyndall, John, 26
Tyson, Neil deGrasse, 162

United States, 13, 161–63; changes in religion, 63–85, 102–18; common sense philosophy, 90–93; Darwinism, 79; diversity of religion, 86–87; evangelical "symbolic boundary," 135; government ethics commissions, 71–72; Jews, 88; megachurches, 105–6', 109, 110–11; mid-eighteenth-century science, 45; secularization theory, 68; social structure, 107; sociology, 59–85; sterilization laws, 80–81; surveys, 120; temperance movements, 135. *See also* public
Unity Church (Unity School of Christianity), 41

universalism, 143
utilitarianism, 113

Venter, J. Craig, 73
Vestiges of the Natural History of Creation, 48
Victorian era, 44, 45, 48, 78, 176n28
The View, Osteen on, 110
Visala, Aku, 99

Wallace, Anthony, 67
Waters, Brent, 73–74
Weber, Max, 50, 58–59, 61, 64, 96
Wedge Document, 83
Weissman, Irving, 75–76
Wells, HG, 58
Wheaton College, 40
"When God and Science Meet: Surprising Discoveries of Agreement" (DoSER and National Association of Evangelicals), 40
When Science and Christianity Meet, 161

When Science Meets Religion: Enemies, Strangers or Partners (Barbour), 29
Whitcomb, John C. Jr., 81–82, 84
White, Andrew Dickson, 1
Wikipedia, 28, 162–63
Wilberforce, Bishop Samuel, 11, 174n18
Williams, Malcolm, 58
Wilson, David, 47
Wilson, E. O., 25, 72
Wolfe, Alan, 105, 109
women, religiosity, 123
worldviews, 174nn11,12; logical consistency, 96–97, 174n12; and truth, 103. *See also* belief systems
World War I, 13, 59, 78–79, 81
Wuthnow, Robert, 98–101, 103, 106–8, 169

Yale Divinity School, 20; Terry Lectures (2005), 20, 25
Young Earth Creationism, 77, 78–83, 94, 120, 196–97n2

www.ingramcontent.com/pod-product-compliance
Lightning Source LLC
Chambersburg PA
CBHW070801230426
43665CB00017B/2447